THE LONG AND THE SHORT OF IT

Roy Fisher: selected bibliography

POETRY BOOKS BY ROY FISHER

City (Migrant Press, 1961)
Ten Interiors with Various Figures (Tarasque Press, 1966)
The Ship's Orchestra (Fulcrum Press, 1966)
Collected Poems (Fulcrum Press, 1968)
Matrix (Fulcrum Press, 1971)
The Cut Pages (Fulcrum Press, 1971; Shearsman, 1986)
The Thing About Joe Sullivan: Poems 1971-1977 (Carcanet Press, 1978)
Poems 1955-1980 (Oxford University Press, 1980)
A Furnace (Oxford University Press, 1986)
Poems 1955-1987 (Oxford University Press, 1988)
Birmingham River (Oxford University Press, 1994)
It Follows That (Pig Press, 1994)
The Dow Low Drop: New & Selected Poems (Bloodaxe Books, 1996)
The Long & the Short of It: Poems 1955-2005 (Bloodaxe Books, 2005)

ESSAYS / INTERVIEWS / PROSE

Roy Fisher: *Nineteen Poems and an Interview* (Grosseteste, 1975)
Robert Sheppard & Peter Robinson: *News for the Ear:
    a homage to Roy Fisher* (Stride Publications, 2000)
Tony Frazer (ed.): *Interviews Through Time and Selected Prose*
    (Shearsman Books, 2000)
Peter Robinson & John Kerrigan (eds.): *The Thing About Roy Fisher:
    Critical Essays on the Poetry of Roy Fisher*
    (Liverpool University Press, 2000)

ROY FISHER

THE LONG AND THE SHORT OF IT

POEMS 1955-2005

BLOODAXE BOOKS

Copyright © Roy Fisher 1961, 1966, 1968, 1971, 1978,
1980, 1986, 1988, 1994, 1996, 2005

ISBN: 1 85224 701 0

First published 2005 by
Bloodaxe Books Ltd,
Highgreen,
Tarset,
Northumberland NE48 1RP.

www.bloodaxebooks.com
For further information about Bloodaxe titles
please visit our website or write to
the above address for a catalogue.

Bloodaxe Books Ltd acknowledges
the financial assistance of
Arts Council England, North East.

Cover printing by J. Thomson Colour Printers Ltd, Glasgow.

Printed in Great Britain by
Bell & Bain Limited, Glasgow, Scotland.

To the memory of

Joyce Holliday

Gael Turnbull

ACKNOWLEDGEMENTS

My thanks go to the editors and publishers of the magazines and volumes in which almost all of these poems have previously appeared, and particularly to Peter Robinson for his help in the preparation of this book, and to Derek Slade without whose bibliographer's eye its assembling would have been harder. This edition includes poems first collected in these books: *City* (Migrant Press, 1961), *Ten Interiors with Various Figures* (Tarasque Press, 1966), *The Ship's Orchestra* (Fulcrum Press, 1966), *Collected Poems* (Fulcrum Press, 1968), *Matrix* and *The Cut Pages* (both Fulcrum Press, 1971), *The Thing About Joe Sullivan: Poems 1971-1977* (Carcanet, 1978), *Poems 1955-1980* (Oxford University Press, 1980), *A Furnace* (Oxford University Press, 1986), *Poems 1955-1987* (Oxford University Press, 1988), *Birmingham River* (Oxford University Press, 1994), *It Follows That* (Pig Press, 1994) and *The Dow Low Drop: New & Selected Poems* (Bloodaxe Books, 1996).

These poems no more amount to a biography than I do; and my habits of working on projects from time to time over long periods and my heterodox approach to the methods I use would make an arrangement that seemed chronological false: so nothing of the kind is here attempted. Dates of composition are given after the poem titles in the index of titles and first lines at the back of the book.

CONTENTS

III

IV

I

Wonders of Obligation

We know that hereabouts
comes into being
the malted-milk brickwork
on its journey past the sun.

The face of its designer
sleeps into a tussocky
field with celandines

and the afternoon
comes on steely and still
under the heat,

with part of the skyline
settling to a dark slate
frieze of chimneys
stiffened to peel away
off the western edge.

I saw
the mass graves dug
the size of workhouse wards
into the clay

ready for most of the people
the air-raids were going to kill:

still at work, still in the fish-queue;
some will have looked down
into their own graves on Sundays

provided
for the poor of Birmingham
the people of Birmingham,
the working people of Birmingham,
the allotment holders and Mother, of Birmingham.
The poor.

Once the bombs got you
you were a pauper:
clay, faeces, no teeth; on a level
with gas mains,
even more at a loss than before,

down in the terraces between the targets,
between the wagon works
and the moonlight on the canal.

A little old woman
with a pink nose, we knew her,
had to go into the pit, dead of pneumonia,
had to go to the pit with the rest,
it was thought shame.

Suddenly to go
to the school jakes with the rest
in a rush by the clock.
What had been strange and inward
become nothing, a piss-pallor
with gabble. Already they were lost,
taught unguessed silliness,
to squirt and squeal there.
What was wrong? Suddenly
to distrust your own class
and be demoralised
as any public-school boy.

The things we make up out of language
turn into common property.
To feel responsible
I put my poor footprint back in.

I preserve
Saturday's afterglow
arched over the skyline road
out of Scot Hay:
the hare
zigzagging slowly

like the shadow of a hare
away up the field-path

to where the blue
translucent sky-glass
reared from the upland
and back overhead

paling, paling
to the west
and down to the muffled rim of the plain.

As many skies as you can look at
stretched in a second
the manifest
of more forms than anyone could see

and it alters
every second you watch it,
bulking and smearing the inks
around landlocked light-harbours.

Right overhead, crane back,
blurred grey tufts of cloud
dyeing themselves blue,
never to be in focus, the glass
marred. Choose this sky. It is
a chosen sky.

What lies
in the mound at Cascob?
The church built into the mound.

In the bell-tower
is in the mound.

Stand
in the cold earth with the tower around you
and spy out to the sanctuary
down to whatever lies dead there
under the tiny crimson
lamp of the live corpse of the god.

Later than all that
or at some other great remove
an old gentleman
takes his ease on a shooting-stick
by the playground on Wolstanton Marsh.

A sunny afternoon on the grass
and his cheeks are pink,
his teeth are made for a grin; happily
his arms wave free. The two stiff
women he has with him in trousers and anoraks
indicate him. They point
or incline towards him. One
moves a good way along the path, stretching a pattern.
The cars pass
within a yard of him. Even so,
he seems, on his invisible stick, to be sitting
on the far edge of the opposite pavement.
Numerous people
group and regroup as if coldly
on a coarse sheet of green.

Parked here, talking,
I'm pleasurably watchful
of the long
forces angled in.

The first farmyard I ever saw
was mostly midden
a collapse of black
with dung and straw swirls
where the drays swung
past the sagging barn.
Always silent. The house
averted, a poor ailanthus
by its high garden gate and
the lane along the hilltop
a tangle of watery ruts
that shone between holly hedges.
Through the gaps you could see
the ricks glowing yellow.

The other farm I had
was in an old picture book,
deep-tinted idyll with steam
threshers, laughing men,
Bruno the hound with his black muzzle,
and the World's Tabbiest Cat.

Describing Lloyd's farm now
moralises it; as the other
always was. But I swear
I saw them both then
in all their properties,
and to me, the difference was neutral.

As if from a chimney
the laws of the sky go floating
slowly above the trees.

And now the single creature
makes itself seen,
isolate,
is an apparition

Near Hartington
in a limestone defile
the barn owl
flaps from an ash
away through the mournful afternoon
misjudging its moment
its omen undelivered.

The hare
dodging towards the skyline at sunset
with a strange goodwill –
he'll do for you and me.

And *mormo maura*
the huge fusty Old Lady moth
rocking its way up
the outside of the dark pane
brandishing all its legs, its
antennae, whirring wings,
zigzagging upwards, impelled
to be seen coming in from the night.

Now I have come
through obduracy
discomfort and trouble
to recognise it

                              my life keeps
leaking out of my poetry to me
in all directions. It's untidy
ragged and bright
and it's not
used to things

mormo maura
asleep in the curtain
by day.

Scent on the body
inherent or applied
concentrates the mind
holds it from sidelong wandering.
Even when it repels
it pushes directly.

Streaks of life
awkward
showing among straw tussocks
in shallow flood.

Neither living nor saying
has ceremony or bound.

Now I have come
to recognise it, the alder
concentrates my mind
to the water
under its firm green.

Fetching up with
leaf-gloss against
the river-shine.

I want
to remark formally, indeed
stiffly, though not complaining,
that the place where I was raised
had no longer deference for water
and little of it showing. The Rea,

the city's first river,
meagre and under the streets;
and the Tame
wandering waste grounds,
always behind
some factory or fence.
Warstone Pool in the fields
I realised today was a stream dammed
to make way for the colliery.
Handsworth Park lake, again a dam
on the Saxon's
nameless trickle of a stream
under the church bluff. The brook
nearest home, no more than a mile,
ran straight out into the light
from under the cemetery;
and there the caddis-flies would case
themselves in wondrous grit.

I'm obsessed
with cambered tarmacs, concretes,
the washings of rain.

That there can come a sound
as cold as this across the world
on a black summer night,

the moths out there impermeable,
hooded in their crevices
covered in the sound of the rain
breaking from the eaves-gutters
choked with pine needles;
the slippery needles wash everywhere,
they block the down-spouts;
in the shallow pool on the porch roof,
arranged among dashed pine branches
and trails of needles,
I found two ringdove squabs
drowned and picked clean,
dried to black fins.

Fine edge
or deflection
of my feeling towards
anything that behaves or changes,
however slowly; like
my Bryophyllum *Good Luck*,
raised by me from a life-scrap and
now lurching static from its pot,
its leaves winged
with the mouse-ears of its young.
I'm vehemently and steadily
part of its life.

                  Or it slides
sideways and down, under my suspicion –
Now what's it doing?

Suddenly to distrust
the others' mode;
the others. Poinsettias or moths,
or Kenny and Leslie and Leonard,
Edie and Bernard and Dorothy,
the intake of '35; the story of the Wigan pisspot
of about that time, and even
Coleridge's of long before:

I have to set him
to fill it by candlelight
before he transfigures it;

with *mormo maura* the Old Lady moth
beating on the pane to come in.

The Dow Low Drop

When the far bank darkens
and the river starts to die
the nondescript
silently fights for its life

*

So out of what materials
shall we be making
our nothing?

*There had been
nothing made.* No
yet about it. No suggestion
something was bound
to come about; that nothing
could then have pictures done of it,
and very like. True nothing
needs hands to build its forms.

*There had been made
that which was nothing.*

So now out of what
materials. Something
harvested, woven, bleached. Or
harvested, pulped
bleached and pressed.

Or chosen for pallor in the ground,
quarried, sawn into straight
sheets, polished;

breathed, even, as a cloud from some
temperature manoeuvre. All
edged with particular tastes.

Is the Mother
back from the mine? White-eyed
out of the footrail, having all afternoon
given shape to certain débris,
certain chunks; having been
final on matters

that offered themselves in darkness
under the birch-scrub slope.

*

Made from whatever material, the blank
skin announces no show.

Empty time.

When it puckers and punctures it slits
straight-mouthed, behaves
as a reversed letter-slot. Almost
everything that tumbles out
is furniture and the like, lived with
but not digested: sideboard,
ironing tackle, things for the kitchen
that match, air-fresheners, seersucker
sheets, candlewick covers,
mugs that match, all
the colours of crispbread; oldish
damp towels, heaters, the mail;
the sweat and push
to sustain all that
through a winter that won't end.

*

Aphrodite from the sky
fallen in Asia
black,
ferried to the island, a sacred
lumpish cone,
smaller than women,

raises the dead and
walks them for a while
without explaining.

My schoolmate, D.,
forty-seven years hanged,
parks the same rented car
as mine directly beside it,
lopes into the courtyard, makes
for the cool museum hall

where she sits, the landlady,
hiked out of shrine-rubble
and dusted down.

He's aged
just as he had to: same
chicken-legged gait, in shorts;
same haircut, grey; grown
the only moustache he could have,
gained a small wife.
And he just might be by now
German or Danish.

He's quieter. A good
career in a science behind him
following a narrow squeak in youth.

I could greet him, dull idea,
if I didn't believe my knowledge.

Died at fifteen, in his delight,
alone in the house,
clothes-line over the banister,
mother's underwear – fine
calculation, could have been finer:
too much buzz. The censors of the day
comforted the boys with *suicide,
impatience, despair, tragedy*. Said
nothing about the underwear.

Hanging yourself's man's work.

     *

Go along and over the level last ridge of the Staffordshire mudstone above
Longnor, and the limestone starts up at you from the Dove, a ragged barricade
of tall crooked points and green humps. The turnpike dives, kinks to cross the
river by lost Soham. *Vasta est.* Far enough north to be harried. The manors
along the Dove wasted, then after King William's days of deep speech, listed.
Beyond the river the road heads up through the barrier, on the bed of the
vanished feeder stream that tapped and emptied the shallow sea's last lagoon.
On the rocks at the grassy lake floor's edge I'm living, in a house built as a
publican's retreat. And across the lake *The Waste Called Dowlamore* rises high
and quick to the first true edge of the limestone upland, the line that joins
Hind Low, Brier Low, Dow Low, Hoard Low. Illusion, the set tilted with its
bushes, walls and crossing cows, and cutting off at the sky where the National

24

Park stops dead also, fresh out of scenery. There's no backside to Dow Low. A straight cut, quarried down hundreds of feet to the floor below base level: the immense Abyss of Jobs. From the rim, a view over all the fields to the east, greened with their own dug lime, seethed in their mother's milk, cratered at Tunstead, Dove Holes, Topley Pike with more prints of New Eleusis.

*

On a day I could hardly be present
a group I guessed at
came to the ridge here again and opened the mound
laying there three rivets, a grooved bronze dagger,
flakes and a knife of flint, a piece of iron ore
and a bone pin. With these things and others
they placed my own dead body that I had

to be food for the journey
all rivets and the like must make.

Under the floor I could feel the deep
spindle of rock within the ridge of rock
narrowly holding us up for ever.

The whole ridge
went. The pillar went
as I went. The rivets, saved.

*

Take out the Commissioners' roads
the lead-rakes, poison-copses
cattle-meres, water-tables
sunk out through mine drains,
pick off the farmsteads and the long
cowshit slips on the tarmac,
all these drawn things. Fade
the inks, depopulate the sky
of everybody but headless light-legs
that stalk under the cloud. Shift it
around. Put it all back, naturally.

*

Cosmogony. That the Mother
vanished from the planet's hide and its surrounding
vapours hung with lights that decorate
and instruct. Went down
in the earth. Brought out of herself
the seemingly straight line, the right angle,
the working in metals, the grenade,
the brick. For all to consider. And
the rest of it, each year a fresh haul.
She provides. Herself in every part
immanent, her light in all of it:
a world of Town Halls with no fathers.

*

That voice you heard in the womb all that while
over your head and down through the ducting,
no matter what it happened to be saying,

stays with you till you die
no matter what you say with it.

*

Not only in desert cliffs,
rock-fares of affront,
cities of single rooms
piled along ravines,

but from afternoon shadows
and the crevices of seats by night
there's a wonderful
growl to be heard.

City

City

On one of the steep slopes that rise towards the centre of the city all the buildings have been destroyed within the past year: a whole district of the tall narrow houses that spilled around what were a hundred years ago outlying factories has gone. The streets remain, among the rough quadrilaterals of brick rubble, veering awkwardly towards one another through nothing; at night their rounded surfaces still shine under the irregularly-set gaslamps, and tonight they dully reflect also the yellowish flare, diffused and baleful, that hangs flat in the clouds a few hundred feet above the city's invisible heart. Occasional cars move cautiously across this waste, as if suspicious of the emptiness; there is little to separate the roadways from what lies between them. Their tail-lights vanish slowly into the blocks of surrounding buildings, maybe a quarter of a mile from the middle of the desolation.

And what is it that lies between these purposeless streets? There is not a whole brick, a foundation to stumble across, a drainpipe, a smashed fowlhouse; the entire place has been razed flat, dug over, and smoothed down again. The bald curve of the hillside shows quite clearly here, near its crown, where the brilliant road, stacked close on either side with warehouses and shops, runs out towards the west. Down below, the district that fills the hollow is impenetrably black. The streets there are so close and so twisted among their massive tenements that it is impossible to trace the line of a single one of them by its lights. The lamps that can be seen shine oddly, and at mysterious distances, as if they were in a marsh. Only the great flat-roofed factory shows clear by its bulk, stretching across three or four whole blocks just below the edge of the waste, with solid rows of lit windows.

Lullaby and Exhortation for the Unwilling Hero

A fish,
Firelight,
A watery ceiling:
Under the door
The drunk wind sleeps.

The bell in the river,
The loaf half eaten,
The coat of the sky.

A pear,
Perfume,
A white glade of curtains:
Out in the moonlight
The smoke reaches high.

The statue in the cellar,
The skirt on the chairback,
The throat of the street.

A shell,
Shadow,
A floor spread with silence:
Faint on the skylight
The fat moths beat.

The pearl in the stocking,
The coals left to die,
The bell in the river,
The loaf half eaten,
The coat of the sky.

The night slides like a thaw
And oil-drums bang together.

A frosted-glass door opening, then another.
Orange and blue *décor*.
The smoke that hugs the ceiling tastes of pepper.

What steps descend, what rails conduct?
Sodium bulbs equivocate,
And cowls of ventilators
With limewashed breath hint at the places
To which the void lift cages plunge or soar.

Prints on the landing walls
Are all gone blind with steam;
A voice under the floor
Swings a dull axe against a door.
The gaping office block of night
Shudders into the deep sky overhead:

Thrust down your foot in sleep
Among its depths. Do not respect
The janitors in bed,
The balustrades of iron bars,
The gusty stairwells; thrust it deep,
Into a concrete garage out of sight,
And rest among the cars
That, shut in filtered moonlight,
Sweat mercury and lead.

Subway trains, or winds of indigo,
Bang oil-drums in the yard for war:
Already, half-built towers
Over the bombed city
Show mouths that soon will speak no more,
Stoppered with the perfections of tomorrow.

You can lie women in your bed
With glass and mortar in their hair.
Pocket the key, and draw the curtains,
They'll not care.

Letters on a sweetshop window:
At last the rain slides them askew,
The foetus in the dustbin moves one claw.

And from the locomotive
That's halted on the viaduct
A last white rag of steam
Blows ghostly across the gardens.
When you wake, what will you do?
Under the floorboards of your dream
Gun barrels rolled in lint
Jockey the rooms this way and that.
Across the suburbs, squares of colour gleam:
Swaddled in pink and apricot,
The people are 'making love'.

Those are bright points that flicker
Softly, and vanish one by one.

Your telegraphic fingers mutter the world.
What will they reach for when your sleep is done?

The hiss of tyres along the gutter,
Odours of polish in the air;
A car sleeps in the neighbouring room,
A wardrobe by its radiator.

The rumbling canisters beat for you
Who are a room now altogether bare,
An open mouth pressed outwards against life,
Tasting the sleepers' breath,
The palms of hands, discarded shoes,
Lilac wood, the blade of a breadknife.

Before dawn in the sidings,
Over whose even tracks
Fat cooling towers caress the sky,
The rows of trucks
Extend: black, white,
White, grey, white, black,
Black, white, black, grey,
Marshalled like building blocks:
Women are never far away.

In the century that has passed since this city has become great, it has twice laid itself out in the shape of a wheel. The ghost of the older one still lies among the spokes of the new, those dozen highways that thread constricted ways through the inner suburbs, then thrust out, twice as wide, across the housing estates and into the countryside, dragging moraines of buildings with them. Sixty or seventy years ago there were other main roads, quite as important as these were then, but lying between their paths. By day they are simply alternatives, short cuts, lined solidly with parked cars and crammed with delivery vans. They look merely like side-streets, heartlessly overblown in some excess of Victorian expansion. By night, or on a Sunday, you can see them for what they are. They are still lit meagrely, and the long rows of houses, three and four storeys high, rear black above the lamps enclosing the road-ways, clamping them off from whatever surrounds them. From these pavements you can sometimes see the sky at night, not obscured as it is in most parts of the city by the greenish-blue haze of light that steams out of the mercury vapour lamps. These streets are not worth lighting. The houses have not been turned into shops – they are not villas either that might have become offices, but simply tall dwellings, opening straight off the street, with cavernous entries leading into back courts.

The people who live in them are mostly very old. Some have lived through three wars, some through only one; wars of newspapers, of mysterious sciences, of coercion, of disappearance. Wars that have come down the streets from the unknown city and the unknown world, like rainwater floods in the gutters. There are small shops at street corners, with blank rows of houses between them; and taverns carved only shallowly into the massive walls. When these people go into the town, the buses they travel in stop just before they reach it, in the sombre back streets behind the Town Hall and the great insurance offices.

These lost streets are decaying only very slowly. The impacted lives of their inhabitants, the meaninglessness of news, the dead black of the chimney breasts, the conviction that the wind itself comes only from the next street, all wedge together to keep destruction out; to deflect the eye of the developer. And when destruction comes, it is total: the printed notices on the walls, block by block, a few doors left open at night, broken windows advancing down a street until fallen slates appear on the pavement and are not kicked away. Then, after a few weeks of this, the machines arrive.

The Entertainment of War

I saw the garden where my aunt had died
And her two children and a woman from next door;
It was like a burst pod filled with clay.

A mile away in the night I had heard the bombs
Sing and then burst themselves between cramped houses
With bright soft flashes and sounds like banging doors;

The last of them crushed the four bodies into the ground,
Scattered the shelter, and blasted my uncle's corpse
Over the housetop and into the street beyond.

Now the garden lay stripped and stale; the iron shelter
Spread out its separate petals around a smooth clay saucer,
Small, and so tidy it seemed nobody had ever been there.

When I saw it, the house was blown clean by blast and care:
Relations had already torn out the new fireplaces;
My cousin's pencils lasted me several years.

And in his office notepad that was given me
I found solemn drawings in crayon of blondes without dresses.
In his lifetime I had not known him well.

Those were the things I noticed at ten years of age:
Those, and the four hearses outside our house,
The chocolate cakes, and my classmates' half-shocked envy.

But my grandfather went home from the mortuary
And for five years tried to share the noises in his skull,
Then he walked out and lay under a furze-bush to die.

When my father came back from identifying the daughter
He asked us to remind him of her mouth.
We tried. He said 'I think it was the one'.

These were marginal people I had met only rarely
And the end of the whole household meant that no grief was seen;
Never have people seemed so absent from their own deaths.

This bloody episode of four whom I could understand better dead
Gave me something I needed to keep a long story moving;
I had no pain of it; can find no scar even now.

But had my belief in the fiction not been thus buoyed up
I might, in the sigh and strike of the next night's bombs
Have realised a little what they meant, and for the first time been afraid.

North Area

Those whom I love avoid all mention of it,
Though certain gestures they've in common
Persuade me they know it well:
A place where I can never go.

No point in asking why, or why not.
I picture it, though –
There must be dunes with cement walks,
A twilight of aluminium
Among beach huts and weather-stained handrails;
Much glass to reflect the clouds;
And a glint of blood in the cat-ice that holds the rushes.

The edge of the city. A low hill with houses on one side and rough common land on the other, stretching down to where a dye-works lies along the valley road. Pithead gears thrust out above the hawthorn bushes; everywhere pre-fabricated workshops jut into the fields and the allotments. The society of singing birds and the society of mechanical hammers inhabit the world together, slightly ruffled and confined by each other's presence.

By the Pond

This is bitter enough: the pallid water
With yellow rushes crowding toward the shore,
That fishermen's shack.

The pit-mound's taut and staring wire fences,
The ashen sky. All these can serve as conscience.
For the rest, I'll live.

Brick-dust in sunlight. That is what I see now in the city, a dry epic flavour, whose air is human breath. A place of walls made straight with plumbline and trowel, to dessicate and crumble in the sun and smoke. Blistered paint on cisterns and girders, cracking to show the priming. Old men spit on the paving slabs, little boys urinate; and the sun dries it as it dries out patches of damp on plaster facings to leave misshapen stains. I look for things here that make old men and dead men seem young. Things which have escaped, the landscapes of many childhoods.

Wharves, the oldest parts of factories, tarred gable ends rearing to take the sun over lower roofs. Soot, sunlight, brick-dust; and the breath that tastes of them.

At the time when the great streets were thrust out along the old high-roads and trackways, the houses shouldering towards the country and the back streets filling in the widening spaces between them like webbed membranes, the power of will in the town was more open, less speciously democratic, than it is now. There were, of course, cottage railway stations, a jail that pretended to be a castle out of Grimm, public urinals surrounded by screens of cast-iron lacework painted green and scarlet; but there was also an arrogant ponderous architecture that dwarfed and terrified the people by its sheer size and functional brutality: the workhouses and the older hospitals, the thick-walled abattoir, the long vaulted market-halls, the striding canal bridges and railway viaducts. Brunel was welcome here. Compared with these structures the straight white blocks and concrete roadways of today are a fairground, a clear dream just before waking, the creation of salesmen rather than of engineers. The new city is bred out of a hard will, but as it appears, it shows itself a little ingratiating, a place of arcades, passages, easy ascents, good light. The eyes twinkle, beseech and veil themselves; the full, hard mouth, the broad jaw – these are no longer made visible to all.

A street half a mile long with no buildings, only a continuous embankment of sickly grass along one side, with railway signals on it, and strings of trucks through whose black-spoked wheels you can see the sky; and for the whole length of the other a curving wall of bluish brick, caked with soot and thirty feet high. In it, a few wicket gates painted ochre, and fingermarked, but never open. Cobbles in the roadway.

A hundred years ago this was almost the edge of town. The goods yards, the gasworks and the coal stores were established on tips and hillocks in the sparse fields that lay among the houses. Between this place and the centre, a mile or two up the hill, lay a continuous huddle of low streets and courts, filling the marshy valley of the meagre river that now flows under brick and tarmac. And this was as far as the railway came, at first. A great station was built, towering and stony. The sky above it was southerly. The stately approach, the long curves of wall, still remain, but the place is a goods depot with most of its doors barred and pots of geraniums at those windows that are not shuttered. You come upon it suddenly in its open prospect out of tangled streets of small factories. It draws light to itself, especially at sunset, standing still and smooth faced, looking westwards at the hill. I am not able to imagine the activity that must once have been here. I can see no ghosts of men and women, only the gigantic ghost of stone. They are too frightened of it to pull it down.

The Sun Hacks

The sun hacks at the slaughterhouse campanile,
And by the butchers' cars, packed tail-to-kerb,
Masks under white caps wake into human faces.

The river shudders as dawn drums on its culvert;
On the first bus nightworkers sleep, or stare
At hoardings that look out on yesterday.

The whale-back hill assumes its concrete city:
The white-flanked towers, the stillborn monuments;
The thousand golden offices, untenanted.

At night on the station platform, near a pile of baskets, a couple embraced, pressed close together and swaying a little. It was hard to see where the girl's feet and legs were. The suspicion this aroused soon caused her hands, apparently joined behind her lover's back, to become a small brown paper parcel under the arm of a stout engine-driver who leaned, probably drunk, against the baskets, his cap so far forward as almost to conceal his face. I could not banish the thought that what I had first seen was in fact his own androgynous fantasy, the self-sufficient core of his stupor. Such a romantic thing, so tender, for him to contain. He looked more comic and complaisant than the couple had done, and more likely to fall heavily to the floor.

A café with a frosted glass door through which much light is diffused. A tall young girl comes out and stands in front of it, her face and figure quite obscured by this milky radiance.

She treads out on to a lopsided ochre panel of lit pavement before the doorway and becomes visible as a coloured shape, moving sharply. A wrap of honey and ginger, a flared saffron skirt, grey-white shoes. She goes off past the Masonic Temple with a young man: he is pale, with dark hair and a shrunken, earnest face. You could imagine him a size larger. Just for a moment, as it happens, there is no one else in the street at all. Their significance escapes rapidly like a scent, before the footsteps vanish among the car engines.

A man in the police court. He looked dapper and poker-faced, his arms straight, the long fingers just touching the hem of his checked jacket. Four days after being released from the prison where he had served two years for theft he had been discovered at midnight clinging like a tree-shrew to the bars of a glass factory-roof. He made no attempt to explain his presence there; the luminous nerves that made him fly up to it were not visible in daylight, and the police seemed hardly able to believe this was the creature they had brought down in the darkness.

In this city the governing authority is limited and mean: so limited that it can do no more than preserve a superficial order. It supplies fuel, water and power. It removes a fair proportion of the refuse, cleans the streets after a fashion, and discourages fighting. With these things, and a few more of the same sort, it is content. This could never be a capital city for all its size. There is no mind in it, no regard. The sensitive, the tasteful, the fashionable, the intolerant and powerful, have not moved through it as they have moved through London, evaluating it, altering it deliberately, setting in motion wars of feeling about it. Most of it has never been seen.

In an afternoon of dazzling sunlight in the thronged streets, I saw at first no individuals but a composite monster, its unfeeling surfaces matted with dust: a mass of necks, limbs without extremities, trunks without heads; unformed stirrings and shovings spilling across the streets it had managed to get itself provided with.

Later, as the air cooled, flowing loosely about the buildings that stood starkly among the declining rays, the creature began to divide and multiply. At crossings I could see people made of straws, rags, cartons, the stuffing of burst cushions, kitchen refuse. Outside the Grand Hotel, a long-boned carrot-haired girl with glasses, loping along, and with strips of bright colour, rich, silky green and blue, in her soft clothes. For a person made of such scraps she was beautiful.

Faint blue light dropping down through the sparse leaves of the plane trees in the churchyard opposite after sundown, cooling and shaping heads, awakening eyes.

The Hill behind the Town

Sullen hot noon, a loop of wire,
With zinc light standing everywhere,
A glint on the chapels,
Glint on the chapels.

Under my heel a loop of wire
Dragged in the dust is earth's wide eye,
Unseen for days,
Unseen days.

Geranium-wattled, fenced in wire,
Caged white cockerels crowd near
And stretch red throats,
Stretch red throats;

Their cries tear grievous through taut wire,
Drowned in tanks of factory sirens
At sullen noon,
Sullen hot noon.

The day's on end; a loop of wire
Kicked from the dust's bleak daylight leaves
A blind white world,
Blind white world.

The Poplars

Where the road divides
Just out of town
By the wall beyond the filling-station
Four Lombardy poplars
Brush stiff against the moorland wind.

Clarity is in their tops
That no one can touch
Till they are felled,
Brushwood to cart away:

To know these tall pointers
I need to withdraw
From what is called my life
And from my net
Of achievable desires.

Why should their rude and permanent virginity
So capture me? Why should studying
These lacunae of possibility
Relax the iron templates of obligation
Leaving me simply Man?

All I have done, or can do
Is prisoned in its act:
I think I am afraid of becoming
A cemetery of performance.

Starting to Make a Tree

First we carried out the faggot of steel stakes; they varied in length, though most were taller than a man.

We slid one free of the bundle and drove it into the ground, first padding the top with rag, that the branch might not be injured with leaning on it.

Then we took turns to choose stakes of the length we wanted, and to feel for the distances between them. We gathered to thrust them firmly in.

There were twenty or thirty of them in all; and when they were in place we had, round the clearing we had left for the trunk, an irregular radial plantation of these props, each with its wad of white at the tip. It was to be an old, down-curving tree.

This was in keeping with the burnt, chemical blue of the soil, and the even hue of the sky which seemed to have been washed with a pale brownish smoke;

another clue was the flatness of the horizon on all sides except the north, where it was broken by the low slate or tarred shingle roofs of the houses, which stretched away from us for a mile or more.

This was the work of the morning. It was done with care, for we had no wish to make revisions;

we were, nonetheless, a little excited, and hindered the women at their cooking in our anxiety to know whose armpit and whose groin would help us most in the modelling of the bole, and the thrust of the boughs.

That done, we spent the early dusk of the afternoon gathering materials from the nearest houses; and there was plenty:

a great flock mattress; two carved chairs; cement; chicken-wire; tarpaulin; a smashed barrel; lead piping; leather of all kinds; and many small things.

In the evening we sat late, and discussed how we could best use them. Our tree was to be very beautiful.

Yet whenever I see that some of these people around me are bodily in love, I feel it is my own energy, my own hope, tension and sense of time in hand, that have gathered and vanished down that dark drain; it is I who am left, shivering and exhausted, to try and kick the lid back into place so that I can go on without the fear of being able to feel only vertically, like a blind wall, or thickly, like the tyres of a bus.

Lovers turn to me faces of innocence where I would expect wariness. They have disappeared for entire hours into the lit holes of life, instead of lying stunned on its surface as I, and so many, do for so long; or instead of raising their heads cautiously and scenting the manifold airs that blow through the streets.

The city asleep. In it there are shadows that are sulphurous, tanks of black bile. The glitter on the roadways is the deceptive ore that shines on coal.

The last buses have left the centre; the pallid faces of the crowd looked like pods, filled by a gusty summer that had come too late for plenty.

Silvered rails that guide pedestrians at street corners stand useless. Towards midnight, or at whatever hour the sky descends with its full iron weight, the ceilings drop lower everywhere; each light is partial, and proper only to its place. There is no longer any general light, only particular lights that overlap.

Out of the swarming thoroughfares, the night makes its own streets with a rake that drags persuaded people out of its way: streets where the bigger buildings have already swung themselves round to odd angles against the weakened currents of the traffic.

There are lamplit streets where the full darkness is only in the deep drains and in the closed eyesockets and shut throats of the old as they lie asleep; their breath moves red tunnel-lights.

The main roads hold their white-green lights with difficulty, like long, loaded boughs; when the machines stop moving down them their gradients reappear.

Journeys at night: sometimes grooves in a thick substance, sometimes raised weals on black skin.

The city at night has no eye, any more than it has by day, although you would expect to find one; and over much of it the sleep is aqueous and incomplete, like that of a hospital ward.

But to some extent it stops, drops and congeals. It could be broken like asphalt, and the men and women rolled out like sleeping maggots.

Once I wanted to prove the world was sick. Now I want to prove it healthy. The detection of sickness means that death has established itself as an element of the timetable; it has come within the range of the measurable. Where there is no time there is no sickness.

The Wind at Night

The suburb lies like a hand tonight,
A man's thick hand, so stubborn
No child or poet can move it.

The wind drives itself mad with messages,
Clattering train wheels over the roofs,
Collapsing streets of sound until
Far towers, daubed with swollen light,
Lunge closer to abuse it,

This suburb like a sleeping hand,
With helpless elms that shudder
Angry between its fingers,
Powerless to disprove it.

And, although the wind derides
The spaces of this stupid quarter,
And sets the time of night on edge,
It mocks the hand, but cannot lose it:

This stillness keeps us in the flesh,
For us to use it.

I stare into the dark; and see a window, a large sash window of four panes, such as might be found in the living-room of any fair-sized old house. Its curtains are drawn back and it looks out on to a small damp garden, narrow close at hand where the kitchen and outhouses lead back, and then almost square. Privet and box surround it, and the flowerbeds are empty save for a few laurels or rhododendrons, some leafless rose shrubs and a giant yucca. It is a December afternoon, and it is raining. Not far from the window is a black marble statue of a long-haired, long-bearded old man. His robes are conventionally archaic, and he sits, easily enough, on what seems a pile of small boulders, staring intently and with a look of great intelligence towards the patch of wall just under the kitchen window. The statue looks grimy, but its exposed surfaces are highly polished by the rain, so that the nose and the cheek-bones stand out strongly in the gloom. It is rather smaller than life-size. It is clearly not in its proper place: resting as it does across the moss of the raised border, it is appreciably tilted forward and to one side, almost as if it had been abandoned as too heavy by those who were trying to move it – either in or out.

Walking through the suburb at night, as I pass the dentist's house I hear a clock chime a quarter, a desolate brassy sound. I know where it stands, on the mantelpiece in the still surgery. The chime falls back into the house, and beyond it, without end. Peace.

I sense the simple nakedness of these tiers of sleeping men and women beneath whose windows I pass. I imagine it in its own setting, a mean bathroom in a house no longer new, a bathroom with plank panelling, painted a peculiar shade of green by an amateur, and badly preserved. It is full of steam, so much as to obscure the yellow light and hide the high, patched ceiling. In this dream, standing quiet, the private image of the householder or his wife, damp and clean.

I see this as it might be floating in the dark, as if the twinkling point of a distant street-lamp had blown in closer, swelling and softening to a foggy oval. I can call up a series of such glimpses that need have no end, for they are all the bodies of strangers. Some are deformed or diseased, some are ashamed, but the peace of humility and weakness is there in them all.

I have often felt myself to be vicious, in living so much by the eye, yet among so many people. I can be afraid that the egg of light through which I see these bodies might present itself as a keyhole. Yet I can find no sadism in the way I see them now. They are warm-fleshed, yet their shapes have the minuscule, remote morality of some mediaeval woodcut of the Expulsion: an eternally startled Adam, a permanently bemused Eve. I see them as homunculi, moving privately each in a softly lit fruit in a nocturnal tree. I can consider without scorn or envy the well-found bedrooms I pass, walnut and rose-pink, altars of tidy, dark-haired women, bare-backed, wifely. Even in these I can see order.

I come quite often now upon a sort of ecstasy, a rag of light blowing among the things I know, making me feel I am not the one for whom it was intended, that I have inadvertently been looking through another's eyes and have seen what I cannot receive.

I want to believe I live in a single world. That is why I am keeping my eyes at home while I can. The light keeps on separating the world like a table knife: it sweeps across what I see and suggests what I do not. The imaginary comes to me with as much force as the real, the remembered with as much force as the immediate. The countries on the map divide and pile up like ice-floes: what is strange is that I feel no stress, no grating discomfort among the confusion, no loss; only a belief that I should not be here. I see the iron fences and the shallow ditches of the countryside the mild wind has travelled over. I cannot enter that countryside; nor can I escape it. I cannot join together the mild wind and the shallow ditches, I cannot lay the light across the world and then watch it slide away. Each thought is at once translucent and icily capricious. A polytheism without gods.

The Park

If you should go there on such a day –
The red sun disappearing,
Netted behind black sycamores;

If you should go there on such a day –
The sky drawn thin with frost,
Its cloud-rims bright and bitter –

If you should go there on such a day,
Maybe the old goose will chase you away.

If you should go there to see
The shallow concrete lake,
Scummed over, fouled with paper;

If you should go there to see
The grass plots, featureless,
Muddy, and bruised, and balding –

If you should go there to see,
Maybe the old goose will scare you as he scared me,

Waddling fast on his diseased feet,
His orange bill thrust out,
His eyes indignant;

Waddling fast on his diseased feet,
His once ornamental feathers
Baggy, and smeared with winter –

Waddling fast on his diseased feet,
The old goose will one day reach death; and be unfit to eat.

And when the goose is dead, then we
Can say we're able, at last,
No longer hindered from going;

And when the goose is dead, then we
Have the chance, if we still want it,
To wander the park at leisure;

– Oh, when excuse is dead, then we
Must visit there, most diligently.

Hallucinations

1

When I think back to the yard of the tombstone maker that used to be on the corner of the lane by the laundry, it seems occupied by strange new arrivals. Four things. Greyish-white, corpse-colour. Indeed, the most arresting of them is the figure of a woman, quite nude, lying stiffly on her side on the gravel between the polished headstones, looking as if she had been tipped there after the limbs had grown rigid. The others are: what appears to be an albino raven lying similarly, with folded wings; a neat pile of coke ash and clinker; and a man's cotton singlet, clean but frayed into holes at the hem. This vest is as such a garment might be, soft and light; the wind flutters it where it lies draped. The ashes too are visibly loose and of a natural texture, though somewhat bleached. But the woman and the bird seem stony hard, like waxworks or petrified things.

The woman is tall and lean, not beautiful. A flat narrow belly, breasts that are hardly noticeable; a stringy, athletic physique. The shoulders are high and square, the face supercilious and a little mean, with a nose that curves strongly over a long upper lip and a poor chin. There is no expression and the eyes are shut as in an unguarded sleep. The hair, quite fair and straight, is fastened close to the head in a kind of plait, such as sternly-reared little girls might wear. It is a body that has been put under strain by the will.

The bird – I do not know so much about birds: it may be a jackdaw, not a raven. It is quite large, with ragged feathers and knobbly claws. But it has a great smoothness and dignity in its lack of colour: the beak and eyes are lightly closed and the head inclined a little forward. This is the least welcome of the four.

The ashes make a roughly conical pile six or eight inches high. They seem to be the product of an unusual heat. Some marble chippings have got in amongst them, and there are faint gleams from streaks of fused metal.

As for the vest, it is exactly the sort of undergarment I have worn in winter through most of my life; though it is clearly of a small size. Cheap in the first place, and now obviously worn to a state where it would be too thin for warmth and too ragged for comfort.

*

The albino raven is unlike any of the birds that live round the town. Yet this petrified freak is the bird of my city, my bird for this place. It would not have come to me anywhere else.

46

The city could have produced it from within itself: it is spacious enough, it has enough secrets. There are suburbs I have never properly visited, or have never managed to find recognisable as I passed through them, districts that melt into one another without climax. In one of these, in a side road out of a side road, this bird might have been bred and manufactured, in a large shed running the whole length of a garden that is cut off by the high wall of an old timberyard or repair shop. By whom? A small family business in the last stages of decay: the father, sixty, short and quick, with baggy overalls, a scrawny mobile neck, a small round head with stiff grey hair brushed upwards even at the back, and little fat lips. The son, nearly thirty, just married; taller than the father, but similar, with a weaker neck and hollower cheeks. His hair is fair, like the brows and lashes of his singularly puffy eyes. The uncle, in his fifties, and unmarried, is crablike and stout, with a lined reddish face and very dark hair, quite wavy.

It is possible they supply pet-shops; or maybe they make garden ornaments of cement or creosoted logs, bird-tables, rustic seats, gnomes, rabbits, toadstools. In some crisis or exultation, or exhaustion, lost for a while to the sense of the world, they have produced my bird without realising it.

What is it? Napoleon. Goethe. A stillborn ruler. Cold, large-headed, enormously wise, completely immobile.

It is important that it was born through these people, or through me, without any sort of Annunciation. If it could have been foreseen it would not have been real. It is unwelcome in the same way that tea-leaves in a cup are unwelcome: it has a similar flavour of bitterness, origin and command. I resent its inscrutability, the suspicion I have that it may be worthless, the doubts I have about whether it is moral or sensual. It reveals no taste whatsoever. In that, certainly, it is like a part of the natural world. I thought at first that it was so obviously literary, so hoarily embedded in symbolism, that I could account it an aberration and so dismiss it, but its urbane banality is clearly something I must have been desiring. With the other three things only I should have been too comfortable, and too lonely: a woman, a heap of ashes, a vest – I could have been a Crusoe within myself. Slowly this bird and I are working on each other. The only rule in our game is that neither of us must appear to change.

2

An orderly underground bar full of men, towards closing time. If I close my eyes, I move from a small, brightly lit room of brown wood and red leather into the crazy caverns of a body. Into a world of spaciousness, and of deep sound that comes in many dimensions. No sight, except a sense of epic underground light on my eyelids. Then odours come, and I am fetched off into memory: memories not of actual things but of imagined ones; or at times I feel that what I am imagining is masquerading as memory. Great wakefulness and pleasure of the senses.

I see beasts trundling along among railway wagons in the fog, with coloured lamps in their heads. A furnace door opens and a blast of voices comes out with the glare. There are gantries and jibs that climb up among one another's girders, threaded with globular lights that glow, bobbing, in the dusk.

I feel my fingers numb. My mind tunes itself approximately to a pitch-level and hears certain sliding sequences of tones, rising and falling seconds, eddying gradually up and down like drunken songs, as the various speaking voices in the room strike the tones in passing. The sequences of voices have a pattern, a long shallow curve, shaped like the arc of a gong. Over the top of this hollow copper music a sudden whistle hops up and down like a paper bird.

I have no sense of walls. The limit of the world is smoke, rolling in the distance.

A Furnace

to the memory of
John Cowper Powys
(1872–1963)

Introtroit

12 November 1958

November light low and strong
crossing from the left
finds this archaic
trolleybus, touches the side of it up
into solid yellow and green.

This light is without
rarity, it is an oil,
amber and clear that binds in
this alone and suggests
no other. It is a pressing
medium, steady to a purpose.

And in the sun's ray through the glass
lifting towards low noon, I
am bound;
            boots on the alloy
fenders that edge the deck,
lost out of the day
between two working calls
and planted alone
above the driver's head.
High over the roadway
I'm being swung out
into an unknown crosswise
route to a connection
at the Fighting Cocks
by way of Ettingshall;

old industrial road,
buildings to my left along the flat
wastes between townships
wrapped in the luminous

haze underneath the sun,
their forms cut clear and combined
into the mysteries, their surfaces
soft beyond recognition;
and as if I was made
to be the knifeblade, the light-divider,
to my right the brilliance strikes out perpetually
into the brick house-fields towards Wolverhampton,

their calculable distances
shallow with detail.

*

What is it, this
sensation as of freedom? Tang of
town gas, sulphur, tar,
settled among the heavy
separate houses behind
roadside planes, pale, patch-barked
and almost bare,
the last wide stiffened leaves
in tremor across their shadows
with trolley-standards of green cast iron
reared among them, the catenaries
stretching a net just over my guided head,
its roof of yellow metal.

A deserted, sun-battered theatre
under a tearing sky
is energy, its date 19□02
spread across its face, mark of
anomaly. And the road
from Bilston to Ettingshall begins
beating in. Whatever
approaches my passive taking-in,
then surrounds me and goes by
will have itself understood only
phase upon phase
by separate involuntary
strokes of my mind, dark
swings of a fan-blade
that keeps a time of its own,
made up from the long
discrete moments
of the stages of the street,
each bred off the last as if by
causality.
                    Because
of the brick theatre struck to the roadside
the shops in the next
street run in a curve, and
because of that there is raised up
with red lead on its girders
a gasworks
close beyond the roofs,

and because of the fold of the
folding in of these three to me
there comes a frame tower with gaps
in its corrugated cladding
and punched out of the sheets high
under its gable
a message in dark empty holes, USE GAS.

*

Something's decided
to narrate
in more dimensions than I can know
the gathering in
and giving out of the world on a slow
pulse, on a metered contraction
that the senses enquire towards
but may not themselves
intercept. All I can tell it by
is the passing trace of it
in a patterned agitation of

a surface that shows only
metaphors. Riddles. Resemblances
that have me in the chute
as it meshes in closer, many modes
funnelling fast through one event,
the flow-through so
dense with association
that its colour comes up, dark
brownish green, soaked and
decomposing leaves
in a liquor.

*

And the biggest of all the apparitions,
the great iron
thing, the ironworks,
reared up on end into the bright
haze, makes quiet burning
if anything at all.

When the pulse-beat for it comes
it is revealed, set
back a little way, arrested,
inward, grotesque, prepared for.

53

Then gone by,
with the shallowing of the road
and the pulse's falling away
cleanly through a few more
frames of buildings, noise,
a works gate with cyclists;
the passing of it quite final, not a tremor
of the prospect at the crossroads;
open light, green paint on a sign,
the trolley wires
chattering and humming from somewhere else.

I Calling

Waiting in blood. Get out of the pit.
That is the sign for parting. Already
the world could be leaving us.

      *

Ancient
face-fragments of holy saints
in fused glass, blood-red and blue,
scream and stare and whistle
from where they're cobbled
into a small
new window beside the Dee;
trapped and raving
they pierce the church wall
with acids, glances of fire and lenses out of the light
that wanders under the trees and around
the domed grave-cover
lichened the colour of a duck's egg.

A pick-handle or a boot
long ago freed them
to do these things;
or what was
flung as a stone,
having come slowly on
out of a cloudiness in the sea.

      *

Late at night
as the house across the street
stands rigid to the wind
and the lamp on its concrete column plays

static light on to it
everything writhes
through the unstable overgrown philadelphus
covering the whole end wall, its small heart-leaves
flickering into currents that
rock across the wall diagonally upward
and vanish, pursued, white
blossom-packs plucked at hard
and the tall stems
swirled to and fro, awkward
in the floods of expression.

A year or two past the gale
I walk out of the same door
on a night when I have
no depth. Neither
does the opposed house,

the great bush,
glory of the wall, sawn back
for harbouring insurrection and ghosts.
Now nothing
the whole height of the brickwork
to intercept expression.

– You'll know this ten-yard stretch
of suburban tarmac, where something
shakes at you; this
junction-place of back lanes, rutted gullies
with half a car
bedded in half a garage,
this sudden fence-post that breaks step;

the street, the chemist's shop, the lamp;

a stain in the plaster that so
resembles – and that body of air
caught between the ceiling
and the cupboard-top, that's like
nothing that ever was.

*

A tune
is already a metaphor
and a chord
a metaphor wherein
metaphors meet.

*

Wastes of distant darkness
and a different wind
out of the pit
blasts over a desolate
village on the outskirts
after midnight. Driving fast
on peripheral roads
so as to be repeatedly elsewhere
I pick up out of the blackness
waving torches, ahead and
over to one side.

And they are white, and lilac,
lemonade, crimson, magenta,
dull green;

festive little bulbs
strung between poles, left out
to buck and flail, rattling
all night,
            receding as I go,
the last lights,
the only lights.
The sign they make as I pass
is ineluctable
disquiet. Askew. The sign, once there,
bobbing in the world,
rides over intention, something
let through in error.

*

Sudden and grotesque
callings. Grown man
without right learning; by nobody
guided to the places; not knowing
what might speak; having eased awkwardly
into the way of being called.

*

In the places,
on their own account, not
for anybody's comfort:
gigantic peace.

Iron walls
tarred black, and discoloured,
towering in the sunlight
of a Sunday morning on
Saltley Viaduct.

Arcanum. Forbidden
open space, marked out with
tramlines in great curves among blue
Rowley Rag paving bricks.

Harsh reek in the air
among the monstrous squat
cylinders puts it
beyond doubt. Not a place
for stopping and spying.

The single human refuge
a roadside urinal, rectangular
roofless sarcophagus of tile and brick,
topped round with spikes and
open to the sky.

*

The few moments in the year when the quadruped
rears on its hindlegs to mount,
foreparts and head
disconnected, hooves dangling,
the horned head visibly not itself;
but something.

*

Waiting in blood.
The sign for parting. The straight way forward
checks, turns back
and sees it has passed through,
some distance back and without knowing it,
the wonderful carcass,
figurehead or spread
portal it was walking,
walking to be within;

showing from a little distance now its
unspeakable girdering, waste cavities,
defenceless structures in collapse; grey
blight of demolition without removal,
pitiable and horrific;

the look that came forward and through
and lit the way in.

*

Gradbach Hill, long hog's back
stretching down west among taller hills
to the meeting of Dane river
with the Black Brook skirting its steeper side,
the waters joining
by Castor's Bridge, where the bloomery
used to smoke up into the woods
under the green chapel;
the hill,
stretching down west from Goldsitch
a mile from my side yard, shale measures
on its back and the low black spoilheaps
still in the fields,
darkens to an October sunset
as if it were a coal,
the sun sinking into Cheshire, the light
welling up slow along the hillside,
leaving the Black Brook woods
chill, but striking for a while
fire meadows out of red-brown soft-rush,
the dark base, the hollows, the rim swiftly
blackening and crusting over.

II The Return

Whatever breaks
from stasis, radiance or dark
impending, and slides
directly and fast on its way, twisting
aspect in the torsions of the flow
this way and that,
                    then suddenly

over,
     through a single
glance of another force touching it or
bursting out of it sidelong,

doing so
fetches the timeless flux
that cannot help but practise
materialisation,
the coming into sense,
to the guesswork of the senses,
the way in cold air
ice-crystals, guessed at, come densely
falling from where they were not;

and it fetches
timeless identities
riding in the flux with no
determined form, cast out of the bodies
that once they were, or out of
the brains that bore them;

but trapped into water-drops,
windows they glanced through
or had their images
detained by and reflected
or into whose molten glass the coloured oxides
burned their qualities;

like dark-finned fish embedded in ice
they have life in them that can be revived.

                    *

There is ancient
and there is seeming ancient;
new, and seeming new –
venerable cancer, old as the race,
but so made as to bear
nothing but urgencies –

there is persuading the world's
layers apart with means
that perpetually alter and annex,
and show by the day what they can;

but still, with hardly a change to it,
the other dream or intention: of encoding
something perennial
and entering Nature thereby.

The masque for that
comes in its own best time
but in my place.

Bladelike and eternal, clear,
the entry into Nature
is depicted by
the vanishing of a gentleman
in black, and in portraiture,
being maybe a Doctor John
Dee, or Donne, or Hofmannsthal's
Lord Chandos,
               he having lately walked
through a door in the air
among the tall
buildings of the Northern Aluminium Company
and become inseparable
from all other things, no longer
capable of being imagined
apart from them, nor yet of being
forgotten in his identity.

All of that is enacted
at the far top
of the field I was born in,

long slope of scrub, then pasture,
still blank on the map three hundred years
after the walkings of all such gentlemen
out of the air

then suddenly printed across with
this century, new, a single
passage of the roller
dealing out streets of terraces
that map like ratchet-strips, their gables
gazing in ranks above the gardens
at a factory sportsground,
a water-tower for steam-cranes, more
worksheds, and,
               hulking along a bank
for a sunset peristyle, the long dark
tunnel-top roof of a football stadium.

All so mild, so late
in that particular change;
still seeming new.
                    Some of it,
my streets – Kentish Road,
Belmont, Paddington, Malvern –
just now caught up and lacquered
as Urban Renewal, halted
in the act of tilting to break up
and follow the foundries out
and the stamping mills,
the heavy stuff; short lives, all of them.

But still through that place
to enter Nature; it was possible,
it was imperative.

Something always
coming out, back against the flow,
against the drive to be in,
                              close to the radio,
the school, the government's wars;

the sunlight, old and still,
heavy on dry garden soil,

and nameless mouths,
events without histories, voices,
animist, polytheist, metaphoric,
coming through;

the sense of another world
not past, but primordial,
everything in it
simultaneous, and moving
every way but forward.

Massive in the sunlight, the old woman
dressed almost all in black, sitting out
on a low backyard wall,
rough hands splayed on her sacking apron
with a purseful of change in the pocket,
black headscarf tight across the brow, black
cardigan and rough skirt, thick stockings,
black shoes worn down;
                         this peasant
is English, city born; it's the last

quarter of the twentieth century
up an entryway
in Perry Barr, Birmingham, and there's
mint sprouting in an old
chimneypot. No imaginable
beginning to her epoch, and she's
ignored its end.

        *

Timeless identities,
seeming long
like the one they called Achilles,
or short, like William Fisher,
age ten years, occupation, jeweller,
living in 1861 down Great King Street
in a household
headed by his grandmother, my ancestress
Ann Mason, fifty-seven, widow,
occupation, mangler; come in
from Hornton, back of Edge Hill,
where the masons were quarrying for Christminster.

        *

These identities, recorded by authority
to be miniaturised; to be traceable
however small; to be material;
to have status in the record;
to have the rest,
the unwritten,
even more easily scrapped.

        *

Mind
and language
and mind out of language again, and
language again and for ever

fall slack and pat
by defect of nature
into antinomies. Unless

thrown. And again
and repeatedly thrown
to break down the devil

his spirit; to pull down
the devil his grammar school,
wherein the brain
submits to be
cloven, up,
sideways and down
in all of its pathways;

where to convert
one term to its antithesis
requires that there be devised
an agent with authority –

and they're in. That's it. Who
shall own death? Spoken for,
and Lazarus the test case. Only Almighty
God could work that trick. Accept
that the dead have gone away to God through
portals sculpted in brass to deter,
horrific. The signs of it, passably
offensive in a cat or a herring,
in a man are made out
unthinkably appalling: *vide*
M. Valdemar's selfless
demonstration; drawn back and forth,
triumphantly racked in a passage without
extent, province of the agent,
between antithesis and thesis.

Sale and Lease-back. Perennial
wheeze. In the body's exuberance
steal it, whatever it is, sell it back again,
buy it in, cheap,
put it out to rent. If it's freedom, graciously
grant it,
          asking in return no more than
war service, wage-labour, taxes,
custodial schooling, a stitched-up
franchise. Trade
town futures for fields,
railroad food in, sell it on the streets.

And as if it were a military installation
specialise and classify and hide
the life of the dead.

        *

63

Under that thunderous
humbug they've been persistently
coming and going, by way of
the pass-and-return valve between the worlds,
not strenuous; ghosts
innocent of time, none the worse
for their adventure, nor any better;

that you are dead
turns in the dark of your spiral,
comes close in the first hours after birth,
recedes and recurs often. Nobody
need sell you a death.

                    *

The ghosts' grown children
mill all day in the Public Search Office
burrowing out names for their own bodies, finding
characters with certificates but no
stories. Genetic behaviour,
scrabbling, feeling back across the spade-cut
for something; the back-flow of the genes'
forward compulsion suddenly
showing broken, leaking out, distressed.

                    *

They come anyway
to the trench,
the dead in their surprise,
taking whatever form they can
to push across. They've no news.
They infest the brickwork. Kentish Road
almost as soon as it's run up
out in the field, gets propelled
to the trench, the soot still fresh on it,

and the first few dozen faces
take the impress, promiscuously
with door and window arches;
Birmingham voices in the entryways
lay the law down. My surprise
stares into the walls.

III Authorities

If only the night can be supposed
unnaturally tall, spectrally
empty, and ready to disgorge
hidden authorities,
summonses, clarifications;

if it can be accorded pomp
to stretch this Grecian office-block
further up into the darkness, lamplit
all the way from the closed shopfronts
and growing heavier; then

that weight of attribution
jolts the entire thing down, partway
through its foundations, one corner heaving
into this panelled basement
where by the bar
the light spreads roseate and dusty.

If all that, then this,
ceiling sagged, drunk eyes
doing the things they do,
stands to be one of the several
cysts of the knowledge, distributed
unevenly through the middle of the mass;
if not, then not.

Brummagem conjuration
for the late Fifties. Not many
hypotheses in play then, even with the great
crust of brick and tarmac finally
starting to split and break up,
the dead weight of the old imperious
racket thrashing on
across its own canted-up wreckage.

Hard to be there, the place
unable to understand
even its own Whig history
for what it was; teachers
trained not to understand it
taught it, and it never fitted. Even less
did the history of the class struggle
reach down or along to the working-

class streets where work and wages
hid, as the most real shame.
                              – Don't
ask your little friend
what his father does;
don't let on we've found out
his mother goes to work;
don't tell anyone at all
what your father's job is.
If the teacher asks you
say you don't know.
                           Hard
to be still there. In the razings
and ripping of the slopes, the draining
away of districts, a quick irregular
stink of its creation coming through,
venerable, strong and foul.

                    *

Drawn to the places
by their oddness;
guided by nobody
to the subterranean
pea-green cafés,
the cafés in the style of lit
drains, the long plunging
high-walled walkway down
beside the railway viaduct
into moments that would
realign the powers if they could only
be distended;

sent by nobody,
meeting nobody
but the town gods.

The town gods are parodic,
innocent. They've not
created anything. Denizens.
Personages who keep strange hours,
who manifest
but are for the most part mute,

being appearances,
ringed eyes,
ikons designed to stare out

at the ikon-watcher, the studious
artisan walking in wait
at strange hours for the guard
to drop. Haunted
voyeur.

What could they ever say?
Wrecked people
with solitary trajectories,
sometimes rich clothing,
moving against the street currents
or lit from above, standing in bars;
always around the places
where the whores in the afternoon
radiate affront.

        If this were art
these beings could be
painted into the walls and released
from their patrolling.

       *

In the hierarchies, however disordered,
it would be warlords, kings and those
with the strength to usurp who went, clean,
to the disreputable, undeniable oracle
to have their own thoughts
twisted back in through their ears in style;

in the civilisation of novels,
the fields racked hard
to shake people off into suburbs
quiescent with masterless men
in their generations, it would be
pacifist mystics, self-chosen,
who would be driven by private
obsessions to go looking
among slurries and night-holes
for what might be accidentally
there, though not instituted; having to be
each his own charlatan.

       *

Grotesquely called,
grotesquely going in, fools

persisting in their folly,
all isolates, supposing
differently, finding differently: priests'
sons with dishevelled wits, teachers
with passed-on clothes and a little Homer,

a little Wordsworth, two or three
generations of Symbolist poets; compelled
by parody to insist
that what image the unnatural
law had been stamping
was moving into Nature,
and, once there,
could not but have its
orifices of question.

         *

Sadist-voyeur,
stalled and stricken, fallen
into that way from the conviction of
not doing but
only looking;

nothing to be shot for,
forcibly drugged or even
set about in the free market
and kicked insensible;
invitations to conform, assumptions
of healing, animal sanity, left
to women's initiatives
in the style of the time; teachers
with slipped-off clothes, drawing back
the candlewick covers of the time,
jerking artistically,
letting faith pace observation.

         *

If this were sanity and
sanity were art, this morning street
outside the old music shop would be
robustly done. Portrayal of the common
people and their commonplace bosses
with classless nostalgia. Courbet
transfigured into every substance of it;
every sensation that surrounds,

passes or emanates
entering the world in the manner of
telling or seeing; with no need
to be lifted by art out of
the nondescript general case because never
for a second inhabiting it; detectable
identities, of gear-shifts, stumblings, jackets,
coming through unimpeded.

*

Birmingham voice
hollow under the dark
arch of the entryway,

by slow torsion wrenched
out of her empty jaw, sunk
hole of lips; no way it could be
understood or answered.

The nearest people. Neighbour-fear
for the children, nine
inches of brick away
year after year from the beginning;

barren couple, the man desperate,
irascible, the woman
namelessly sick, tottering
in extremis for years, bald, spectral,
skin sunk from sallow
to sooty brown, wide eyes set
straight ahead, yellowing,
walking dead. Early

learning. And the dog,
dung-coloured whirl of hatred
too quick for a shape, never still,
slavering and shouting
to hurl itself against the garden
palings repeatedly. A welcome
for my first free steps among the flowers.
Slow-dying woman,
her life was primordial and total,
the gaze-back of the ikon; her death
modern and nothing, a weekend in the Cold War.
The dog must have brained itself.

Had the three of them been art, it would all have
been beaten pewter, dulling
in low relief,
              or the grey
sculpture-gibbet of an *enclos paroissial*,
exemplary figures of misery hobbled
to a god bent on confusion,
mercilessly modelled,
glistening when rained on.

His widowhood
was modern and quiet, his death
art: upright in his armchair in the daylight,
facing the door, his eyes
oddly narrowed and suspicious, just
as they were in his life.
He was silvered. It was done.

            *

Once invented, the big city
believed it had a brain; Joe
Chamberlain's sense of the corporate
signalling to itself with millions of disposable
identity-cells, summary and tagged.

Right under all that, the whole
construction continued to seethe
and divide itself by natural law; not

into its tributary villages again,
but winning back Dogpool,
Nechells, Adderley Park and the rest

in the cause of a headless
relativity of zones, perceptible
by the perceiver, linked by back roads,

unstable, dividing, grouping again
differently; giving the slip to being
counted, mapped or ever recognised
by more than one head at a time.

Vigilant dreaming head
in search of a place to lay itself.

IV Core

Dead acoustic.

Dead space.

Chamber with no echo
sits at the core, its place
plotted by every force. Within,
a dead fall.

Grave-goods that have motion
have it on their own account,
respond to nothing.
The chamber whose location knots
an entire symmetry
uses none.

Heterogeneous,
disposed without rhythm,
climax, idiom or generic law,

grave goods send word back out.

                    *

That sky-trails may merge with earth-trails,
the material spirits
moving in rock as in air,

it's down by just a step or two
into the earth, mounded above at the sky,

and the floor obliquely
tilting a little
to the upper world again.

We're carving the double spiral
into this stone; don't
complicate or deflect us.
We know what we're at.

We're letting the sun perceive
we've got the hang of it.

Write sky-laws into the rocks; draw
the laws of light into it and through it.

On the door under the ground
have them face inwards
into what might otherwise seem dark.

*

Inside a total stillness
as if inside the world but nowhere
continuous with it,

a warehouse with blocked
windows, brickwork and staging
done matt black
and cleverly lit to resemble
a warehouse
put to night uses;

suspended in there, moving
only on its own account,
the image, *deus mortuus*,
death chuckling along in its life,
uncanny demonstration, one edge
of clowning, charlatan,
the other huskily
brushing against nothing,

in the outermost arm of the spiral,
where it disintegrates,
gives itself up, racing
to flake away,

he is once again passing
close to his birth; Hawkins
on his last go-round,

declining solids, genially
breaking apart, brown man
with papery skin
almost as grey as his
beard and long hair,
the look of a hundred winters
down on his shrunk shoulders

that shake with a mysterious
mutter and chuckle across the mouthpiece,
private, bright-eyed, hung
light in his jacket, shuffling
on wrecked legs,
the old
bellow, the tight leathery sound
shredded, dispersed,

the form of a great force
heard as a monstrously amplified
column of breath, with
scribbles of music across it.

*

Without motion, or sign of motion,
or any history of it,
a polished black basalt
pyramid, household size.

Reflective hornblende faces, wedges
that seem ageless but not old;

here flown as fugitive
from all exegesis.

*

Peachy light
of a misty late afternoon
strokes, with some difficulty
for all they're above ground, the bared
cheekbones of certain villagers;

has to get round
the bulk of St Fiacre
and through the tall open stone-framed
window-spaces of the modest lean-to
ossuary by the wall;

and has to
pick them out in there
from among shovels, vases,
wheelbarrows, watering-cans;
and go in to them by
their personal windows.

They're on a shelf,
the last half-dozen or so,
up out of the way,

housed in a style
between hatbox and kennel,
tin, or matchwood, painted
black, painted pale green,

skull-patterned,
lettered, *Chef de M.* ——,
Chef de Mlle.——, and dated. First
quarter, twentieth century.

        *

Over on Barnenez headland
the long stepped cairn
heavily drawn
across the skyline
has itself seen to be on watch,

powerfully charged
with the persons of certain
translated energies,

the wall of masonry courses
spiked with them, passages,
a bank of ovens in a tilery,
their dispositions
by no means symmetrical;

their buried radiance
variable, heavily shielded,
constantly active; of fearsomely
uncertain mood and
inescapable location.

v Colossus

The scheme
of Adolphe Sax

that there should be
a giant presence in the sky

rearing above Paris,
slung between four
towers taller than Notre Dame;

blaring into the rain,
a vast steam organ
in the style of the technology and the time,
its truck-sized player-cylinders fed to it
by locomotives;
                  all found in the heart
and its logic, just as Piranesi found
what was appalling but unbuilt.

Le Notre, L'Enfant
surfaced closer to the possible.
Paris was spared
the sight of the colossus
rising in a forest of sticks, the way
sections of Liberty in the foundry-yard
towered behind the houses,

and also the inevitable doom of it, cannonaded,
rusted and sagging, enormous
broken image of the Siege.

        *

And up comes the Grand Fleet
from the floor of Scapa Flow,

pale-bellied, featureless, decomposing,
bloated with pumped air,

breaking the grey surface, hulk after hulk,
huge weight of useful iron

slithered across, cut into,
sold off: worn tanks of fire

that trundled through the sea,
both sides' dirty coal-smoke
blown the same way in battle.

                    *

Clarity
of the unmoving core
comes implacably out
through all that's material:

walls of battleship scrap,
the raising up of Consett
along the skyline,
the taking of it down again.

                    *

Mansions of manufacturers strung along ridges
upwind of prosperity built in infernal
images below,
                    well out of it, but not yet
out of sight.
                    Were they
mansions in Paradise, looking out over Hell?
Were they mansions in the better parts of Hell?

Question evaded by the model
chief residences of the model factories,
set upon slight
elevations of the Middle Way.

                    *

This age has a cold blackness of hell
in cities at night. London
is filled with it, Chicago cradles it
in ice-green glitter along
the dark of the lake. Birmingham Sparkbrook,
Birmingham centre, Birmingham Castle Vale
hang in it as holograms. For now

Puritan materialism dissolves its matter,
its curdled massy acquisition; dissolves
the old gravity of ponderous fires
that bewildered the senses,
                    and for this
glassy metaphysical void.

Something will be supposed
to inhabit it, though it is not
earth, sky or sea. There will be
spastic entrepreneurial voyages twitched out
from wherever its shores may lie.

*

Mercurial nature with a heaviness to it
flies with an eye to sitting
down somewhere and being serious.

With a heaviness to it, an opacity
saddening its flight.

Haunted look of stalled energy, of rights
impatiently or contemptuously surrendered.

VI The Many

Transit of Augusta Treverorum
to Trier; a location
busy with evolutionary forms long
before the brain-birth of 1818.
First, a grid-city, fit to support Constantine's
huge palace and basilica, working
as it was designed to do, its defences
anchored to bastions;
the size and operation
generating the structures of the first rank.

The size vanished; the operation
ceased. On all sides
the general case
collapsed, and the nettles grew out of it,

and the beasts fed there and let fall
their dung. There will have been scrub,
and mounds, and the rest of the new
general case of reversion,

out of which still rose up
spaced widely and without relation, certain

of the great masonry contraptions
that gave no proper
account of how they'd been arrived at.

Next, the shelter of each of those things
generated a settlement of scufflers,
scratchers of livings. Pragmatic
tracks linked one with another; in due time
the separate nuclei touched their
forces together and fused

to a mediaeval city which, conceived,
closed off. It walled what it was. It sat

smaller than the Roman city, quite
differently shaped
and oriented; entirely grown
out of the landmarks of that city,
and ignorant of it.

I see such things worked rapidly,
in my lifetime; hard for the body to believe in.

                    *

Mercurial nature, travelling fast,
laterally in broken directions, shallow,
spinning, streaked out in separate lights, an
oil film dashed on a ripple,
its plural bands
drawn out and tonguing back on themselves,

in an instant is gone
vertically on a plunge, on a sudden
switch of attitude,
                    without ever
pausing to drop its flight,
compose itself, gain weight;
                              dives
narrowly deep, as far down
as anything;
                    plunges unaltered,
slips away down
in twisted filaments, separable
argumentative lights.

                    *

Parable of the One and the Many. Presences
flaring out from the wet flints
at Knowlton ruin,

multiple as beans, too small and irregular
to distinguish or call names. Divide;
survive.
          Some god, isolated
by a miscalculation, cut off
from his fellows, hauled in
across the bank to clear the green
ring of its demons; churched over;
and in his time forsaken.

They ate him,
and drank him,
and put his little light out and left.

                    *

The stones are waters
the stones are fires
dragged in a swirl across the core,

these slopes their after-image
fixed into the longest
fade they can secure;

ice, and sunlight, and blackened
crusts, lichen and heather sweeps
tilting off, one through another.

Draining through peat-hags,
Dane River, by its weight sucked out
from a mile of upland bog

to pour down, stained
through a crumbling, matt-black, moist
ravine of soft, firm

stuff that could be fire;
peat scattered with coal glitter,
mineshafts in a trail before

the drop into pastures.
These moorlands
hang down in swags from the sky,

from graves in the sky,
companies of lives lifted up;
Stanton Moor, Knot Low,

Shutlingsloe,
tilted, eroded cone,
mutable, as the lands turn on it,

as if it were a cloud shape
or the massing of a mood, emerging
to be directly read.

Over away from Dane
Axe Edge sends down the Dove,
gathers the Manifold
and lets it slip
through complexity;
the hills in their turns tantalise

and instruct, then the learning
dissolves. There's no
holding it all. Steadily

as the star-fields swing by,
this land-maze
brushes against, and stirs

somnolent body-tracks, unmapped
traces in the brain.
Axe Edge

thrust up towards the anvil-cloud
full of rivers, the skyline
inky and dark. Under

the evening, the hoof-strike flashes.

                    *

Landscape superimposed
upon landscape. The method
of the message lost
in the poetry of Atlantis
at its subsiding to where all
landscapes must needs be
superimpositions on it. All landscapes
solid, and having transparency

in time, in state. Odysseus old —
what to do with him?
— sent out to have his hardened
senses touch against lost reality.
It is called water that he passes through.

       *

The boys are swinging firecans
along through the dusk;

rusty cans, bodged with holes,
with long string handles, coals from the grate

and whistled through oxygen to make
red-eyed pepperpots, clustered

fire-points, raging away in a trail
of acrid chimney smoke in the street.

       *

The land, high and low,
has been scattered across with fire-pots;
brick, iron, lidded, open to the sky,
the glare streaming upward
in currents and eddies of sparks, blackening
the look of the rim, the district,
even by day, requiring that it be
strong; that it shall one day split itself

       *

The true gods, known only
as *those of whom there is never news;*

rebellious, repressed; indestructible
right access to the powers of the world;

by tyrannies given images; given
finish, given work; and in due time

discarded among the débris of that into
private existences, into common use,

deliquescent, advancing by a contrary
evolution to the giving up of all

portrayable identity, seeping unevenly
down to a living

level, pragmatic
skein of connections from

lichens to collapsing faces
in drenched walls, exhalations

of polish and detergent
in palace-voids of authority,

patches of serene light in the skulls of
charlatans making tea in swamp cottages,

evidences that dart into the particle accelerator
unaccountably; and others

caught unawares in the promiscuous
rectangles of the Impressionists,

and ready to come back out to us
through the annexation-frames
of a world that thought itself a single colony.

*

Coming home by the road across Blackshaw Moor
in a summer dawn with the ridge just showing
grey above the plain and out of the white mist;

a red eye goggling high in the dark rocky
crest of Hen Cloud, a lamp in crimson canvas
up there somewhere. That skyline
was mad enough already.

*

One particular of Poseidon: the bronze statue
through whose emptied eyeholes
entire Poseidon comes and goes.

VII On Fennel-Stalks

They have no choice but to appear.

We knew they existed, but not what they'd be like;
this visitation is the form that whatever

has been expected but not imaged takes
for the minutes it occupies now.
                              Just after sunset,
looking out over the thin snow,
the moor vegetation, stiff canopy,
showing through it, greying. Wind
getting up, dragging smoky cloud-wisps
rapidly across on a line
low in the sky.
                    Another wind,
steady and slow from the north, freezing
and far higher; and with it,
rising from behind the ridge, gigantic
heads lifted and processing along it, sunset-lit,
five towering beings
looking to be miles high,
their lower parts hidden, their lineaments
almost stable in their infinitely slow
movement.
               Relief at the sight of them
even though they seem to mean
irrevocable dislocation. Creatures
of the Last Days, coming to the muster.

Apocalypse
lies within time; as these beings
may or may not so lie; if they do,
their demeanour could equally match
the beginning of all things. It's the same
change. There's a choice of how to see it.

For them, no such choice. Self-generated,
and living perfect to themselves
in some other dimension, they have it
laid on them to materialise in the cold
upper air of the planet;
and arriving there
they can take on only the shapes
the terms of materialisation impose.

Visibly not as they would wish to be,
they're self-absorbed. The human eye
watches them shrewdly, albeit
with the awe it's been craving; sizes them up,
how to ride them.

*

Cargo-cult
reversed. There have always been
saucers put out for us
by the gods. We're called
for what we carry.

In barbarous times
all such callings
come through as rank parodies,

refracted by whatever murk
hangs in the air;
even the long pure
sweep of the English pastoral
that stretched its heart-curve
stronger, and more remarkably wide

merely to by-pass
the obstruction caused by a burst
god, the spillage
staining the economic imperative
from end to end with divinity.

*

Mythos,
child of action, mother of action;

hunger for action understands itself
only by way of its own

secretion, fluid metaphysical carrier
that makes, where it collides, cultures,

and where it runs free, myth,
child of action, mother of action.

*

There can be quaint cultures
where a poet who incurs exile
will taste it first,
                    puzzling half a life
at the statues in the town park and those
particular shin-high railings there;

afterwards, fame and disgrace.

Succeeding a single blink of passage
through a beam of power
on the road between fortunes; between
province and metropolis,
art and art, fantasy
and amenity.

                    *

The snails of Ampurias
ascend
            as the canopy of air
upon the ruins
cools after sunset.

They infest
                the wild fennel
that infests the verges of the road
through what have become wide
spaces above the bay.

The snails ascend
                    the thin clear light,
taking their spirals higher;
                            in the dusk
luminous white, clustered
like seed-pods of some other plant;

quietly
rasping their way round
                        together, and upward;
tight and seraphic.

The Cut Pages

The Cut Pages

Coil   If you can see the coil hidden in this pattern, you're colour-blind

Pale patterns, faded card, coral card, faded card, screen card, window fade

Whorl   If you can see this word and say it without hesitation you're deaf

Then we can get on with frame

Frameless   Meat-rose, dog-defending, trail-ruffling

Dodge

The Redcliffe Hotel? Forget it

Coming in on the curve. Cross under the baffle. Dropped through, folded in the flags

Street work. Across purposes and down flights. Only male shades flit

Fronded and without reference they evade substance but evidence vestiges

The detective in the driving mirror

Dying to get out. But is exposed to the open at all events

'The Detective in the Driving Mirror'

Put down your stethoscope and let me look. Vestiges through the venetian blind, I see. Wall-corner, bird-supporting coping. Who were you stethoscoping?

Dwindles to a cut

Washes of screen. Men are fluttered. Houses are being thrown away wholesale. Butchers are on air

If you can see the numeral 88 in the pattern. The Old 88; the wallpaper piano

Leviathan Lane. Home of the Works. Appears to have rolled over and huge stretches of its ghastly grey underparts come into view

Stem of a spiral stair depending through glass light, in going down, in confined but neatly stacked office and reception space

There is one flung out. On that one the light is sharp. There is no half-light; only the grace of diffusing what is full

They try to get in through the frosted glass, their spidery dark hands show almost visible as themselves as they scrabble. They come only at one oblique off-centre place; they can't succeed

Accretions after origin. Atypical hazards. All we are worrying about is our own distress at their frustration

Communitas. On the march. March a path to march on

I owned a patch, they marched on it. What march is that? My tit

Flying purpose, the waves hit the opposing shore, then forge back through their own fantails

Seem to be taking place

Hello kitchen

Whahgaar. No lid on the light, no expectation. Make yourself into a corner. Let it rush

Pouring into the subway from all sides. Down the approaches: a quick glance at their feet, and down they go

Most things stay transparent

Launching into doors. Do they have doors in the District? Some

Now they've fixed it so that you can't

He paints words with the past

Give us something, give us something

If I do, you'll regret it

The defective mirror plucks at a glove. It is passing, it is passing the mirror. The mirror's defect is to pluck what slips

Tumbled. Strewn. Built. Grown. Allowed

I was going to say it but I won't. You can be going to say yours. I was going to say it because I knew it

Click

The second day. Was that the first?

Hats are in evidence, but precious little else. I mean the men aren't

Spread. Examine the spread and report back to spread-head Coaling at intervals along the line

Yes, forming into lines, little clusters of lines, little directional urgencies of line-clusters, unexpected accelerations of urgencies

Yawning into urgencies unprepared

Slats and shades, heads and shoulders, afternoons look at afternoons

Lengthening, passing over, surfacing over. You're not recoverable. Take only what you need. Why travel heavy if you can travel light?

Stop this one. My shoe. No, it's gone

Spread. By close proliferation so instantaneous, no more than a tight rustle, it seemed pre-existent. Nothing could move. Nothing should want to

Three smiles

Three smiles from the same

Three smiles from different people

All footways lead up from this bollard

Sliver

Edge-on presenting itself. And a conspiracy to stop a person getting a clear idea of where his various limbs are; in what and with what mobility

Yes, the spirit of it all

They're on the run, scurrying past to the edge of town, and back again. We're not. It's their turn, whoever they are

Don't say *engulf*

Cross marked on the pane, cut into the glass. Small shining scratches

Traces. So much isn't the railroad, so little is. We dot by traces

Breathe again, we dot so small

Stepping-stairs, leading round, leading to another platform with its rail from which we

Free our spread

far through you will it come, sweet red,

sweet stream of blue

River of artifice

Inhuman curvatures

Don't say. Engulf

Little character. Little distinction

Beating under the crossbeam

Scatter.

Throw.

Bright.

Scatter.

Elastic belt disaster. Over a space with plucking out past the edge

Bend your back to the curvature

Bristling, and with extreme rapidity

Enamel panels passing, as if of use to the adjacent effort

Bluish network of flicker, running across the dark fluid surfaces, finding them

Stretch, power-leak and dispersal. Then a radial diagram of the next order

Decorated. This light falls through the dirtiest air in the world

He will not refer, but will act: the other refers constantly but will never move

Memories speciously manoeuvred to angle in on a point, projected to another's memories: the dupe memories connect, the best miss, and leak, given form to no purpose but one they fail in

Fantasy. Beaten thin from inside and like a panel

A round red metal chicken used for holding lubricating oil. Surrender

I have no obligations to fulfil before going with you

The ratchet passes

It follows that dropping further – everybody takes counsel

Summoning all the scratches into pattern

In time

Get him to kick his lumber overboard, whatever he's made with it. He knew it was lumber: his optimism for it was weakness

Lumber like that is hard to disintegrate back into the flux

Has it moved on from us? Has it moved off us? Are we out from under it? In under something else?

Sideways, diagonally through a posed photograph, caught only in a momentary record of chaos

The sunlight ran a rail and burst from the end

Sedentary

Manoeuvre

Into the height of the proposals. All is silently, without sensation, burned back to the circumstance

Find somebody

On a rise again, on what's filled. Every deception imaginable is likely. Every circumstance imaginable is deception

This life I have grown to think of as my own

And this

Corrugated sheet holds what was decided. Easy to see, hard to move

Grow in long startling stabs and develop at their ends. Then more. Any direction

Things dropping behind the back of sight are clearer than those I see

Something is here. It is tongued. It has fallen to its place

Return too often to the place of the swing bridge: then let the bridge swing the place. There are other places. The swung place is gone

Roll. The quickest way. Sideways and up

The particular lineaments – and I thought they were the general lineaments

That is tall

Settling about, tall

Closing, tall. Smiling, tall

Like opening wave with no feature to be on, but on all features, and not remaining; not succeeded either

To origin, which is another patch of sun. We are shown another patch. Not the one. Was the one we tried to look for not the one, whereas this is? Perpetually displaced. Or is this what can be seen, the surrogate, while the true one cannot be perceived?

Skirting it. We must have crossed it many times. Hard to say. There is nothing that has to be done with regard to it

Monstrous love

Shaggy fragments sailing out of the background

Into the drop-sheet, or past it. There's a sheet hangs to catch things, but maybe it doesn't. Nothing sticks

Ferretting, by the handfuls, in among what was left. Not one scrap demands to be kept more than the other

The opening is much deeper, but it doesn't matter

Everything is changed. Without warning. Everything was a warning

The slipping foot. The cry. The gap trapped in the opening

Sedbergh. With all the escape roads removed, obliterated

Altered. Men alter. Are altered

Everything in the street runs to the end, to the open space where there's always movement

A type of sky at the street's end where there seemed to be shapes of giant arches, as if from that particular place on the world changed into one where there were such arches

Some war long before. Not one of the wars of time. In the dream-time. Some war learned of before time was learned. The operators of the war were of their own world, not an earlier generation of this

Rose-stuff, the variations: whisked, turning

Back, fanning up the line, past the starting place, back on another track, with much motion, slow progress. To be seen, at all costs

Not located in ice, or mud, or flat plane. In air or glass. Counter-system that won't engage in a dialectic

Far. It is far from us. No. We are far

With that, everything has come to us in a cluster. Turn it inside out, and step out of it. Call for another

Separations, a rhythm of trenching the moving mass, that reforms round the suggestions. The rhythm separates. The spaces are alive

Always falling to be away, never on the rise

Away, travelling: to come upon whatever rises, distends, is bland and broad in the ruck

Voyage is through partial things, mixtures, edges where tangled solidities give on to broken-up vacancies

Stump. Ampetus stump

The ceilings ran on, through arch after arch. The floors had been furnished anyhow, with islands and dams of clutter

Have you seen anybody?

They're everywhere – of a kind

The text of fury, with oncoming plumes, the orb of darkness, the fire-feathers

Yes. Those are the steps. Down around the outside of the curved wall. No, it's not in nature; you're right

Friends surround me

Lower than the treetops all about, there is the ground, the false floor. Always to be going down, arrested and spread, only to run wide, looking for an edge to what's down

Red blush, swelling at the middle and mottling across

Perpetual Check depends on the alternation of moves between the players. The opponent has no way of selling you an extra move, whatever price you offer. But there's some aspect of the game that's in a position to make the offer, and there's a price it will accept

Price!

Interviews, breaking away into riots round the house. Stripped up the wallpaper, all the old intentions

The mill opens everything out above, white frames, the bright things open. It's all right. The good will die, they will come to us. Spread of the sails, the angles where they meet at the boss, the places where they straddle to the full, the places from which they could be broken inwards towards each other

Elm. The mouth

Separated, it still had life, the break looking like nothing and all that was alive in it sticking out brightly. The wilting bitter and sharp, curses with no possibility of contradiction

What a wish is. Like a broad nipple. Like a place in the trees, distant, boxed-off, dull. I want that because it's mine

Nowhere to head for. Nothing to be done. This discontinuity is my discontinuity

One patch of town has noticably more wires about than any of the others. Only coincidences

The head of it: up into the height. A hardening of style, but nothing more

When I am going I shall wish – what a wish is. The elm

The wrong side of a door, the ladder standing away from the wall at the top

See how the leaves are rusted all across the field

The return. Full point now that was origin. And on through it in a new direction. Loss. And the deposit of loss, the lit buildings, the land and the sky. Left here they cannot be, or say, what is gone

A long plume was lying

Nobody has to have a face. Nobody who has a face can keep it. They can never be recognised again. There are no voices asking to be remembered

Undifferentiated

Enclosed. At least by treaty or agreement. Framed, unmistakably

A journey by car through many streets, seen through several windows, by more than one head

No one is found. The steps are empty in the sunlight. The place shouldn't be left empty: not all that plant

The hotel on its toes. A revolving door, multiple mirrors. Narrow site, warehouses to either side

Flat white sodden lifegiving encounter

Stripes of bitter orange on the new flag

Hard rivulets of emerald come round machine-drawn curves to hairy

Mastered but not enjoyed

Only with bands to drive

Sabotage of the arrangement. Was inevitable. Now all the friends are free

Shadows that work levers in the hot afternoon

In all the hot afternoons. You can go to them. They come from hard facts before and after. From no tree; from no kindness

Always there is work. With underwear, with doors, with pots of food, with plants

A long way away the sun crawls past the windows. Daylight sleep in a trough

Big shoulders. Support her moderate head

Turning the place again, it finds trees and a pond. A dead crow like a fish burnt in the pan lodged in a bush by the water

The blind is lowering all the time and the world dives with it, answering with brilliance bursting from the glass

Red hook, red smoke powder. The comedian with dusty stockings and flat belly drum

Soft white pointed peppers

Wire print arrangements rushing through, fence disputes on order

The holes are made, reamed about till the core's exposed. The answers will drop in

Laws for the empty. Patterns for the free

A leaf shape hangs like a wheel against the light, with rings of holes cut in it. Stemmed and attached to others, and springing from a dark main stalk. Many such heads hanging about the stalk

Past a simple shed

On to blue bricks, flat

Against blue bricks, standing

A flight of domes below

There is addition, there is flight. There is the simple state that is always tilting, easily but always. If you go with it you can hold, if you neglect to you're thrown

Clothing rich but fusty, beaded with hard things. Kept in the bottom of a room, dusty velvet, dusty sun

To rely on the spongy disc in the floor, with its concentric ridges. The floor holds if the disc gives. It gives and presses back

It will be barbaric, the middle channel between the squares

Cannot be said

Cannot be caught

Gone into a detail. A forked detail. A cluster. A generality

Sold out; and the price thrown after it

Cold canvas; naked in the cold canvas, vulnerable to thought but protected in every possible way by everybody

By certain people. Certain knees, feet, hands, necks, ears. Faces, never. Voices in discussion. The word was corrupt. The word corroded

The plant seemed more permanent than the man

The sun is written on from the other side

Miraculous urine, streaming among the ice. The boot, the snaky hulls against the murk. Deep tanned brown of the swept pavement between the snowfields. Earth solid with black fire, sky with grey fire

Soon

The streams ran through the garden round the house and in under the balconies. In some of the rooms there were channels of running water bridged by plank walks from which the plants trailed

Serpentine roads in such bare scrub they weren't hidden one from another. More roads than there were reasons for

Holding the hair over the distance

Silence. Silent water. Feed the sounds into the silence. Sun. Grey sun. Track sun

The painted wheels hum in the early morning. Grey pigeons are lit from beneath

The rim. To a great distance. Eaten back to the least, nothing but the bare curve. Utterly without excresence

Subject. Measure a subject. See which way it sticks out. How it's fixed, and to what

Cracks appear everywhere, large and small, in all directions, on every surface. Wonderful

When the discomfiture is over, when the laughter is over; when the gas is the plain air

There will be flakes

There has been secession: but there are flakes

Every single taste is sweet and hard, there is no contrast, no rough, no dull. One after another after another they come, solid waves. The information

Embedded, an enormously complicated wheel with many gadgets built into and among its heavy spokes. The clay very bland

Nothing has passed. Those strawberry-like plants have pushed red stalks right across the road and rooted in the cracks

There is a banner to be dropped from a beam, a soft flaming thing

It looks at the world. What faces there are are jailed. That's bad luck

The range of things becomes apparent. Then another behind it. There are ranks of ranges

Out of the bell, distance

Out of the bells, nearness

Tickle of grass

Assorted weed, pebble

Glass drops. They pile up in the bed

Have they thought about it yet?

One plate has bolts instead of rivets: the entry port

With corrugated sheet bodywork, vertical boiler and nodding camel-head jib, nosing through the groundsel on the track. Alien thing, framed in solidity

Catering for most of what comes, letting what comes late split away in its own inadequacy. Catering for more than can possibly come: taking advantage of the leeway to garnish everywhere with ice packing

Cubes of light looking in on us at noon. Sunken floor, recessed. This is the moment when secession should stop. We're set down

A terrible corrosive rain scores down, eating the vertical grain. Everything stands. Everything stinks

The blue is of stained earth, a soft shine on it, and a stink

Hairy leaves of the poppy hang over the stones

The last ones coming in, the damps rolling up out of the evening. Pads of this and that lie about

A place for spiny flourishing stuff. Part of the fun? How to make a place. No leasing-out the job

Tempestuous in the container, the simple brown sliding contents, having only one way of moving, one direction, the continuous slide

There's no choice. There's everything, but no way of choosing. Nothing comes away. *You* come away, pulling things with you. No choice for you, no choice for them

But seen very close, so close that to move a fraction would give the sensation that the head's trapped, breath in danger, it's a tent. The light is given, on trust. The breath is given, on trust

Away, in air, in depths of fire with no sensation but the sensations of air

By paddle and by screw. To grow

Squaring out, wherever you can, wherever there's space, pause, leisure and resource. It pays

Only a little way under the surface it's passing all the time, in its own orders

Breathe. The mast for breathing. Stay-wires against the flatness of breathing

The cold came round in a crescent

A field of points thrown over what they dropped, kicked, dragged through, dirtied and lost

Yellow oil leaking through a rag binding the tube, seeping and then starting to drip. Loss was no problem, and neither was mess

The horizon's only a few feet away, rigid, and with fronds waving on the sky

Sam us again

The orders haven't been given. The orders that could be given just don't exist

Throwing. Throwing

Every separate end has its placing on or in what looks to be a common element. This is extensive but may in turn lead, if the trace can be found, to just one of these separate ends

100

Centre. They brought a centre and set it up here, but it wouldn't take. It was rejected, and went off sideways. No sign of it now

Corner. If you start from inside and travel out it's all corners.

Pistols across the river. They're part of it. The shooting is horizontal corrosive

Red lights for peace. Peace tails

Faith. The little red lights sailing over the precipice into the shadows

Marsh, set with tree islands, is beautiful. The eyes take in what cripples the step: there's no comparison, the two sensations don't seem to be in the one body

To be changed. Stricken, but peaceful deep in the face

Getting ready up. Getting ready out. Getting ready down

Stripes shoot along, then crane up at a shallow angle, then level out, a bit broken in progress

Lovable old clown face. The red nose, the spots of colour on the cheeks. That pouchy mouth with camel-lips and teeth, wet with spittle. The big eyeballs are pink with blood-vessels. A succulent smile of resignation, too much for a smile

Seeing the old face through the loose strings. Almost a shock. Will it stay? What will it bring?

Carrion, the breeze blows on the carrion where it lies in the field. It comes, the breeze keeps it at a distance, the pale sun plays over it

Precise pinnacles, threaded between with hairs, and on the hairs, spit blobs

There'll be a body at the very end, a smiling acquisition round a smiling navel

In the angle of the frame over the gulf full of sunlit mist. The frame is modern, the ritual is modern. Every gulf will have its use. Plastic gold capitals swimming up, picked out by the sun

Whether the sparkle smells, the dead pink petal clings, wrapped round, to the finger

The top undone, and some way down, to make a swell in the shape. Like that, nothing can be done, it's no use asking. And the whole goes slowly by, turning and tilting on some nonde-script pivot, chosen by offsetting

There is no process. There are many changes

Refer to the space beyond the reeds. The space has been seen, passed through. Since then it has been replaced by another

Deafened by the alarms, hearing no alarms; inventing all sounds by carving the walls of silence

Substitute.

The breadth.

Turn him round.

Ham him a bit

Tracks high above, right to the tops, moving figures all over.

Patterns on the backs of hands. Scrub at the answers. They keep coming up, lead under chalk. Suggest. Let it keep coming, on the stretch, on the possibility of check, the soft twist into the next

Row of numbers, quick print, magenta ticket roll, fingers on the teeth inhibit whistling

This was a man, a dog without a skin. He does not die, or come to us. But he was trying to come to us. It was no escape: a passing event that had to be witnessed

Once the hiding place had also swallowed up the last of the pursuers into its winding and blind ends, the pursued ones started dismantling it around the pursuers, who were thus driven in deeper and deeper, like hares in the corn

Feet on the ground, browbones to the sun, jaw held up with spit

It needs nothing. It can have what it likes

Pelletted

Pellets grow, and grow a fine fur

Giant bricks. Good. Never mind how they got there

The chase. The chase! Print

Pastoral, kneedeep in pastoral, juicy green. Loads of marble, loads of care

Great square wings in which romantic visions of a softened city pass in coloured openings between black framings. Growing by pushing outwards into a stretched pallor; and sending itself away

A filbert set in the sunlight. Could be baleful but it doesn't have to be

They come like red trellis under everything, lanky stretches that turn up all over the place. They're intrusive, but there's no sign of any damage they've done

The bills are put, the

wheels on the walls,

wires dangling

There's no sign of anything. They're the sign. Maybe it's just that the time has come round. But some things have been flowing backward

Korean chrysanthemum, flattened into a fan. Rushing in, seeing it, falling on his knees, struggling on his knees to justify it

He must have come from somewhere. Terra Cotta Brick

Sham signifiers, wearing the palms bearing the bays, keeping the places patrolled, walking the dogs' dogs. There seems to be

British Bakelite could rise again

Standard in the sunset, with the separate rays

Woman went off with a conical idea

The lost Tucker

Friends assembling by proliferation and pushing out, rolling beadlike towards, expanding, lightening, scattering, without

Slash, with hanging in free air. There's laughter in the slash. Under it, a deep cinder bed

Somebody has hidden the accuracy. In with the corrosives

Ridged, cloven, branched. Set about with fine white hairs

The only remaining red. Started the surfaces

West was where the snow bunched itself for falling

The palm leaves come as pads

Scent of Mungo

Tobacco matting

The creatures

and their curve

Locked fringes. The signals are alive and dead. They happen but their purpose is stung away

Scramble into the

Sediment up above, tracking

Sloping deep fires where they have never been

They have been everywhere, we share the world. Watering

Sand hung in the sky, ready to start something

Sweetly coloured but without glow, boil and shudder

And dot away

And to shade with

Leathery plant

Semblance, by light codes, the gogglings

Speed of the dark, immense speed of the dark. Of the weight of the dark

One corner was flattened into the mount, the other bent out and standing a few millimetres proud

The Ship's Orchestra

The Ship's Orchestra

The Ivory Corner was only a wooden section of wall painted white, at the intersection of two passageways. To the left of it was the longer corridor; to the right at once there was the washroom door.

Ivory Corner for leaning against, the white pressing the forehead, the wood's vertical grain flickering beneath it up and down across the horizontals of the eyelids.

Washroom door swings, has weight, has rubber silencers. Limbs overhanging it from the Ivory Corner get foggy, the elbow gone, winging; a hand spread on the panel beside it stays brown and dry and shiny.

Always the chance of meeting that walking white suit with a big orange on it for a head; the white yellowed a little, as if through some sort of commerce with urine.

Then it was her black (purple, juice) net dress, rough to the touch, things grew so big in the dark. Or lacquered hair, dry and crisp as grey grass. Want it to come away in handfuls, and she be meek, and satisfied, as far as that. Plimsolls, the smell of feet in a boy's gymnasium. Learn to live with it.

Merrett calls his saxophone a tusk. What shape is the field of vision the eyes experience? Its edges cannot be perceived. A pear-shape, filled with the white plastic tusk, rimmed and ringed and keyed with snarly glitters, floating importantly. Where? Against a high, metallic and misty sunset, the sky like Canada in thaw, and Billy Budd's feet dangling out of heaven five miles up, through a long purplish cloud.

Potential fracture of Merrett's saxophone: by stamping, quick treading, sudden intemperate swing against an upright. In section rather like the break in a piece of dry coconut. No, it would not be likely to bleed. Just the steward brushing up bits of powdered saxophone from the saloon carpet, and Merrett, if surviving, looking out to sea.

Behind the rubber-stoppered door, the birth-basins.

Then it was her back, so broad and curved and deeply cleft, doughy and dry to the touch, like some porous cushioning that could not feel. The desiccated hair, yes, distinctly loose; all my senses precarious. I thought of the sheets as black, all hard things there are as ebonite, the indulgent back as very faintly luminous where I touched it; yet I was aware of something brusque in the air: a scented bonfire.

At times the sea rises uniformly to become much of the sky, harmless, translucent, golden-grey, with the great sun billowing down under the keel and flaking off itself from ear to ear. A wake of hundreds of scooped-out grapefruit halves.

Amy, too, in some of her moods, calls her trombone an axe. And the piano, whether I play it or not, is one of the kinds of box. Tusk, axe, box together joined. White baby grand box in scalloped alcove.

Janus, old door-god, your front face is alabaster, fringed with tooled curls, your cheeks and frontal prominences agleam; but a petrified, pitted arse, rained on for centuries, is all that confronts what's on the other side.

Dougal never actually speaks of his bass, even. But Joyce, the girl on drums, doesn't know too much yet. Judge the moment right and we can get her to call them anything. Tubs. Cans. Bins. Bubs.

A waterfall of orange-coloured deckchair canvas, from top to bottom as far as I can see either way without moving my eyes. And a long scroll – I can see the bottom of that, it is weighted with a short pole – covered with dimly printed instructions and transit data. Between these two, the projecting angle of two white-tiled walls at intersection. A narcissistic young passenger – I did not notice of which sex – has just left the picture, dressed for sunbathing.

Consideration of a porthole. Not punched or cut, but made by enormous controlled suction of plane surface away from chosen point of orifice; to be banded, clamped, bolted, glazed. For Merrett to regard the sea, his head resting as if provisionally on his small Napoleonic shoulders. Dougal has spoken to each of us in turn, to say 'Four days at sea, and they haven't asked us to play.' I believe he has also written these same words in a diary, the only entry so far. Dougal concerns himself a great deal with this question of our status, and Amy at least is beginning to be suspicious about his musicianship. This may be because, however obscurely, Amy is American, and is plainly a negress; being black, stringy and big-mouthed, although she wears her hair straight, while Dougal is equally plainly a late British Empire seaport (Liverpool) Spade; tall and medium brown, with quiet eyes and cropped ginger hair and a neat moustache of the same colour. There isn't a leader in fact; we're just a Foster Harris orchestra and if the ship people get any trouble they just wire the office behind your back. But Dougal has to bother.

The white suit with the citrus head ambles by, negotiates the steps with care. It seems benign today.

The taste of the first mouthful of whisky is a thing that creaks, like straining wood, but doesn't quite split.

About five of us, then, and something of an assortment. The coloration problem touches Merrett and me more lightly, in that we are, fairly decidedly, Caucasian, although I can tell already that there's a need for one of us to feel Jewish at times, and we pass this rôle back and forth tacitly. I am sallow and fleshy, with something of a nose, while he is more ruddy, with black hair and a pout. Both of us come from nondescript families; both of us are called Green. He is a Londoner. Both of us are circumcised, too; but so, as it happens, is Dougal. The other oddity is this Joyce, from Nottingham, who looks very young. She must be about seventeen, but doesn't look it: little face, rather pasty (has been sick, though); long blonde hair she can't quite manage; longish nose and big (relatively) dark eyes. Round-shouldered; sometimes a bit damp-looking under the arms. She hasn't unpacked her kit yet. Cans. Bins. Bubs. All five of us double violin.

Think of what all the people you see taste like and you'd go mad: all those leaping, billowing tastes through the world, like a cemetery turned suddenly into damp bedsheets with the wind under them. So the possible taste of a person is a small thing, just a flicker of salt, putrescence, potatoes, old cardboard across the mind, behind the words, behind the manners. And the actual taste, if you go after it, is something that's always retreating; even if it overwhelms, there's an enormous stretch of meaninglessness in it, like the smell of the anaesthetist's rubber mask in the first moments – it ought to mean, it ought to mean; but how can anything mean *that*? There must be a taste about me that could be sensed by others. Somebody as skilled as a dog could recognise it as mine; yet I cannot. If I try to get it from myself I just get the double feeling of tasting and being tasted all in one, like being in a room with an important wall missing. Hold hands with myself as with another person; the hands disappear from my jurisdiction. Looking down, I see moving effigies; the hands that feel are some way off, invisible. There is an image of me that I can never know, held in common by certain dogs.

White wall goes up to a white iron ceiling with big rivets. Windows higher up for a bent gaze. A grey canvas sky with the smoke streaking back from the funnel. This is like those afternoons on shore when everything seems to exist for the window panes. Somebody drumming on the grey canvas roof in my head.

Furniture all over the bandstand and the dance-floor still. The captain was soothing to Dougal, said, 'I can read music very fluently myself, you know.' If you gutted this little white piano here, sealed it and caulked it, it might float.

Joyce's hair by her ears and jutting over her forehead; her nose; the slightly separate gazes of her eyes: something clawlike in all these, latent and neglected. She and the others have been talking and I heard her say she was good at gym at school. Plimsolls, steamed windows; rhythm brushes in the desk.

It splits my head! The great green-glass snout of the sea, the liquid thruster, like an enormous greengage sweet, with bubbles of air in it and the trails of sharks. Presses down into me, through my skull into the back of my nose and throat; peppermint, novocaine, cold and numb. The sky, chalk-blue, squats over it, shaking, pushing. How did I come to be so far down, how did I come to be beneath the ship, to be like a figurehead embedded in the keel? In the flesh of the whole of my right side, from scalp to ankle, there is growing a wet chain, caked with rust. It's not painful; but when I move I can feel my flesh shifting minutely against it. Its tension is different from the tension of my flesh. The old schoolmistress sits at her high desk in the chair with its own footrest. Beside her is a big extension loudspeaker with sunset rays across it in fretwork. Piano music comes from it, and the beating of a tambourine. The old schoolmistress sings, swaying in her chair. The lights are on in the classroom. The little boy lies on the floorboards.

A person is a white damp thing – and here's Amy, who's black and dry – a white damp thing, greyish in some lights even when alive. You could inject salt water into the human body. An all-over emetic. Ha ha. Seminarist. Plankton. Bathyscape. Handkerchief.

Impossible to believe the sound in a piano is so far from the pianist's fingers. I know the keys are ivory boxes filled with wood. In the key of E they seem filled with the pulp of teeth; in G with butterscotch. When I play alone the music is never without a voice or a body.

Lizards, we are all lizards, or will be: khaki-green rubbery lizards prancing agape on a plinth covered with plastic sheeting, over which the cold water is kept running, out of respect for our nature. And we shall not feel sorry for one another when the blunt scissors jag at us and the cold fluids trickle sluggishly out.

Old man up on the boat deck in the morning sun. Sheltered from the wind, wrapped into his chair with a rug. Flattish hat, with the crumpled brim turned up; muffler, sunglasses. Little old man with a clean brown monkey face, mouth like a sloppy purse, livercoloured lips; hands spread out, spatulate, fingers pressing into the rug. He said to me: 'You are a pianist. I am a masochist.' Merrett came up and said, 'Old man, we are going to pick you up by the knee-caps and throw you overboard while nobody is looking.' 'Gentlemen,' he said, 'I am not a homosexual; you misunderstand me.' Etc.

Is it good to feel, under the skin of the chicken as you hold it from running for a moment, the muscles you are going to eat? Oh, questions, questions. How can you crucify a man with a giant orange for a head? The orange falls off once the body slumps down between the strained arms. The shirt collar feebly tries to mouth the last words; you replace the orange, it falls again. You can't put a nail through the orange to hold it to the cross; that's another story. Stand holding it up all afternoon, and the shamefulness of the detachment in the dusk, when he's cold.

A huge yellow oil-drum afloat in the waters of the bay. Sunlight.

Throbber, she said, you're my throbber. And you're my gummy, was the reply. My gummy; my guggy gummy. Now you're my thrubber, she said.

I have known this all along.

Astringency, the prickling of the scalp, flexing of the feet, rotation of the wrists, passing the hands round the confining surfaces of the room where one is. That done, the thought of the scalloped alcove where the band might play. Combed plaster in swirls of rough relief, a deep pink rising from the floor to meet the powdering of gold that thickens and conquers at the zenith. Floor projection forwards, a curved apron, no higher than a tight skirt can step up from maple to black linoleum pitted with marks of casters, drum-spurs, bass-spikes.

Swung from the arms of the gaslamp that was the only light in the street; a street greenish black, among factories. The long linen sack was twisted round and round and was unknotting itself in slow revolutions, with all the weight at the bottom. As it turned, the moisture caught the light, coming through the fabric from top to bottom, but not dripping. Kick.

I am in a poster. This is how the whole thing's meant to appear, obviously. Somebody has been at work on my perceptions, cutting them as giant rudimentary forms out of very thick softboard with a fretsaw, and painting each one a single colour. Although they're only two-dimensional shapes they're thick enough to stand squarely. The ship's superstructure, away over me here in the sunlight, is huge and straight, and of an immensely comfortable white. It's not at all complicated. People, the sky, the sea. The cataract of orange deckchair canvas, the scroll; these are present, and a march of relief-built letters you would need a ladder to climb. An E, an A, a T. You don't have to go and eat. This *is* Eat. Scaffolded, boarded, painted. This is the provision, this is the activity itself. Maybe I have hands a yard wide, a smile like an excavator, nothing matters. The dimensions of the components are not determined by the component subject. Fine. The directors of the shipping line, Foster Harris, the captain of a distillery can be seen queueing by the ballroom door to take credit for this ordering of things. They are small and neatly photographed against the placid outsize expressionism of this set. Then there's the sun. This is Eat. It says it is, so it is. Things seem what they are, believe it.

Looking at this world that is like cake, this fifth day at sea, I realise that Amy, Merrett, Joyce and Dougal are probably happy people, to whom a day like this is nothing strange. And I was thinking of them lying down below on their straw, sniffing and shifting about. Joyce on her straw. Merrett on his straw. Joyce with her clothes too thin to ward off prickling, Merrett with nowhere to put his glasses and his trousers too tight to lie down in comfortably. Dougal on his straw, lying on his thin shoulders and knobbly buttocks, scratching, scratching, his long fingers always squeezing at his skin. Amy on her straw, hard and glossy, waiting for her belt, her dress, her skin itself to split under the strain of not caring. In fact I know Dougal and Joyce are playing draughts, Amy reading magazines, and Merrett lying benign on his bunk playing cat and mouse with a hangover. Snug little figures in the big poster. We are getting to be like the passengers. They should let us play, perhaps; treat us in some little way as if we were a band of musicians. Little way, big way: the dimensions of the components are not determined by the component subject. It doesn't matter. I see, coming up a stair, through a door, round a corner, up an open companion-way across a deck, through a door and out of sight, going, the actor who must be going to take the part of me in the immortalisation of these days – their 'rendering'. Bigger than I would have expected, and a bit old-world. Tuxedo, black hair, suntan, highpowered eyebrows, searching brown eyes; boyish manner preserved in maturely male bulk (shruggable shoulders, big back). Glasses in breast pocket, presumably. Do Merrett, Dougal, Joyce, Amy, see their actors and actresses today? Probably not. Why did I have to see mine? I didn't want to spoil the poster by appearing as myself. Why not? This is Eat. Take what comes.

Throwing up in the washroom the other day I had a vision of a dark pink, double-tailed mermaid. I haven't been seasick this trip, so far as I know: this was the little drunk I went on with Merrett and Amy to get settled in. There's a binary phase in this kind of vomiting, especially marked if your balance is fairly good. A strong consciousness of two ears, two shoulders, two knees, feet, elbows, sets of fingers gripping the edges of the basin; these two sets of characteristics existing each on its side of the room. Between them is a void, a gully; and that is the vomiting. It was in a sort of clear sky above this gully that I saw the mermaid; just at the moment when the idea of being sick rises to the ears, brims and fills them like a sea, the sight goes and the sudden assault on the pharynx arrives, and the invasion of the facial expression. She was floating Botticelli-fashion against a greenish watery sky and some way up from some very stylised olive-green waves. The two tails, in obvious concession to the binary thing, pointed to left and right, and were, at the extremities at least, green as the waves. For the rest, apart from some rather nondescript-coloured hair, she was coloured this remarkable deep pink, uniformly, without variation of tone: lips, nipples, finger nails, the one eye she had open, everything. It was the pink of scouring paste or a rather sickly tulip, a little bluish, yet very bold. Although clearly breathing, and even moving a little, she looked like a figure in a primitive painting whose artist, while realising that flesh wasn't white, hadn't got down to details. She was a burly girl, with fat rubbery cheeks and round arms; looking out of her left eye at me as though she had never seen anything like me before.

Amy has begun to play: the first of us. I can hear it through the wall. She has got out her trombone case, removed the instrument, and is blowing it. Long notes, staccato series. Methodical, clear, accurate; says nothing. Amy is a killer, a musical shark. For those who want that kind of treatment. She'll not bother with me. She must be feeling low, to have to play.

111

Soon there will be a meal. The food will pity me, I shall pity myself. Healthy, ambulant, I am about to be fed with cosy food that tries to make up for my being far from home, my being a great big boy criminal. The seat will be soft, the things clean, my last mess mopped and laundered. And until that big soothing spreads towards me the little notes of the trombone hammer away, like brass shell-cases on a moving belt. It is the sort of time when something very large and wide and silvery, like the capsized hull of a vast ship, can begin slowly to rise above the horizon.

Reasons. The ship is a unity. Enclosed within its skin of white paint it floats upon, and chugs across, the unified ocean. Some would think of it as having the shape of cleavage, a narrow leaf: to me it is a flat canister bearing another canister and a similarly cylindrical funnel, the basic canister shape being eccentrically elongated. This is because the vessel's speed is not great and, whereas there are those who would see the superstructure as a vague and mutable spectre above the hull, it is that hull that appears ghostly to me, while the funnel never altogether leaves my thoughts. At any rate the ship is a unity and does one thing: it proceeds on its cruise. Not only does it have a structural and purposive unity; it has a music which proceeds with it, sounds within it and makes signals of the good life. In among the musicians is the tough glass bubble of the music. Reasoning, now. The musicians don't play. No bubble. The ship is not a unity. It is not white. It is grey, indigo, brown. Thin girderworks of green, and orange even, and coils of pale yellow piping. It is not a series of canisters; it is a random assembly of buildings which, though important-looking, have no proper streets between them. It does not float; its parts are arrested in their various risings and fallings to and from infinite heights and depths by my need for them to be so. The funnel cannot be said to crown the firm structure; rather it juts rakishly over inconsequential forms and looks when the sky is dirty like the chimney of a crematorium suspended above the waves. The ship does not proceed on its cruise, but opens and closes itself while remaining in one spot. The ocean is not a unity but a great series of shops turned over on to their backs so that their windows point at the sky.

O captain. Is it the captain? O first officer? Is it the first officer? Etc.

Such heavy straps and buckles for so young a girl to wear! Such a stiff casing and mask, such mechanical magnification of the voice to stridency! Such a channelled street, with iron pavements for her to strut down, so young!

Monitors, those curious warships there used to be. Little vessels that each carried one enormous gun. Restless home lives of their captains.

The rings of winter, the circles of winter. Why? The hoops and bands of frost. Cooperage that fetches the skin off. Why circles when it goes cold? There are times when you can live as if in a round pond, keeping on moving even when it freezes. And overlapping ponds all round, across the gardens and the streets; making up the sea when the land stops. The rings are there but nobody can ever see them.

Think of Joyce's mother. An accordioniste, maybe, toothy, gilded somewhere, and with a hollow at her throat you could rest your nose in after a hard day's work. To turn her child into this, what can she be? Yet the girl thinks of herself as a jazz musician; talks about Blakey and Roach, or mentions them when pressed. Think of Amy's mother. Difficult. Think of Merrett's mother; of Dougal's mother. Of mine.

He was in a garden all walled about and set amid the sea. And he came into a place where there was a soft-faced flower like a cup on a single stem; the bloom a little larger than his own head and its top a handsbreadth taller than he. And soon the flower lay down on a low bed that was in the place and gave him to understand he should lie on the bed beside it. And he did so. Whereat the flower lay close with him and softly folded him in its leaves, as well as it was able. And he was aware of a marvellous scent from the flower, and would have swooned, etc. And forthwith the flower made great to do to unloose the fastenings of his garments, even to the buttons of his braces. And right hard the work proved, whereas the flower had not fingers but the points of its leaves only. So in this wise passed a longer while than that of all that went before.

The rings of summer for that matter. Carry on.

This is what it is like on the land. She: she holds court facing upstream, on a handrailed plank bridge over the yellow floodwater of a ditch cut into the clay to hold a gas main. The gas and the clay stink like dung in the cold; pink smoke jets from a vent high in an isolated building some way off. The place is surrounded by white canvas screens, damp and grubby. Over her waved dark red hair is spread a muslin dishcover with a bead fringe. Angry brown eyes, pasty skin in folds down to the dewlaps and scrawny neck. Head raised, wide mouth pulled into disapproval. She sits straight-backed in the old cane armchair, propping herself on one elbow. One leg is crossed over the other and the fluffy slipper points elegantly. Apart from the slippers, the dishcover and a pair of baggy pink drawers, she wears nothing.

Merrett, Dougal, it is you and I who have put her there; struggling in our leather breeches through the mud of the site, carrying her at shoulder height in the cane chair; Joyce, Amy, in dungarees and waders you were there too. We must be together in something. Far off across the wet land there are conical fires perhaps and men turned into meat.

The rings of summer would be visible if they existed. The powder we used to make orangeade from, cast in big circles on the ocean, and the circles widening and fading as the powder sinks, in curtains through the depths. And in the empty middles of the circles white things could rise, and float, and disappear. Whalebone spars, cakes of soap, plastic saxophones, tennis shoes.

I saw it from above at dusk as I looked over the rail. On the deck below, it sat hunched, the white suit full of blurred shadows. The head is larger, puffier,

113

more yellowed and sad, and it shows indentations which have not filled out again and which seem to be the product not of blows but of violent fondling. I think the end will come, probably by further violence, during the night, or tomorrow at the latest.

My head. The huge shimmering cloud-filled canister that supports it by describing its furthest limits is shaking irregularly in the night breeze. There is light on the waves, and the ship is a dark factory.

Ivory Corner, white and shining phosphorescent, a tongue that licks me slowly as I approach, from toes to scalp, and extinguishes itself at my back.

I have talked to many people today. I have talked a great deal. The question of our not being asked to play has gone cold, even among ourselves. We are accepted everywhere as what we have become. People go off to bed early in the silence. The absence of music is somebody's urbane whim, and they respect it. Maybe there is somebody slow who will notice, tomorrow or the next day, and be indignant, just as Dougal was at first. But think now of those dozens of silent black aridities moving about the ship, going into cabins, losing momentum, sleeping, turned inside out in the dark like rubber gloves.

There's a labyrinthine system, running all through the ship, of whatever it is that rules by default the minds of the incurious. Slippery wet blackness, invisible by day. Sacs, coiled tubes of it, linking all the people, deck to deck, dream to dream.

I once actually met one of those men who say to you, 'As a matter of fact, sexual thoughts and activities play a very small part in my life.'

Pink smoke jets from a vent high in the wall. Ibis-coloured. In the yellow ditch float bottles of clear glass.

At sunset Merrett grew frightened and stopped drinking. He tried to tell Dougal and me stories about himself. We listened quietly, for I had not been drinking and the stuff seems to have no effect on Dougal. Merrett, in the red sunbeams, talked and laughed with us, while the coming of night alarmed him.

Then it was her black net dress, rough to the touch, and the warm dry scent everywhere catching the breath; and it was the grey desiccated hair floating and filling the room, the dress and the hair up to the ceiling, the room a skirt, the hair in the ceiling corners with the smoke; hair from her scalp, legs, belly. Useless to open my eyes, I was blinded with touch. But her skin was nowhere; the body was away. She had filled the room with her dress and the dead hair. Pouflam! The fire caught it.

She is among the hollyhocks, she is on hands and knees among the rhubarb, she is legging it over the low fence in the dusk. She still has the black dress.

114

She still has the grey hair. I see it behind the petrol pump where she is standing, her back to it, pretending to hide. She is too mad. She doesn't really feel what happens to her. I insist that she must. Who made her mad? If she were really to go bald her breasts would become beautiful, etc. I have to be sentimental about her, for her own safety.

I wake, and ebony poles are across me from wall to wall, a few inches above my face. No farther apart than the bars of a baby's cot. There's a grey dawn light travelling the cabin; it goes. No. Sleep again, in this paper leaf. I have wet myself, I have died. No. In my sleep they have anaesthetised me and with their toothless rubber jaws they have gnawed away my genitals entirely. Cleaned me up — I hear one of them still mumbling it. I dare not touch yet. The grey light, the white light, the dull disc of waking. Not yet. In the night Amy comes to me now. She strips her hard black body, a piece of furniture, and presses it down on me where I lie as if she would break my bones. And with the expanding mandibles that have replaced my privates I clasp her and contain her sadism for hours without motion, until she lifts herself off, quietened, though still taut. Her straightened hair sticks up in a crest as she digs her fingers through it. She fastens her white towelling robe and gives me a dog's snarl of a smile as she goes.

Amy does not come to me in the night.

My actor goes past, treading lightly, his big shoulders affable. He greets me; I respond. He has useless-looking hands of course. Who will play for the sound-track, will there be any soundtrack, etc. As well as his own breakfast, he has eaten mine.

Visceral pipes of white porcelain, huge things, in banks and coils, too wide to straddle. How to get lost in the morning. They reach up in stubby loops and descend far beneath, the systems crossing, curving round, running in parallel. Some plunge vertically through several levels then divide and disappear; some come creeping through the interstices of others as if squeezed before cooling. At the top, the light strikes hard and bright, softening and blurring at the next levels.

Deep down there is only the little light that drips deviously through the chinks. Every so often there is an open end, pointing upwards.

Potential fracture of the pipes.

Hope-pipes, love-pipes, fright-pipes, thought-pipes, loss-pipes, hate-pipes. Pipes of coarseness, pipes of sanity. Pipes of confession. Pipes of purity, pipes of sanctity, pipes of flight. Riding-pipes, rubbing-pipes, sliding pipes, wiping-pipes, confronting-pipes, adoring-pipes.

Potential fracture of the pipes. Virtually impossible. Only single-handed with a light sledgehammer, squatting on the topmost U-bend and clouting at the pipe until it cracks and shows the ochre stuff it's made of. Then bashing at the necks down to the levels, smashing across the fat conduits that curve down, caving in long sections of horizontal pipe from above, then standing in the channels and striking out at the sides till the brittle catwalk underfoot collapses; the débris all the while shuffling its way down in shards and dust into the open mouths and between the pipes to the bottom of the whole system. Descending, the need for clearing the rubbish from the pipes to get a foothold; the monotony of the straight stretches; the strength of the main joints. Arrival at the level where the débris no longer shifts, but has accumulated to this height up from the floor; and how far down that is, under rubbish and unbroken pipes, it is impossible to discover except by reaching down to it. Then the task is to probe for the buried pipes, shattering them among the surrounding fragments, never being able to clear their surfaces any more, but hammering at them blind through what covers them. The excavation of hollows to work in; the seepage back of the broken pieces down the slopes. The laceration of the boots and gloves, the sensation of the feet sinking deeply into the jagged shale; the pipeless walls of the system's container staring inwards at one another, feeling the new light down themselves towards what is at the bottom.

Then it was that man learned to fly. Unfolded from the middle of his waistband by the pulling outwards of a black cord was the creased brown paper bird-form, crackling in the sunshine and peeling itself out bigger across his belly and chest, pushing his shoulders back and flap-wrapping around them. The tail that flattened itself across his thighs; the paper membrane that stopped his nose and mouth, closed his eyes and clapped wind at his ears in immense distance. The railway that ran southward across the smooth ugly sea.

Dropping from the sky and going fast, a cone of paper or some composition fibre, white tipped with red. Disappears below my lower lids, behind whatever is there for it to disappear behind. Effusion of aeronaut; part of a trombone mute; spiritual part of man-made cat.

The paper membrane that stopped his nose and mouth, closed his eyes and clapped wind at his ears in immense distance. The hand that at the same moment walked its long fingers up the back of his neck and through his hair, prodding quite hard, treating his head as something unlikely to burst, letting the pointed nails pivot in the skin as the fingertips turned over. Joyce.

Joyce, who looks at people sometimes as if she lived in their bodies and had just moved a few feet away to get a better look. When her life invades her daze. Too soon yet for anybody to tell her.

Her looks, not her life, invading the daze. The life's not powerful enough to alter without the looks. But in that pasty little face the mouth is going to be wide, with an upper lip that pulls back at the corner. The brows will be thick over the irregular eyes and the nose long and straight, with a knobbly end. Some of her postures foreshadow these changes.

116

The mouth. Fills the area of vision, is very close. Soft, the woman's mouth, impossible to tell whose. Colours fade towards vapour. Closer, there is nothing but the lips, their joining line rising and falling along their shapes, the wrinkling in of the surfaces towards the line. Slowly the line retreats, the lips part, widen; the teeth can be seen, the gentle tongue, not quite motionless, the spaces of the mouth, capable of holding a clear note of music. The breath must taste of cold water. From the right Merrett walks on, the lower lip level with his knee. Seeing the open mouth, he peers forward; then, putting his hands into his jacket pockets, steps carefully over the lower teeth and into the mouth, ducking his head. He walks cautiously about, looking up, down and around; but does not go anywhere out of sight. He ducks again under the top teeth, steps carefully over the lower, and comes out. Then he goes on his way. The mouth stays open.

Somewhere there's going to be some music. I haven't the courage myself to clamber over what keeps me from the piano, to plunge my fingers into its clashes of sound. And what I play isn't what I mean by music. Breath music. Slow opaque music. The ship has come close, drawn itself up my body and continues to rise. Yet it is, though fitted to me, nevertheless very big and stretches far away from me above and below and on all sides. And all the compartments of which it is made are full of milky sounds ready to knock against the bulkheads and echo all through the vessel.

The captain's hat revolves, returns, revolves, returns, never completing a revolution. The captain breakfasts above the clouds, on thoughts invented for him by Dougal.

Great glycerine drops of water trickled down the girl's bedraggled hair, were caught in her eyebrows, ran down her nose and off its tip. Down her checks and neck, cascades. All over her chilled lumpish flesh, the big grey eyes looking down at it, the wide mouth curving, the tongue licking the drip in from its corner. A rivulet between the breasts, spreading across the steep belly. Twisted streams down each breast and falling from the cold plug-nipples. Water standing in separate shiny drops on her big thighs.

Corridor of grey mucus. A kidney bowl of it behind each door.

Over the white linoleum floor the nurse advances with the orange gladioli arranged in a spray, then goes off behind whatever she goes behind. A tap forcefully turned on. The nurse is mature, ladylike, and of fair complexion.

Dougal tranquil, nodding down there in a canvas chair, his cuffs rolled back, the gilt strap of his wristwatch gleaming. His cigarette, cocked between his fingers, burns down. Then which of us is worried?

Shirt cuffs folded back, right above the elbow, whites of eyes showing. Let's go to church to see the dog given its fix.

Merrett said last night that his alto would dent rather than fracture; and that he also had in his trunk an ordinary plated metal tenor, not so handsome, but capable, he said, of cracking a man's skull if you hit him hard enough with it.

Blue fog. Electric cigars. E-flat horns wired in series. *Camions.* One eye at a time, one eyebrow at a time. Dougal dozes. For Dougal to have his proper beauty the circumstances of his life – waking, going to sleep, washing, eating, defecation, micturition – need to be regarded as clinical conditions, their operations supervised by trained nurses.

The two little scrubbers hugging each other in Merrett's bed in the hotel, both of them snivelling and complaining; and Merrett, in shirt and trousers, lying rigidly under the covers on the edge of the bed. Scene from Merrett's first professional job, as clarinettist in a traditional band touring out of London. The bed, Merrett's and the banjo-player's; the idea, the banjo-player's. Nocturnal disappearance of the banjo-player.

All this disposal business, these basins, enamel buckets, plunging tubes, embalming sluices, constant jets, sterile bins, sealed incinerators, consideration of where the banjo-player might have gone that night, of the abolition of words taped to our memories, of the storage of one night under another night, the earlier ones gradually fading as the multi-track builds up beyond the bounds of desire; all this question of the attenuation of substance to concepts. Are there in the ship's mortuary yellow-soled feet with the toes sticking up and facial lines of resignation showing on them in their stillness? Where are our instruments? They luggage us, they follow us, they squat behind us when we're not looking. The facts are these. Merrett's plastic alto in case beneath port-hole. His tenor locked away in his trunk. Dougal's bass, in cover, standing behind the door of the small room behind the bandstand. Joyce's drums, boxed and cased, in the same place. In Dougal's cabin, two violins in fabric cases edged with leatherette and an acoustic guitar in a polythene bag. In Amy's, the polished trombone, with chasing all round the bell, its mouthpiece set against Amy's lips, while she blows long notes, very quietly. In the corner, a small guitar and amplifier. In my cabin a stack of folders of standard invertible reversible orchestrations, song copies and manuscript paper. The white baby grand piano, locked, its lid down with crates of tonic bottles stacked on it, in the scalloped pink and gold alcove. Disposal.

Potential utter disposal of the instruments, itemised disposal (as stamping on the violins, hammering the drums flat-sided, sawing the piano into slices like a ham, turning the trombone into an artificial flower, fighting a duel with the guitars, shredding the bass with pliers and chisel) being too crude and guilty. An engine is necessary: a hangar stretching some miles in all directions, with every part of it, outside and in, painted matt white. Semi-opaque panels to admit much diffused light. The instruments fitted into white foam rubber containers sealed laterally and set in further containers sealed longitudinally, these last being cylindrical and of uniform size, about ten feet in both length and diameter. As many as possible of these cylinders; all must be uniformly weighted, and each must have an identifying number stencilled on it consisting of a number of digits equal to the total number of cylinders, only one digit on each cylinder varying from the norm established in the first numeral, and the varying digit not to be in the same position in the sequence on any two cylinders. Filling the hangar, a continuous white tube into which the cylinders fit and in which they are moved pneumatically at a steady speed. Further details of solvent tanks, sludge filtering and caking, moulding of cake into casing of fissile explosive device, recording of distribution of post-explosive material, public opinion poll, suspension of communications for necessary periods, change of languages, etc.

Without the instruments: we can all share a taxi and spend the afternoon at somebody's sister's wedding party. Wellington boots, exuberance, ducks and drakes on the park lake with crumby plates.

How the sloping shed of a Saturday evening in England falls over Joyce, over me, over Dougal, Merrett, over sad Amy. We do not play, we are people. Dougal embraces Amy in a delivery van, Merrett and I go to a gymnasium just before it closes. Joyce is one of the little girls who giggle at us as we go in.

This is what it is like on the land: on ground where disused vehicles are dumped, a woman has given birth to a child in a giant aeroplane tyre.

On the land the oil-refineries strain to escape from themselves along the river banks but cannot move, and the sky on its conveyor comes round and round again.

On the land the men swarm over the new concrete obstacles and fill the spade's ravines with their ebullient bodies. Let us build again!

The ship's orchestra is at sea. Crammed into a high and narrow compartment in a heated train on a penal railway, we loom out of the shadows at one another in our full dignity at last, between the brownish light of the windows on either side, light that fails to reach right into the domed ceiling of the compartment. The light paints over Merrett's glasses and covers his eyes. Amy's cheekbones are luminous in the tobacco shadows; our heads reach up close to one another, preternaturally large from narrow shoulders and stretched bodies. We are about to agree.

Perhaps the little white piano has useless dampers, and however good the others are my playing will be a continuity of shining brass water, shaking idiotically. Have the others wondered whether I can play? Pianists who go about alone usually can. For my part I have seen Dougal stowing his bass behind the door; have heard him scat odd bars; I have heard Merrett blow a few sodden flourishes on his alto when he took it out to show it to me as soon as we were drunk; I have not seen Joyce anywhere near her drums, but I have heard her humming to herself. I have heard Amy's short notes, and her long notes; and what appeared to be a series of arpeggios of the chord of the fifteenth, with the fifth, seventh, ninth and thirteenth degrees flattened in various combinations as the afternoon proceeded. Some of them slowed her up a little, but it would have been an achievement even for a woman who was sober. Amy has stayed drunk in order to break Joyce in, it appears.

All the same, we're about to agree. The guards are laying the jumping chains out in the sunlit courtyard. The lizards scuttle for shelter. The weeds that have had links dragged roughly over them straighten up slowly.

The old man on the boat deck, sitting wrapped in his rug, turned his sunglasses towards us and, seeing us all together for once, suggested to Merrett, Dougal and me that we ought to dress as women. It took him some while to make clear what he meant, and when he had finished he sat laughing and laughing, his mouth open all the time. Amy was much amused too, and wouldn't let the idea go. It turns out that she is the only one of us who has actually been married.

The white suit going round the corner into the washroom, shuffling with a stick. The length of the corridor away, and the light bad; but the head appeared to be bandaged.

My body explored slowly by squares of differently coloured light. Odd sensation. The little slanted rectangles alter the sizes of the parts of my body they touch from moment to moment and leave a black creek of me in among themselves, that waves and shakes itself about in pursuit of them. The flapping black unseen part of me: a unity.

A covering of sacking over me, that I needn't move. Beyond it there is a room distempered pale green. Smell of soap. Inside the sack, in here with me I think.

The big standing dog. The silent dog. The chimney is stuffed up, the cracks round the doors and window sealed. The brown dog, motionless, grows to completion within the room. Nothing to consider there but its rough matted coat, its deep flanks.

The porthole of enormous strength has come among us and stands, turning this way and that to be admired. Adversative at all times but turning, turning always to make peace. The big standing porthole. The brown compartment. Our soap-sack, our own, the scent of which guides us back to ourselves in the night. The dog's huge stale smile, its mountainside of coat; the silence of its smile.

Hear the lining of the chaps part here and there from the gums, the saliva and air making sound in there. Sound that peels back behind the bulkheads, across ceilings; up and down the backs of the legs. Sound fitted with a glass eye.

Inside the wet aeroplane tyre: when there are enough strips of bacon rind we shall weave him a little coat.

Sound that moves beneath its clear brown glass, propelled by full sails; that carries reservoirs of ink beneath its waist; that shadows itself as it goes. Sound that swallows pearls into twilight the colour of beer.

Slippery sound, retarded till it fractures into many transparent wedges, then into countless pools of travelling light, within each of which great black streets stretch themselves before the windscreens of lampless vehicles, travelling fast. Sound that polishes the stinking dust and makes it stand up in the night, before the wardrobe mirrors, while the gloves deflate, crinkling in the dark.

The sound of hundreds of feet of film, split from their reels on to the store cupboard floor, being trampled in the dark by the animal shut in there.

If Merrett, Dougal and I dress as a woman, become women, will Amy and Joyce have to become men?

There'll be no need.

In the domed compartment, so ill-lit, where the spilled celluloid crinkles out of sight under our shoes, Amy's knees touch mine as the train sways; Dougal's knees touch Amy's and mine; Merrett's knees touch Amy's and mine and Dougal's; Amy's, Merrett's, Dougal's and my knees touch Joyce's as the train continues to sway. If only we could all play together on one single instrument!

Ivory Corner for Joyce; on the white paintwork a big lipstick mouth to kiss her. Ivory Corner for Amy: padded hooks, to hold her up by the shoulder-straps.

Ivory Corner for Merrett: with a heavy iron disc to press down on to the crown of his head when he stiffens upward. Ivory Corner for Dougal: Joyce, standing stark naked and freezing cold, with her eyes shut, at two in the morning.

To be somebody else: to be Amy. Like this. The men push me out of the wash-room if I go in there. Grabbing my elbows, knee in my butt, hand shoving my head forwards at the door. One pulls the door open and the others shove me against it so that the white edge of it comes between my knees, splits the skirt, strikes up my belly, and my teeth and nose come hard against it. This is to make the black ape-woman swear; the bitch whimper for her fix.

What do they think I want? The sea coming up my street, fast, kicking up my nose, making my calf-eyes roll at the sky, splitting me with an explosion of green glass foam? The rifles laid across me in a heap, where I lie naked, the cold bolts thumbing my rifle-coloured skin? To go around smelling of dead flowers again? I don't know what size of things I want.

Anybody, mummify me. It doesn't matter which of them I am.

The little shrivelled black monkey, growing smaller and smaller. The blue above: morning in Sky Gulf. The monkey's owner knocks nails into a piece of board to make music for it.

And the alabaster kingfisher plummeting upwards through the grey photo-print of the water for minutes on end, out of sight. Dedicated.

She's wet all over, with a thin film of something slightly viscous, almost like very watery cement. It must be dropping from somewhere overhead. Cold sweat out of the metal. Not so much on the hair though. Glistens: phosphorescent, the sheen wavering as she breathes. Her lips are lightly stuck together with the stuff, and the eyelids too.

Why has Joyce been crying?

The single instrument would have to be an inflated ring, like a tyre-tube. When it's wet whatever rubs across it raises a squeal. Each of us to have an undefined territory on the circuit. Not really a tangible thing even though it's our common body; but it's as if there was an invisible sphincter in the sky somewhere, with a fivefold answer to our touches.

Buckle the lamps in close to the ribs, rub salt on to the pale peaks of the shoulders, clasp stones wrapped in rag in each armpit; paint the mouth of the navel with lipstick. Pin newspaper cuffs round the nipples and the groin; whether it is a man or a woman is immaterial, but shave the legs and forearms in any case. Whoever it is will need to stand up throughout. Thin white steampipes run down the pink wall.

I am something that has been pushed out of Amy's body, though I cannot remember it. I have no legs, though I have the idea of legs, and I have no arms or hands, though I can conceive of them; but I can move my head this way and that, where I lie. She knows I have come out but she doesn't know where I am.

It would upset her very much to learn that I can move my head in this way, and I shall take care that she never finds out. My eyebrows are beautifully thick and curved, incidentally.

A thin brass ring goes bouncing down steps noisily. And still the orchestra is about to agree.

Bandaged, I am something that has been pushed out of Merrett's body in his sleep. Although I can run and jump I have no head at all. I think I am yellow.

What appears to be human hair hangs in long ropes, caked with runs of white sediment, from the gantries the ship must pass under to get to the sky again. Just a few of these ropes of hair, fairly easy to avoid.

There is dangling in the little concrete laboratory, too, from surprised fingers. Twisted black, like monkey limb or hair set in bitumen, stuck to itself and dried, and easy to tear. Blander to taste than anyone would think; its smell of sweet banana spreads everywhere.

Flakes of skin on the gantries, flakes of cellulose adhesive coming off in the evening sun. Flakes of grey paint. That grinning dog that eats everything.

There is hair fringing some of these girders that is soft and fair, and combed out. Eyelash hair that curls in the sunlight and flickers in the wind. Once: a belly rubbed with lemon peel. Somebody's.

Cold in the afternoons, cold in the evenings. There is one eye now, stitched open with wire. Flocks of children fall away when I rub my fingers, and ranks of square houses. How big my fingers are.

What does she think when I rub my tanned fingers down the white doorpost, altering the surface; or across one another? What does she think I am doing? Children with dirty faces, inquisitive mouths hanging open; they are always silent. These fingers I rub are hard, the skin feels dead. What does she think they are?

Trapped somehow, arrested in this doorway, dropped on to one knee, this hand that troubles me resting on the other, thumb and fingers crossing, rubbing. Otherwise peaceful. But arrested here. And I am aware of Amy watching me from very close. She has made herself like a rubber moon. And Dougal; and Joyce behind him. And Merrett squats close to me, looking at me like a friend. They are taller, and everything is narrower, bulkier, softer. As I feel them watching me I become incapable of watching them at all. I wonder what they see when they look at my fingers moving.

The light on the black arms of the big machine shows the edges up hard. The iron arms go down across darkness, into broken light, back through darkness and up again, their edges hard. A sizeable piece of worn-looking white cotton stuff is being passed to and fro inside the machine, but it doesn't get dirty.

The face of the stretched undervest. I am not plagued by it, but I know it is there, and its opposite, and its less obvious variants. What is the opposite of a face?

Now there's this trumpet-player, Henrik, come out of the sickbay at last. He looks at me when I'm down, too, friendly, though I never visited him. Cadaverous, sallow man, with cropped grey hair and big moulting brown eyes that weaken his mouth as they move.

I cannot tell how it is lit. In those moments when suddenly I am trapped or down, and they are looking at me, I am aware of nothing but their compassionate eyes. And when it is gone I cannot imagine how the scene was lit. Not by daylight. Something beyond the doorway and the dark panelling.

Horsehair, the padding of an old chair, pulled out in a flat tangle. Sometimes a man's star stains like a cigarette burn on yellow wood.

Suffering and love in Henrik's eyes. A thinking love. Temptation to make him happy, then outwit him.

What does she think when she knows they are close to me?

There is clear brown glass, there are pink flowers, there is the dark panelling. The distance of late afternoon sun.

A long hand with a tremor rests on the metal arm of a black machine. The thumb rubs drily across the iron, across the side of the forefinger.

A journey. Between Amy's breasts by caterpillar tractor. And back again.

The white porous earth-cloud that passes me through itself, and through; that brings forward more of itself to grow round me, the sounds of factories muffled above my head, beneath my head. To subside through this cloud-bread that puts blind and deaf distance about me.

If she knows they are close to me, she knows she, too, has come close. She sees what Henrik sees when he talks to me.

While Henrik talks to me the others talk to my actor up on deck. With Henrik there is clear brown glass, there are pink flowers, dark panelling. On the land too, there are these things.

A couple of hours before dawn the dry, porous grey fog, webbed with black net. Caked carbon of burnt hair on the lace, sweet smells of the garden at night.

Morning. The actor watching me whenever I go up on deck.

I have been to this convalescent woman's cabin twice already, once in the afternoon, once in the night. She knows I have nothing to do. Her reddish-brown hair is dyed from grey, I think. She's sallow, and rather bony; not exactly elderly, but careful about how she moves, and a little deaf. The first time, the late afternoon sun beat up off the sea through the little curtain; the second time, the faint light from the wall fitting spread out across the panelling without reaching the corners. She watches everything with her brown eyes – doesn't like closing them. In the cabin she says very little. When I'm not with her I don't need to think about her at all. I like a pretty silk frock she has, patterned in grey and red.

The old man on the boat deck no longer says anything as I pass. I go up close and peer at him. Behind the sunglasses his eyes are shut. His hands are folded over his stick, their slight tremors shaking it.

In the swimming pool the actor goes idly along on his back, the sunlit water patterning his breast and belly.

There was a little old man I helped to nurse while he was dying. His paralysed legs grew soft and feminine, his whole body coy. In the coffin he was rouged and decked out in satin frills and ribbons.

The skin of her bared upper arms is pale and flabby, though she is thin. My fingers and my thumbs detect the muscles under the skin. There is a vacancy on her body that her pretty scent does not cover. Across the vacancy her brown eyes follow me.

The water supports the actor, the sun nourishes him, the air delights in his body. The water sprinkles him with stars as he wallows playfully on his back, dipping from side to side.

Suppose she wears nightdresses like the heavy shiny pink one always, not just when I visit. That would be no joke.

The actor's nipples are like the soft oval tops of little puddings flavoured with the palest chocolate, buried in his breast. His flesh absorbs, creamy and riddled with muffled journeys. He is cumulus. The thought of his flesh is a thought rubbed with oranges, painted with honey.

Will she darn the seam we burst open under the arm or will she leave it torn till next time? I know where she keeps her glasses when she takes them off, I can't pretend to myself that I don't. Am I kind to her? Would I be flattered to see the other men she has settled for before me? I think I should not.

The smell of leather passes heavily on the wind to starboard and disappears ahead.

She seems to enjoy me as if she were enjoying something I should not myself like: a shiny, sticky iced cake, for example. That is the newness. If I go many more times she will start to notice me.

Two late afternoons, one after the other. Some repetitions, some variations. Not enough data to set patterns. I play all the time with the simple yes–no toy of whether I go for the second midnight in succession or leave the first to stand as an emergency. Plenty to think about. Nothing gives me a lead.

He flames under the waves in flakes like the setting sun. His navel is an ancient mouth. His teeth strengthen his followers' fingertips as they brush them across his opened lips. His feet, etc. His privy member, handsomely formed, is still as a lizard.

There are circles of beauty across his body. Smiles of beauty across his shoulders. All this has been prepared for: white canvas screens stand about on the deck, flapping tightly in the sun.

Patted dry, he puts on his crisp white jacket again. His fingers, made for smoking cigarettes, settle his collar. He wears his glasses.

Joyce is taller than I thought she was.

Why should they have been doing it in the washroom instead of the sick-bay? Behind the rubber-stoppered door. I had assumed him dead without expecting a funeral. So many other ways. Disposal. But to glimpse the white suit, yellowed, crouched on a stool by the basin while the nurse and the sick-berth attendant were taking the bandages from the head.

The captain has gone down into the depths of the ship; into slippery wet blackness, invisible by day.

I could go to her in the mornings too. Or instead. Perhaps somebody else goes in the mornings. But I was the first, yesterday. She'd had no time after being so ill to get anybody else.

Bent over on to the porcelain it looked at me without any change of expression. Placid, interested in what was happening. Discernibly a human head, bald, with one big eye looking at me. Where the dressing peeled away I could see the contusion, the spontaneous breaks in the skin, the wounds that looked too tired to bleed. All the time he concentrates on his head.

For a moment, a great shaking glass sheet for a window, with the blurred pink figure of a man shouting at me through it. But I cannot hear a sound from him or from the wind that distorts him so.

Dougal comes past. I tell him to avoid the washroom. He thanks me.

She wants to make me forget. That is what she says, starting to notice me. In the darkness, slippery nylon wrinkled against my face, my head full of cold scent, I feel self-pity coming on.

What is it she thinks I can remember? I can never remember enough. Against her side I rub the chain I feel growing in me, but she misunderstands. I want to be kind to her.

Above us, below us, the ship spins slowly in the night, grinding quietly. From a porthole, Merrett surveys the waters with distrust.

White plastic fibrils appear here and there in the darkness of the ship. They stretch and snap and bud, then break quickly and disappear.

The water comes over, brimming, golden-grey, with nobody to notice it. Full of pale light towards the surface. No more taste to it than to a human body. Broken thistles afloat in it. Lapping softly down the plates of the hull it finds its level again.

In the dawn light, something dark hopping from one wave trough to the next, keeping level with the ship, just as a sunbeam sometimes does. Nothing to bother about.

The ship draws in again the coils of piping that trailed beneath its hull in the night. Far from land, we sail in shallows where grey cylinders and globes lie under the water, near enough to the surface for their rivets to show.

I go below, and feel the ship above me turn, turning, trying to find the night again.

This is what it is like on the land: the town-gods, with coloured rings painted round their eyes, drive their cars down to the water's edge and stand in them watching the ships go by.

Protection has its grip slowly peeled off all of us, and off all our things. We're left glistening and tight. What it is that will taunt, what is it that will lunge?

On the land there are big old sheds of corrugated iron, their reddish-brown paint much faded. Cinder paths behind them, and tough grey-green weeds.

The white iron ceiling, the ivory corner, the washroom door. They have finished in there. The room has been full of steam; the mirrors and walls are clouded over. Damp soiled dressings in the bin. They have gone away. I wonder whether they have forgiven him.

With steam in my glass, a wet clock with fingers that keep slipping back, the effort of propping my shoes against a slippery tiled wall, things are unsteady. Iron ladders lead down, you can see feet, waists, heads moving about. Wiping the moisture off a chromium rim of this chromium-rimmed thing gives a narrow strip of mirror; and glinting, scissor-eyed, they look in from it at what's going on. Two or three of them, not recognisable. Here there are many black shoes, shuffling, swivelling, some of them women's. Wearing at the linoleum.

I smell methylated spirits. Dougal there, just behind me, lying as if dead. He's stripped to the waist but his trousers are neat. Amy, kneeling beside him, pours the stuff on to wadding and wipes his chest and throat. People tread on them in passing. Ducts up into the air, down into the dark. More feet, blackshod, bare pink, thudding close to me along the metal wall beside my ear or across the thick reeded glass lid through which I look up into the bright fog of daylight. High up in it, billows of orange smoke seem to be going past.

II

The Collection of Things

I encountered Sikelianos
unexpectedly, in the early evening.

It was in the bare, ungardened patch
around what must have been
his house, or summer place,
or his museum: shuttered,
builders' gear all about; a chained goat;
a telegraph post with a streetlamp slung from it;
Sikelianos
on his plinth in that scruffy, peaceful spot,
surveying the Gulf of Corinth
in the haze below, marble
head and shoulders a little grander
than human, flushed
by the sunset's glance across
Delphi's red-tiled roofs. He was
one more fact. Not a provocation
to any fervour, to any damage.

On a side track along the hill
there was damage: two bullet-holes,
small calibre,
crazing the glass front of a shrine,
erect kiosk of rusted
grey sheet iron, a worn offertory slot
under the locked, tended
display-case. Which contained,
undamaged, a green glass lamp,
oil for it in a pop-bottle,
a torn-out magazine page with a stained ikon.

And another place, below and behind
the poet's head, had a cracked gold
high-heeled slipper. It was an almost empty
grave under the cypresses, cut
shallow and dry in the churchyard rock,
most recently used, for a short spell,
by a woman of the generation
of Sikelianos. Nothing left in it
but the marker recording her death
at ninety, two or three years back,
and a plastic posy, some small bones, the shoe.

Sikelianos is gathered in,
called down from every corner of the air to condense
into that shape of marble, rendered to
a decent, conceivable size
and emitting among the hills a clear quiet
sunset tone that owes
no further obligation at all
to detail, description, the collection of things.

Timelessness of Desire

Into the purpose: or out.
There is only, without a tune,
timelessness of desire.

don't open up the way
this town shines in through glass
and the days darken;
there's nothing better,
not one thing better to do –

What's now only disproved
was once imagined.

In the Wall

The trails of light all start
from unstable origins
that drift in the dark
in every direction

They coil and wave
into the frame

which is the dark

They make loops of lemon,
of brilliant angelica, streams
of shimmering ruby water

And they stop dead. Arrested,
it turns to a wet street.

Drive at the barrier again. It makes
a night, wet with brilliances.

Brilliant with the power of arrest.

– Or stale, muffled, the senses
having no edge:
feeling for the underside,
wakeful. The name
is Charlatan. A trodden place,
a city: the feet have been

everywhere – on the pillows,
across the benches, on to the walls.

Deep under the viaduct arches
the bare earth is barren;
no rain or daylight. It is dead
dirt. The naked foot,
the soft parts
have been set down here too.

          Central
to the world, a toilet cubicle
under the street:
             a judas-hole
in the door, spikes round the top,
a white crisis-chamber.

In eight or nine distinct
dried brown spattered arcs
somebody's blood has jetted
the whole height of the tiles.
                              He's quite
gone away now.

In the walls

town gods and household gods
used to stare
                    out of ringed eyes

seeing
what was never to be said

lacking, in any case,
discourse.

A scent with no face
in darkness:

sallow beyond the skin
and through to a lily-of-the-valley odour
sallow satin

lifted in the voice

not looking but breathing fast

shifting little and quick
more sensible than sense allows;

a raid into the unalterable.

Household god
on a hall table,
stage-lit from a streetlamp
through frosted glass:

eyeless, topless clay head,
true human image
thrown up in Leisure Arts,
holds evenly within his form
a loose mess of papers

Can't speak.
Can't read.

The Mouth of Shade

The mask behind the face
can't see: slants of dark
barely dividing puckered
lids. Wolf cheeks
sunk, taut, mouth fallen,
empty pit,
straight to the base of the lungs
whose pumped-out air
lets the mouth say what it likes
without closing. Talkative,
sure of itself by the minute, but
lacking memory; whatever comes
through next, from wherever.

How stale it sounds; how sudden
with life a moment later,
kicking down deep
into the shoe, knowing
the total ropes. Metallic
flash in the eye-slits,
then emptiness. What's left
in there to make it work?

A form. And the insignia, worn
nobody knows how long; hung loose
and comfortable, always kept fresh
for whatever the show turns out to be.

The Square House, February

Mounted on all four walls the neat
wide windows framed in white
idly take pictures of the weather
over my shoulder or
out of the corner of my eye then
play them long after

up there against the long desk
watching the snow
come into Staffordshire
by way of the Cheshire Gap and Crewe:
how the flakes topple
softly among the low dark branches
patterning passing shadows through
the silvery veil of net on the pane
and how they will do that for most
of a dark afternoon
settling hardly at all

Near Garmsley Camp

Under great heat we're searching
the slopes above Kyre brook
for antiquities: earthwork banks,
moats, mounds. There's a need
between us to discover something.

We're in a strange descent; curving
through a young plantation, aspens
or white poplars, spaced leaves
on straight pale poles, stage trees,
a wood.

      Beyond that, the track
baffles, turns into nothing or anything,

but best, at the bottom of the wood
a field-gate chained shut
and an unmarked meadow, thickly
hedged round, and floating above itself,
floating a foot above its own grassy floor
as a silky, flushed
level of seed-heads, lifted
on invisible stalks and barely
ruffling; a surface cloudy and soft enough
to turn the daylight;
                except where
close at hand you and I can

stare sidelong through it and down
into the measurable depth of clear air
and watch winged creatures swim
high and low through the stems.

Thus far down, and seeming
further; translucent patch set into
what seems the opaque ground. Above,
the bright opaque haze of the afternoon
has hilltop trees, towers, telegraph poles
rising into it as if into infinite
distance;
           but visible for miles
a man stands sunlit and hammering
high on Edvyn Loach church steeple,
trespassing in the air claimed for spirits
by the stone push upwards, and giving
the game away; an entire man standing
upright in the sky.

Suppose –

Suppose that once in a while
It still works, just as it used to.

Somebody unwraps it among the teacups,
Curtained from street flashes
By afternoon clatter,
A crowd of faces and feet,
That sort of thing;

Opens it, finds a poem –
The old flat arrangement,
Dry track of half a voice –
And lets it drift on his own thoughts,
Like a simile.

As a mirror, held to face another,
Deepens it with recessions
This used idea, abandoned
And pinched up into caricature,
Monitors and shakes the new.

Between them, a guttering freedom,
Just enough light to ask questions by:

Why Aleksandr Blok, the beautiful,
Dealt out humbug,
Still made sense –

Discovering the Form

Discovering the form of vibrancy
in one of the minor hilltops,

the whorl of an ear
twisting somewhere under the turf,
a curve you have to guess at.

In a house out of sight round the shoulder,
out of ordinary earshot,
a desperate mother, shut in with her child,
raves back at it when it cries,
on and on and on, in misery and fear.

Round on the quiet side of the hill
their shrieks fill an empty meadow.

Provision

The irritations of comfort –
I visit as they rebuild the house
from within: whitening, straightening,
bracing the chimney-breast edges
and forcing warmth, dryness
and windows with views into
the cottage below canal-level.

For yes, there's a canal, bringing
cold reflections almost to the door,
and beyond it the main line to Manchester,
its grid of gantries pale
against the upland and the sky;
there's a towpath pub, where the red-
haired old landlady
brings up the beer from the cellar slowly
in a jug; there's a chapel
next door to the cottage, set up
with a false front and a real
boiler-house, and –
rest, my mind – near by there's
a small haulage contractor's yard.

Everything's turned up here, except
a certain complete cast-iron
housefront, preserved and pinned
to a blank wall in Ottawa.

This comfort
beckons. It won't do. It beckons.
Driving steadily through rain in
a watertight car with the wipers going.
It won't do. It beckons.

At Once

I say at once there's a light on the slope among the allotment huts. If I leave it a moment unsaid it'll set solid, and that only the beginning. But, said, it has gone.

The wonderful light, clear and pale like a redcurrant, is set off by a comfortable mist of winter afternoon over to one side of it among the allotment gardens.

Appearance of mist. The light in its glass. The witnesses were built in about 1910 in the shapes of houses. The stream crawls past the bottom of the slope, edged with vegetables and crossed by planks. You can approach.

The light is in the earth if anywhere. This is already the place where it was. We've hardly started, and I want to do it again.

Dusk

The sun sets
in a wall that holds the sky.

You'll not
be here long, maybe.

The window
filled with reflections
turns on its pivot;

beyond its edge
the air goes on cold and deep;
your hand feels it,
or mine, or both;
it's the same air for ever.

Now reach across the dark.

Now touch the mountain.

After Working

I like being tired,
to go downhill from waking
late in the day
when the clay hours
have mostly crossed the town
and sails smack on the reservoir
bright and cold;

I squat there by the reeds
in dusty grass near earth
stamped to a zoo patch
fed with dog dung,
and where swifts
flick sooty feathers along the water
agape for flies.

The thoughts I'm used to meeting
at head-height when I walk or drive
get lost here in the petrol haze
that calms the elm-tops
over the sunset shadows I sit among;

and I watch the sails,
the brick dam,
the far buildings brighten,
pulled into light,
sharp edges and transient,
painful to see:

signal to leave looking and
shaded, to fall away
lower than dulled water reaches,
still breathing the dog odour
of water, new flats, suburb trees,
into the half light of a night garage
without a floor,

then down its concrete stems,
shaded as I go down
past slack and soundless
shores of what might be other
scummed waters,
to oil-marked asphalt
and, in the darkness, to a sort of grass.

III

Epic

'Stranger, in your own land
how do men call you?'

'I will tell you. Men call me Roy
Fisher. Women call me
remote.'

The Making of the Book

'Let the Blurb be strong,
modest and true.
Build it to take a belting;
they'll pick on that.

Then choose your second gang –
the first, led by your publisher,
you already belong to,
its membership involuntary, if free –

for the other, set up an interesting
tension between the acknowledgements
and the resemblances; but in the photograph keep
the cut of your moustache equivocal.

Write your own warrant. Make plain
in idiot-sized letters
for which of the others you'll take the blame – Yes:
it's *necessary* to belong;

several allegiances
are laid out for you ready.
And remember, though you're only a poet,
there's somebody, somewhere, whose patience

it falls to *you* finally to exhaust.
For poetry, we have to take it, is essential,
though menial; its purpose
constantly to set up little enmities.

Faction makes a reciprocal
to-and-fro of the simplest sort – and characterless
but for an 'aesthetic' variable,
inaudible to all but the players.

And this little mindless motion,
that nobody but the selfless and Schooled-
for-Service would ever stoop to,
drives the Society.
It's a long story:
but the minuscule dialectic,
tick-tacking away, no more than notional,
in obscure columns,

at length transmits itself
mysteriously through Education –
which pays off the poets too,
one way and another –

out beyond Government,
past Control and Commodity
even to the hollowness
of the seventeenth percentile, the outermost
reaches of the responsible.

If the reviewers fall idle, everybody drops dead:
it's as simple as that.

– Go, little book.'

A Modern Story

A prophecy (1981)

Being past fifty, with suspiciously few enemies
and just about enough achievements

I was sat in my garden, watching over my grey peas,
when there came to me – not in a flash, but more like

a sunken boiler, slowly and implacably surfacing of its own
volition – the finest of all my ideas! It felt even then

as though it might be one of the five best
projects for a literary work in England at that moment

and, do you know, I was right! The Arts Council Literature Panel
awarded it one of their five bursaries: seven and a half thousand pounds I got.

But when the cheque came it gave me Writer's Block. Four days.
Five. Six. After a week, I no longer knew myself.

In what I can only call now a fit of distraction
I – founded a Poetry Competition, with my bursary money as the prize.

Though mad, I was canny, mind. I first sold my elder son
my project, cash down, to pay for the ads.

Then everything suddenly got very fast. Thirty-two thousand entries
came in at one pound fifty a time. That's forty-eight grand

and a handling problem. To help with the mail
and the critical rough sorting I was able to take on

four unemployed Ph.Ds and three newly-redundant
publishers' editors under the Government

Work Experience Scheme, and to give my younger son
a Youth Opportunity. And when it came to hiring the judges

I asked a few friends I valued for their fairness and cynicism
to guess who they'd inevitably be. It warmed my heart

to be able to prove them right. Then, three weeks before closing date,
I saw how I could use my Small Business Starter Allowance to double the
    prize money,

and that announcement brought in a late crop of entries, six
thousand or more. There were no problems

such as the judges giving one another the prizes; they gave them
to next year's judges as it turned out, but nobody knew that at the time.

So: with part of my fifty grand profits, and the unstoppable weapon
of thirty-eight thousand stamped addressed envelopes targeted on poets,

I quickly put in a bid for a chain of South Coast vanity presses
that had overreached themselves and needed the gas bill paying.

At which point an easy-voiced man telephoned and asked to see me 'about
    England'.
I thought he was the Inland Revenue and invited him round with caution.

He was tall, very affable, a little cold – Anthony Bate could have played him:
his conversation was light, oblique and wide-ranging.

He gave the impression of a man in some way *authorised*
yet there was something in his drift that was erotic

though in no way you could specify. At length I was seized by the idea
that, while taking care not in so many words to say it,

he was proposing to sell off to me, very cheap,
for me and my friends to do whatever we wanted with, a piece of England

the Arts Council Literature Department! The staff. The files. The goodwill.
He leaned back, and looked into my eyes. The figures took me only a second

'No deal,' I told him. 'I'm a straight business man now, not a gangster.'
He gave me his card. I presented him with one of my books, edition of two
    thousand, remaindered.

'Bing-Bong Ladies from Tongue Lane
or
This Introduction Needs No Poem

(a tribute to Cy Roth)

Bing-Bong Ladies: self-style for the emergency cleaners in a major supermarket chain, summoned by a two-tone bell to deal quickly with shattered mayonnaise jars and the like. As in, 'I've had two bing-bongs already since nine-o'-clock.'

Tongue Lane: a road on the edge of the Fairfield Estate, which is attached to, rather than part of, the spa town of Buxton, Derbyshire, but harbours the more active part of its population.

Cy Roth: wrote and directed, not necessarily in that order, and possibly simultaneously, the film *Fire Maidens from Outer Space.*

I am indebted to Peter Revell for the information contained in the first of these notes; and to Ronnie Scott for the form of the work's alternative title.

So now'

Sets

If you take a poem
you must take another
and another
till you have a poet.

And if you take a poet
you'll take another, and so on,
till finally you get
a civilisation: or just
the dirtiest brawl you ever saw –
the choice isn't yours.

The Poetry of Place

A resident of Rutherford, New Jersey,
happens to have for sale, at collectors'
price, a wheelbarrow,
old, but not old enough, red,
but too red: painting it up,
he's obviously not seen the shade
quite right. His greed makes him
a hasty reader. Glazed
with varnish, it'll do. Whoever buys it
gets to see the room where the original
things with ideas in them are.

On   Not

Emparalysed   not
speaking space   neither
that   was space
now letting   no light in
but sending   from the dark
unusable   flocks of shine

And I'm far away in
Absentia, beyond all the shine.
A land in names only,
where the Community Coast extends
from Jutty Point to Cut Dog Island
and the steam ferries take their names
from the pubs that own them –
The Spark of Decency; The Chutney Plum.

Whole days idled away, everyone
unmistakably on the Skib Bib
at the best, shunning shifts
at the Potato-cake Works, instead
reading animal stories –
*Dire Tom, the Diatom; The Short
Sharp History of Hardfart the Aardvark –*

or drinking in the Dancing Belly
where the Four Crouched Poets of Splad
still endure reproach; while
out in the square the equestrian
statue of Edward the Afterbirth
looks coldly on. But I'll

be back soon enough from the Deep Nectaries
with more news of the truth, never fear.

On the Neglect of Figure Composition

Prelude

Hundreds upon hundreds of years of Lapiths
versus Centaurs; Sabine women abducted
by ferocious male models in nothing but
helmets and little cloaks, the corners
curled on their privates; such fading
mileage out of archaic feuds. It all passed.

But I propose a fresh Matter of Britain,
the parties to be as follows. First,
all those who have come to believe
our profoundest guidance to be
the person and style of His Late
Majesty King Zog of Albania: yes, Zog
of the white yachting uniform, of the pistol
for shooting assassins,
of the plump
princesses, in matching
rig, and sharing his peculiar
gift of being able to make himself appear
rancid when photographed.
                              All British Zoggists
mimic his dress and demeanour, his small
upturned moustache, the proud
suspicion of his eyes. In times of truce
they hold conventions at weekends
in the hotels of our former

manufacturing towns. They dress up,
eye one another, make wild plans.

Most repugnant to them are
the Ianists; once no more than a small
quasi-theological dream, but lately
more numerous, and moving in the land –
though not, it must be remembered,
given much to travelling. For an Ianist
is far more likely to project, or simply telephone,
his outlook and will, for implementation,
to another in the desired locality; they are
a sort of conceptual cavalry.
The heart of Ianism

lies in a constant meditation upon
The Real Ian. The Real Ian
is neither sportsman nor entertainer
but a part-time polytechnic lecturer
called Trevor Hennessy. He teaches
at two polytechnics, one
in the Midlands, the other in the Home
Counties; and he is not
explicit. Ianists are the most implicit
of all known people.

Sketch for the First Exhibition of the New Heroic Art

'Ianists and Zoggists Resting between Engagements, in Rocky Terrain'

'The Spirit of Queen Geraldine, Borne on a Cloud, Encourages Flagging Zoggists during a Skirmish near Burnley'

Diptych: 'Members of an Ianist Cell Brushing their Crests / Appraising One Another's Crests'

'A Zoggist Cohort of the First Rigour Surprised by Ianist Irregulars'

'Five Ianists Scorning to Interrogate a Captured Zoggist'

'The Zoggist College under Snow'

'Ianists Driving Randomly-Coloured Ford Escorts in Formation on the A1 near Peterborough on a Fine April Morning'

'The Zoggist Acceptance of the Surrender of Weybridge'

'Suburban Panorama Incorporating Zoggists Enacting *Enforced Exile in Reduced Circumstances* and Ianists Enacting *Unacknowledged Supremacy*'

'A Modest Zoggist, Borne Unwillingly in Triumph on his Comrades' Shoulders'

'Zoggists in their Cups'

'Condemned Ianists, Already Blindfolded, Exchange Comments on the Turnout of the Zoggist Firing Party'

'Zoggists Hiding in an Ianist Laundry'

'Ianists Relaxing with their Women. They Sit Silent in a Circle Drinking White Rum while their Women Dance Quietly to Records in the Other Half of the Room'

'*The First Time in his Whites.* The Mother of a Zoggist Cadet Proudly Puts the Finishing Touches to his Uniform'

'An Ianist Foraging Party Mingling with the Crowds in Sainsburys'

'Oxford Zoggists in the High'

'The Passage of The Real Ian through Purley by Night'

Paraphrases

(for Peter Ryan)

Dear Mr Fisher I am writing
a thesis on your work.
But am unable to obtain
texts. I have articles by Davie, D.,
and Mottram, E.,
but not your Books since booksellers
I have approached refuse to
take my order saying they
can no longer afford to

handle 'this type of business'. It is
too late! for me to change
my subject to the work of a more
popular writer, so please Mr Fisher
you must help me since I face the alternatives
of failing my degree or repaying
the whole of my scholarship money...

Dear Mr Fisher although I have been unable
to read much of your work (to get it that is)
I am a great admirer of it and your landscapes
have become so real to me I am convinced I have, in fact,
become you. I have never, however,
seen any photograph of you, and am most curious
to have an idea of your appearance,
beyond what my mirror, of course, tells me.
The cover of your *Collected Poems*
(reproduced in the *Guardian*, November 1971)
shows upwards of fifty faces; but which is yours? Are you
the little boy at the front, and if so have you
changed much since then?

Dear Mr Fisher recently while studying
selections from a modern anthology with
one of my GCE groups I came across your interestingly titled
'Starting to Make a Tree'. After the discussion I felt strongly
you were definitely *holding something back* in this poem
though I can't quite reach it. Are you often in Rugby?
If you are, perhaps we could meet and I could
try at least to explain. Cordially, Avis Tree. PS. Should we
arrange a rendezvous I'm afraid I wouldn't
know who to look out for as I've never unfortunately
seen your photograph. But I notice you were born in 1930
the same year as Ted Hughes. Would I be right
in expecting you to resemble *him*, more or less?

                    – Dear Ms Tree,
It's true I'm in Rugby quite often, but the train
goes through without stopping. Could you fancy standing
outside the UP Refreshment Room a few times so that
I could learn to recognise *you*? If you could
just get hold of my four books, and wave them
then I'd know it was you. As for my own appearance
I suppose it inclines more to the
Philip Larkin side of Ted Hughes's looks...
See if you think so as I go by...

Dear Mr Fisher I have been commissioned
to write a short
critical book on your work
but find that although I have a full
dossier of reviews etcetera
I don't have access to your books. Libraries
over here seem just not to have bought them in.
Since the books are quite a few years old now
I imagine they'll all have been remaindered
some while back? Or worse, pulped? So can
you advise me on locating second-hand copies,
not too expensively I hope? Anyway,
yours, with apologies and respect...

Dear Mr Fisher I am now
so certain I am you that it is obvious to me
that the collection of poems I am currently working on
          must be
your own next book! Can you let me know –
who is to publish it and exactly when
it will be appearing? I shouldn't like there to
be any trouble over contracts, 'plagiarism'
etcetcra; besides which it would be a pity
to think one of us was wasting time and effort.
How far have *you* got? Please help me. I
do think this is urgent...

The Passive Partner

'Just tell me straight: did you go to bed with him?
I mean, *did you have sex?*'

                      'Well – sex
was had.'

'Oh God.'

'But – ah – very heavy weather
was made of it. Climax
wasn't reached. It's
been forgotten until it was
raised by you just now.'

Freelance

As always, it's the dreams that make the best sense of it:
powerful blasts from the base of the brain
send mind-litter scurrying for oblivion,
Some of its tangles, for a chance of survival,
fusing into desperate narratives, the nearer
the knuckle the better the chance.
                                    Crick,
I'm relieved to be told they're nothing but
phantasms of disappearing waste, guaranteed
not to be meaningful.
                        So I'm glad I'm not really
hired to take a class in Creative Writing
at a bus-stop in Barcelona; glad
I've not started up a winter-long Tuesday
WEA class in som far-flung hole in the night,
then forgotten to turn out for the next ten weeks;

and especially glad that I haven't after all
entered myself for a school exam
where a section of the English paper commands:
'Write a short sequence of poems. *Either*
a sequence entitled 'Clean' (six poems)
or a sequence entitled 'Dirty' (two poems only).'

Critics Can Bleed

His passion for the books
warms them

His warmth
softens them

Then his wits
work them.

The Dirty Dozen

Dirty Nature,
Dirty sea;

Dirty daytime,
Dirty cry;

Dirty melody,
Dirty heart;

Dirty God,
Dirty surprise;

Dirty drumlin,
Dirty design;

Dirty radiance,
Dirty ghost.

On Reading Robert Duncan and Hearing Duke Ellington

Jumpin' Punkins

Jump in
drunken punkins
dunken deep in
Duncan's
pun–can.

Masterpieces in My Sleep

Masterpieces in my sleep. A suppressed
novel by John Cowper Powys,

the core of its mystery
a high green mound that covered
legendary rumour.

At its climax
old Powys with his one
visionary eye
raised up a beam of energy
that blasted away St
Alfeah's, or whoever's, Tump
with a great cry and revealed for an instant, Yes!
the buried church, complete, the lost chapel
and the mound
within the mound; all seen
clear for first and last
as they vanished. For
the sake of the transfiguration
he annihilated the evidence
beyond all commentary. Maybe
that page of the text itself
never had empirical existence. I talked
in the dream with a divine,
worldly and humorous, the prime
scholar. He couldn't even *mention*
that apocalypse; it was something
deeper and more frightful than an embarrassment.
But we spoke easily
of the round grey nondescript mere
the author had left undisturbed
right through the action
in a dull meadow off to one side. 'It's
the only true *Pool*
in the whole of our literature!'
cried the scholar. Both claim and pool
seemed still to be
there to be agreed with.

The Poetry Promise

We promise our readers we will be:

Ensuring Quality	All our poems will have been workshop-tested to Award Winning standard
Maintaining Quality	Every poem will also be independently retested before you see it to ensure there has been no loss of quality before the poem reaches you. Every poem is designed to represent value for the time you spend reading it
Nurturing Answerability	Every one of our poems is authenticated as being drawn directly from the writer's personal experience or thoughts
Reducing Waiting Times	We are committed to progressive reduction of the time it takes the penny to drop after you finish reading a poem
Demonstrating Relevance	All our poems are at the very least relevant
Sharing Frameworks	We guarantee our poems will not contain any words or concepts with which you are not already reasonably familiar
Equalising Opportunities	All our poems will undertake to stir your feelings in a general way while taking care to respect any religious or cultural beliefs you may have
Dealing More Fairly	Each individual poem will be completely co-terminous. It will not contain either too few words to join up its meaning adequately or so many as to make it appear to be up to something else
Developing Access	All our poems are so designed as to be suitable for reproduction in fire, water, fur (non-animal), and on condoms
Observing Guidelines	All poems will be written in guidelines

'Poetry You Can Count On'

The Nation

The national day
had dawned. Everywhere
the national tree was opening its blossoms
to the sun's first rays, and from all quarters
young and old in national costume
were making their way to the original National
Building, where the national standard already
fluttered against the sky. Some breakfasted
on the national dish as they walked, frequently
pausing to greet acquaintances with a heartfelt
exchange of the national gesture. Many
were leading the national animal; others carried it
in their arms. The national bird
flew overhead; and on every side
could be heard the keen strains
or the national anthem, played on
the national instrument.

Where enough were gathered together,
national feeling ran high, and concerted cries of
'Death to the national foe!' were raised.
The national weapon was brandished. Though
festivities were constrained by the size of
the national debt, the national sport was
vigorously played all day
and the national drink drunk.
And from midday till late in the evening
there arose continually from the rear
of the national prison the sounds of the national
method of execution, dealing out rapid
justice to those who had given way
– on this day of all days –
to the national vice.

Hypnopaedia

As I expounded *The Man With the Blue Guitar*
my students outwitted me.

Eyes glazed, or averted, they declined
to pick up a single question,
forcing me to drone on alone. I was so boring
I fell asleep.

Then a little way off
through the opaque white screens in my head
I started to make out a voice.
It was expounding *The Man With the Blue Guitar*.

Startled, I awoke, talking. Seven stanzas it had taught
without any prompting from me. Though curious,
I still didn't have enough gall
to check its performance from anybody's notes.

Irreversible

The *Atlantic Review* misspelled Kokoschka.
In three weeks he was dead.

Ninety-three years to build a name –
Kokoschka – but he felt
that fine crack in the glaze.

Then he 'suffered a short illness';
that's what the illness was.
Irreversible.

John Ashbery should watch out.
Hiding as John Ash in Haight-Ashbury
won't help in the clash
of Haight-Asch with John Ashbury;
it's got to happen.

I'm just the maker
of mutant poems. In one
sails became *snails* – try it. With me
Organic Form overproduces. Here's
my poem *The Trace*, that's started
to feed off itself, and breed:

– silky swallowed hair
that dried and was
flying in a fan –

Now it's *dined and was*
flying in a fan –

– sulky squalid whore
that dined and was
frying in a fin –

For *Trace* read *Truce*;
for *Bruce*, *Brace*:

– crying in a fit –

Chisellers! cut deep
into the firm, glistening
sand –

Norseman, pass by!

Stop

Spent all his life
playing for time.
All of it.

Envoi

At nineteen, suspecting my living might depend on it,
I started pretending to be grown up.

On my sixtieth birthday, suspecting there might be
unhealthy truth in Vonnegut's admonition,
we become what we pretend to be,
I kissed the pretence goodbye.

       Whereupon
people I loved found it easy to give me toys,
while others, pleading the nation's poverty,
found themselves suspiciously unable
to find me money any longer.

      Madam or Sir,
I beg you, turn out your toys and convert them
to cash for the reasonable hire of your poet. (Unless
you prefer to provide your own, exposed rhymes carry
a small additional charge. Metres come free.)

IV

Kingsbury Mill

If only, when I travelled,
I could always really move –
not take the apparatus,
teeth and straps,
the whole thought-mangle.

I think of Kingsbury mill-house,
first fresh thing east of the city
past the filter-beds:
having to slow the car
over a packhorse bridge,
seeing the mill,
whitewashed brick in the meadow

Feeling the load of what's behind
like steel bars caving in a lorry-cab
racketing onwards through the pause.

Linear

To travel and feel
the world growing old on your body

breathe and excrete
perpetually the erosion that makes the world

a caravan the little city
that has the wit to cross a continent

so patiently it cannot help but see
how each day's dust lay and shifted and lies again

no forgotten miles or kinks
in the journey other than cunning ones

to pass through many things acquisitively
and touch against many more

a long line without anything
you could call repetition

always through eroded
country amused by others and other worlds

a line like certain snail tracks
crazily long and determined.

Butterton Ford

— But the street is the river —

Not much of a river, and
not much of a street.
Not much call for either
down this end.

They may as well double up,
let the stream slant out of the hill
over the cobbles in a thin race;

a footway for flood-time,
with a little bridge with overflow holes
cut in the coping. Keep the pressure off.

The Thing About Joe Sullivan

The pianist Joe Sullivan,
jamming sound against idea

hard as it can go
florid and dangerous

slams at the beat, or hovers,
drumming, along its spikes;

in his time almost the only
one of them to ignore

the chance of easing down,
walking it leisurely,

he'll strut, with gambling shapes,
underpinning by James P.,

amble, and stride over
gulfs of his own leaving, perilously

toppling octaves down to where
the chords grow fat again

and ride hard-edged, most lucidly
voiced, and in good inversions even when

the piano seems at risk of being
hammered the next second into scrap.

For all that, he won't swing
like all the others;

disregards mere continuity,
the snakecharming business,

the 'masturbator's rhythm'
under the long variations:

Sullivan can gut a sequence
in one chorus –

– approach, development, climax, discard –
and sound magnanimous.

The mannerism of intensity
often with him seems true,

too much to be said, the mood
pressing in right at the start, then

running among stock forms
that could play themselves

and moving there with such
quickness of intellect

that shapes flaw and fuse,
altering without much sign,

concentration
so wrapped up in thoroughness

it can sound bluff, bustling,
just big-handed stuff –

belied by what drives him in
to make rigid, display,

shout and abscond, rather
than just let it come, let it go –

And that thing is his mood
a feeling violent and ordinary

that runs in among standard forms so
wrapped up in clarity

that fingers following his
through figures that sound obvious

find corners everywhere,
marks of invention, wakefulness;

the rapid and perverse
tracks that ordinary feelings

make when they get driven
hard enough against time.

The Only Image

Salts work their way
to the outside of a plant pot
and dry white.

         This encrustation
is the only image.
         The rest –
the entire winter, if there's winter –
comes as a variable that shifts
in any part, or vanishes.

         I can
compare what I like to the salts,
to the pot, if there's a pot,
to the winter if there's a winter.

The salts I can compare
to anything there is.
Anything.

The Memorial Fountain

The fountain plays
         through summer dusk in gaunt shadows,
black constructions
         against a late clear sky,
water in the basin
         where the column falls
    shaking,
rapid and wild,
         in cross-waves, in back-waves,
    the light glinting and blue,
as in a wind
         though there is none,
               Harsh
skyline!
         Far-off scaffolding
bitten against the air.

166

Sombre mood
in the presence of things,
                no matter what things;
respectful sepia.

        This scene:
        people on the public seats
        embedded in it, darkening
        intelligences of what's visible;
        private, given over, all of them –

Many scenes.

Still sombre.

As for the fountain:
                nothing in the describing
beyond what shows
                for anyone;
        above all
no 'atmosphere'.
                It's like this often –
I don't exaggerate.

        And the scene?
        a thirty-five-year-old man,
        poet,
                by temper, realist,
        watching a fountain
        and the figures round it
        in garish twilight,
                        working
        to distinguish an event
        from an opinion;
                        this man,
        intent and comfortable –

Romantic notion.

A Sign Illuminated

In honour of something or other – poor
King Bertie's crowning; the Charter Centenary;
1938 as a whole – the city

decreed that on several occasions there should emerge
from the Depot on Kyotts Lake Road an Illuminated
Bus. On a published route

it would slowly glide through every
suburb and slum in turn. Crowds
might turn out. So it came

crusing on summer evenings, before
the little boys went to their beds, its lights
plain in the sun from as much as a mile off;

those lights were its headlamps and certain thin
patterns of domestic bulbs
all over the coachwork. What the city had picked

was one of its own
retired double-deckers. They'd sliced off the top,
blacked the windows, painted out the livery;

it was a vehicle so old
that the shadowy driver sat exposed above the engine
in an open cab. Among the little boys

were many who knew the design and the period
registration plates. In the sunset light
they could take it all in: this emblem

that trundled past all the stops; possessed no
route number, passengers or conductor; was less
than a bus, let alone less than lit up.

One World

When I last saw them they were eleven
born on a council estate
halfway to the next town,
sold into the lowest stream
at five or so: you can recognise
a century of Brummagem eugenics
in a child. It was a school
where three out of a hundred
passed for Selective forms
in a worker-zone Comprehensive.
But not these. It was late:
apart from their other troubles
they couldn't read.

I was no help. Most days
they scared hell out of me: I taught
pacification and how to play.
I lived for the moment and trusted nothing.

By now some are dead. I read of one
suicide and one broken skull.
The rest will be going on thirty. About them
I know I can generalise without offence.
But to name names: if John Snook,
Ann Pouney or Brian Davidson,
Pat Aston or Royston Williams
should of their own accord and unprompted
read over this and remember me – well
if they're offended they can tell me about it.
It would be good to know
We all look at the same magazines.

The Poet's Message

What sort of message –
what sort of man
comes in a message?

I would
get into a message if I could
and come complete
to where I can see
what's across the park:
and leave my own position
empty for you in its frame.

Mother-tongue, Father-tongue

As I get to the age they were at when I last heard it
it's talking more often in my head

Funny. I ay got that pain no more

and I'm slipping this grammar back on

Then him as was the head one come in and he told us

when I mutter to myself. Not when anybody

He'd had something come to his leg

could hear. They might think I was
joking. I'm not.

*And I've had a letter off him today, so I've wrote him
straight back*

'So did you always talk like you do now?'

I talk as I write

170

It's one of them like you like

I write as I talk

They've give him like a Sistifikit

Norman-French-Latin
catches the teeth;
Not mine. Feel
The syntax, ignore the phonology

You hadn't bettoo!

Rugged. It did the job

This what I'm doing's for her

right through life and out the other end

Her's one of them ladies as has been married twice

– I'm getting quite fluent again

There'll have to a welt be put in it though

Aren't I?

Summat o' that. Ah.

Meaning yes

Ah.

The Sidings at Drebkau

(September 1989)

By the road at Drebkau
the line copies itself sideways.

Parallel silent freight trains
stack themselves there
under a rolling low sky
that gleams on to the massed iron
and slides on over the plain
into Poland, levelling across
German villages with Polish names,
a forty-year-old border, a Poland
shakily written on a map of Germany.

Branch-lines that curve away
to the gas and coal combines of the hacked
forest and the flayed plain, haul out
brown coal to put a foundry-stink
into country towns, age them
brownish-grey, deaden their eyes
behind the scatter of cyclists, the school bus,
the row of flagpoles that hoist the community
a modest official height from the floor.

A land with the lights turned down,
hugging its powerless good sense to itself,
what governs it long since flaked away
into fantasy; this decency
won't leave an image bold enough
to be remembered by people who need it.

Even such image as there is
equivocates: simultaneity,
dilated out of nature by a monstrous
pair of hinged wars, seems to be dragging
some of us back through time to our lost, dirty cities;
yellow haze, poisonous rivers; home.

The Slink

Round behind Harecops and up across Archford Moor,
a slope of hedged fields with a road up or down.
Zone of a few dozen acres. No focus: instead,
the appearance of being inclined to judge. The
judgement, understated.

Helpless awareness, wholly alert. Having the
discomfort, day and night, of a thread of language
passing through, pulled against it, reversed, re-
run; never breaking, never belonging.

Borne constantly over to one side, to the shelter
not of primary buildings – opera-house, cathedral,
law-palace, prison – but of the blankness of the
bare ground artists didn't render by more than a
wash and a few spacing figures who rummage there
or float, as the sun goes down and pediments shove
shadows.

Constantly to the left, as far as the isolated row
of shops, beached tram. *Saltender's*: boarded up
and the boards kicked in. *Cliff's*: incinerated,
the painted woodwork squared into satiny black
scales. *Adward's*: empty, a dump.

Just beyond night-fire's limits, burnt fur.

Seized slowly from the left: trapezius gives up
on the body, shapes only for itself. Locks off
the ribs, winds tighter with each step. Stops off
walking straight.

Self-portraits and Their Mirrors

Harsh in the face
caught in a double
ice of daylight, a
mirror beside a window

Face
destroyed by the affront
in its own enquiry

The eyes staring at the eyes
staring and the features
actively scattering
away from that one
failure as if
suddenly caught
in hypertrophic growth
with no face to belong to.

Going

When the dead in your generation are still few,
as they go, they reach back; for a while
they fill the whole place with themselves,
rummaging about, inquisitive,
turning everybody on; bringing
their eyes behind yours to make you see things for them.

Now there are more, more every year,
sometimes a month packed full with them
passing through, first dulled, preoccupied, and then
taken quickly to silence. And they're gone, that's all.

Day In, Day Out

Escapist realism,
flight for a day
on a determinist train,
the wear on the track tuned
to one fugitive's weight.

Likelihood
of a certain emotion at the flight's extremity;
great unlikelihood of its failure
to be conjurable: the mark
being that which the one available shot
can't but hit.

Given that,
a brake that drags and catches
scrapes a thin colour on to the certain emotion;
dresses it.

The Sky, the Sea

The sky, the sea
and the beach:

at evening
there is a man left
on the glistening fade,

heading for the beach house
under a wind
that scrubs all sounds away.

There is a driftwood fire in the hearth,
the smoke pulls down on the roof;
there are two of them there,
it is simple;
and into the dunes
their window faces its white eye.

It is simple: the house
in the eye of the wind –
all else is ground, the long levels
sustain it, the small
knot in a grain washed clean
to silken grey –

All of it is plain:
the house also featureless, a Puritan
bungalow, bleached but strong;
and beyond what has to be done
there is nothing; the dusk
free to come down,
filled with cities of division.

In the Visitors' Book

'Fish and parsley sauce got cooked
behind a first-floor landing door, some
hours before each visit. An unseen
neighbour would lay out scent-
trails of unease across the stairs
to mark the climb to something I knew
to be strange, however orderly. Up there,
clear hospital-inmate views down into
miniaturised garden strips with pools
while giant aircraft lunged
grey-bellied from behind the roof,
sagging on out of sight
towards a runway. Views, and talk,
friendly, but less inquisitive
than the ghost of the unknown woman's cooking.'

The Mark

Yet with no peace of mind
with clouded eyes and haunted
when pastures tilt as sunlit
sheets. Wind hitting low

What it is, milk, not white
but lifted to a shine
under the metal cup that clasps
a lamp on straggled flex

Orchards going down,
dark end of October.
A limp on the path between
byres and barns

By seeking about, slow hunt
by scent, sun in a cloth;
peace on a different tongue.
By wearing down

Squatting in bright blacklead
in the hearth, named a man,
faces the room, sputters,
smokes, won't satisty

Why not utter a strange
notion, just as its minute
threatens to pass? A thing
that smells no advantage

but has to be spoken out
from special clothing,
heavy, fresh from the cupboard.
The thought is nobody's

Wearing down, worn down, worn
away. Other forms
inhabit the whole skin, abandon it,
struggle against air and die

Worn down. Brushing against health
harms it, a shove, a flush,
dragging, a discomfiture. Bought
in advance, with small change,

with walking away small time
nearly to nothing. Less
than could serve. The lamp
drilling away what's too little

Fallen out of calculation,
visible when remenbered
the hour lies in the ground,
white body, pointing the way.

Releases

One Sunday afternoon by the shuttered corner shop heavy flies, bright green and blue, swarmed on the fish boxes. Culling them with a rolled paper you lived close to them. Dead, they filled up the Maltese-cross grooves in the slate-blue paving bricks.

The gantries of the travelling cranes hit back at the sky in the afterglow.

All structures are mysterious, however the explanation goes.

In a place like that, virtually everything is a structure.

Wherever the floor or the crust of the ground is opened, indoors or out, there is revealed some part of the continuous underwork; a tarry pipe, a gas main, a pot of still yellow water.

Grammar of my journey through the streets, through the rooms and halls. I sense my movement always as forward and express it so. I ignore my ability to turn left or right. Or to glance, or to think, aside. My whole tortuous track warps into a single advancing line. This warping hardly shows in the stations of my path, even the unspiral staircase, but it has many consequences in what lies beyond or beside what I travel through. All the same, I'm prevented by definition from knowing what those consequences are like. If I even think about them they swing into place directly ahead of me, and in doing so they straighten themselves up.

The greater part of my life is past, and I seem to have done nothing. Yet I've achieved rather more than I've attempted, so that means I've kept my standards.

It's amazing what you can say if you try.

Forgive me, but on the hillsides over Abergavenny the houses are too many, too high and too white.

Far into the jigsaw puzzle there are blobs and flecks of whitish grey in the dark inks of the hillside. The puzzle shows anarchy and nature to the child. It's not for solving, it's for the disordering of feeling. Some piece of going on substance, sky-stuff, skyline-stuff, some locus with no qualifiers of its own, is the heart of the world's energies. Some reason, at the mercy of the laws of a puzzle, assigns those energies. The puzzle helps teach a fascinated resignation: any pavement, any dwarf wall, any old inside leg The best isn't necessarily best.

The double-fronted shop perched next to the road bridge over the main line cutting, its shutters peeling down to the greeny-blue undercoat in the sun. Shadowy, with an old Kelvinator ice-cream machine and many groceries, but with plenty of space above them. Not a popular shop. Nobody could ever lay a story on it. The story would recede, disperse, fail to answer when called.

Coming down the hill by the park early one summer evening on the top deck of a bus, seeing the warm roofs, the horse-chestnuts and limes, stretching out from me, spreading under me; deciding this was the first thing I needed, and the strongest. What I thought was not what I knew was there, but I stayed.

On leaving, photographing a few houses, street corners, the railway bridge, on a bright afternoon, in case they're about to go. Colours welling suddenly through all the shapes that had never seemed coloured at all.

Toyland

Today the sunlight is the paint on lead soldiers
only they are people scattering out of the cool church

and as they go across the gravel and among the spring streets
they spread formality: they know, we know, what they have been doing,

the old couples, the widowed, the staunch smilers,
the deprived and the few nubile young lily-ladies,

and we know what they will do when they have opened the doors of their
         houses and walked in:
mostly they will make water, and wash their calm hands and eat.

The organ's flourishes finish; the verger closes the doors;
the choirboys run home, and the rector goes off in his motor.

Here a policeman stalks, the sun glinting on his helmet-crest;
then a man pushes a perambulator home; and somebody posts a letter.

If I sit here long enough, loving it all, I shall see the District Nurse pedal past,
the children going to Sunday School and the strollers strolling;

the lights darting on in different rooms as night comes in;
and I shall see washing hung out, and the postman delivering letters.

I might by exception see an ambulance or the fire brigade
or even, if the chance came round, street musicians (singing and playing).

180

For the people I've seen, this seems the operation of life:
I need the paint of stillness and sunshine to see it that way.

The secret laugh of the world picks them up and shakes them like peas boiling;
they behave as if nothing happened; maybe they no longer notice.

I notice. I laugh with the laugh, cultivate it, make much of it,
but still I don't know what the joke is, to tell them.

Homilies

What seems a random clang in the offing, then clangs akimbo that bring on
dark. Darkness with no rest in it, nor any call to agree it's boundless. Nor any
will to do that. Behind, beyond the dark, outside it, dull skin of the yurt that
holds it in swells and wrinkles in the air. Some turn to it, open their clothes
and press their belly-buttons to it to draw its wisdom through. And so they
do, though for most the thrill fades. Then a clang that seems no part of the
dark comes striking up from the side, then another striking down. None of
this has any business being in time but now there's a push.

All starts are false. Admit it. That point could be worked to death. Not now,
though. Not here. Question is pragmatic: whether or not the false start stains
the whole of what comes after it and makes rubbish. Not always. Beyond the
start the blur straightens up and clears, the stain fades and all's right as rain.
So a whitewashed cob corner's looked for and there it is. Go behind it, tap it,
see if it shakes. The sun stays steady, or its absence, this calmly-taken grey
afternoon storm around broken planks of a coop with paint peeling off in strips.
Eyes look out through the gaps. And for the end it's treat with truth, a toss.

The main shifts having made their moves, with the lesser ones popping out
from under wherever they can and everything settling down at last, there's
nothing you need to do but arrange the books then go outside and die. If you
find you can no longer spell, just orange them. Make nice orangements. Then
go outside and die. It'll be fine.

A sign, it stood fair beyond belief. Sign, as it happens, of a ghastly and wilful
misunderstanding but from old habit unable to say so. Or, indeed, to say
anything at all. So turn to the texts and notes: so crazed and shattered, as it
also happens, they can be made to work only as bits of signs. Brecht for a
while kept a sign over his desk, its text: DIE WAHRHEIT IST KONKRET.

Aside to a Children's Tale

This dead march is thin
in our spacious street
as the black procession
that stumbles its beat;

our doors are clerical
and the thin coffin door
winks on a wet pall,
a frozen sore;

and four men like pigs
bear high as they can
the unguarded image
of a private man;

while broken music
lamely goes by
in the drummed earth,
the brassy sky.

Some Loss

Being drawn again
through the same moment

helpless, and to find
everything simpler yet:

more things I forgot to remember
have gone; maybe because I forgot.

Instead there is blankness
and there is grace:

the insistence of the essential,
the sublime made lyrical
at the loss of what's forgotten.

The Time, Saturday

1

After years of sour flatus,
mind-lunges, sudden but dwindling
rages, he swells,

when his knob-nose and
his stomach tell him he's
finally where it's to be had,

into his recrudescence. Having
no use for proportion,
structure, space,

he finds his genius lodged
in a place thick with himself.
A one-end street, a steep

wall-headed pitch with rubble, where tarmac
gives out and the scattered bricks
breed. Terraces worn,

filled with faces. Saturday sunset,
smoky. An old Buick taxi, *Pride of the North*,

charging up the ruts. Hangs in, idles
like a cement-mixer, goes dead. Not all the people
assembled to witness the recrudescence.

are drunk. Some have a permanent intentness.
One woman only totters, another
keeps herself crouched. Recriminations

go slanting off. Not all the speeches
get spoken, or could be. He's well-
buried into brick-ends, oil-cans, glints of declining

sun on tea-set gilding; dust and sand
rubbed ruddy into his skin.
In him a god of opaque

grandeur lays claim on spirit, breathing
through gnawed-down hard-bake Roman brick
mortared with puke. Almost there comes

the clamping-on of cracked, rust-stained
marble cladding, the brandish
of a torn-out privet bush.

2

An hour into the cool and the dusk
with a move to a nearby
hall, and it's fading: the air

already too thin for anything
but ordinary breathing, and a group
standing statue around him at haphazard

angles under headroom. Among them
a caretaker, calling
music back down from the rafters.

3

Things falling flat. Everybody
who's left and can bend
gets into a drawer, folds down.

Off-centre under the low ceiling.
Strip-lights with shades come on. Talk
slopes back up, back down.

4

Well after midnight the set,
still rubble, barely heaves, its cleaned-off
cubicles lit by numerous

low-flying moons that negotiate
passageways, manoeuvre through windows.
In a tidy corner, a room suddenly

filled with one, a great roofless
shout: 'GAO!' – one of the most
secret names of God. The lights

suddenly drain away upwards.
Near by, another voice: 'Got to get
some of these wet moons seen to...'

Corner

Dark projecting corner
of shiny mahogany
standing out
among shadowy walls.

Beside it the face
gleams. Somebody standing

or halted in walking out.
A teacher –
          there are no
teachers here, no lessons.
It's not a teacher.
          Somebody –
the settings are made
to show faces off.
People have to expect to be seen.
They can clear themselves of enigma
if the settings allow,
if the enigma –

Keats's death-mask
a face built out from a corner.

It you're living
any decor
can make a wraith of you.

The Square House: April

Dawn birds at noon
on a still pale grey
April day with a tractor
behind the wood and aeroplane sounds
hidden in the sky

What light there is
sets them off
even the single magpie
hung like a parrot tail-heavy
in the sycamore

The ringdoves are rising rising
out of the gardens
heads high and startled
between phoenix wings

There's something in the fluid air
something in nothing
in the null
middle of the day

They are in it and I
witness it. In the channel of
air between my window and the wood
the finches are jumping like
lice among the bushes

The crest of the hen blackbird
carrying débris to her nest and
perched on a post halfway
is a luminous emblem
a great head
of last year's silvered Honesty
springing high from her beak

At a certain height
almost in the cloud
the rooks marshal and manoeuvre
in the something they sense.
They are in it. I
witness it. It is in
me.

White Cloud, White Blossom

Sandy wall and trees
locked to the sky

small country
buckled iron fences
ducking in the grass

leaf print shadows,
fingers on a soft big belly
out in the sun

old bricks patch the mudhole
where cows come through the hedge,
dead swags of bramble shake on the wire,
under the elders
dry twig beds lie

steam from a mash boiler
blowing down through the wood

white cloud, white blossom

The Open Poem and the Closed Poem

1

To come out ready capitalised, with outlines,
cross-beams and a display,
and this terrible year
moralising itself at my feet, right
from the frozen clutter at its beginning
through to this hundred-
and-ninth day since I last
opened this writing notebook
or thought about what was in it;
having written *Roller* and lost it
and forgotten it, and *Wonders
of Obligation*, and forgotten every word of it
until asked, and *The Red and the Black*
and forgotten even the title, and *Releases*
and forgotten I'd ever written it
or what it was; and climbed the mysterious
pip of a hill over Oakenclough
in the snow and mud
and wrecked my shoes, and
forgotten where I'd been to wreck them
until reminded, and having run
my new car twelve thousand miles without
memorising the tyre pressures,
and having lost my room for manoeuvre
to the monetarists, and having
walked Avebury and forgotten all
but the shape of my understanding of it;
to have things clear, the circumstances
answerable for a start, so that it's plain who's talking.

2

Winking drop on the lens
shatters a soft
fog of lamplight in the dark
that hides how close
overhead the wet balks are;
where you're standing, the way
you're standing
makes the signal, what gives
the wires to shine, a handsbreadth
at a time, rapidly sliding
through the thick of the wall, the bank,

black peat that holds
flakes of thrush-egg. Underfoot
in the shallows every unevenness
crawling with rust, alive
with rust. Foot of the signal.

They Come Home

To win back the parents
from the passage-laws;
bring them home together,
bury them under a tree;

spread their bone-dust,
that now stares back at the sun
for the first time and not for long,
two colours of dry limestone,
female and male,
met for the first time, your
fingers and mine mixing your dead
in a layer across the topsoil,
set with corms,
aconite and crocus,
directly under a double-winged
trapdoor of live turf;

by no means separate the dead
from anything.

To have them
won back, by awkward custom;
lifted free
of the crematorium counter
and out from the poor
vestige of common ceremony;

left to our own devices, holding them,
each in a stout paper bag that
covers a squarefaced container
of dull plastic, coloured like
milky cocoa, with a toning beige lid.

And the last journey of all, of necessity
by way of the car-exhaust workshop;

they travel, your foot steadying them upright,
together on the floor, concentrated,
come down to owl-size in their jars,

and they stay there for an hour without us,
lifted up high on the greased, shining
hydraulic pillars under the workshop roof-lights,
closed in my grey-green car
while its rusted and burnt-out piping gets
yanked off and replaced. They come home
over a new smell of hot metal.

By no means separate
from anything at all.

Jars and their paper bags,
name-labels,
go to the bin, with the clearings-out
from the discontinued kitchen;

each has still
a whisper of human dust that
clings to the plastic,
the boundary a mad
regress beyond the microscopic.

They're going again in a day or two:

to be in part twice-burned
in city flames; eight hundred
degrees of the lance-burner
under the oven's
brick arch, and then whatever
blast of the municipality
lifts the remainder haze clear of Sheffield
and over the North Sea.

V

At the Grave of Asa Benveniste

(with Fleur Adcock and for Agneta Falk)

Churchyard woman coming quickly from under the wall:
You're looking for Plath. No question-mark.

no short way out of it but
follow the finger, stand
for a spell in the standing-place,

be seen, then duck off sidelong
to where under your stone
you're remarked on less:

Asa, translucent Jew,
your eyebrows arched
so high as to hold
nothing excluded that might want in,

it's proper to come your way
by deflection. Exquisite poet,
exquisite – will the language say this? –

publisher; not paid-up for a burial
with the Jews, nor wanting

to have your bones burned,
ground up and thrown, you're here

in the churchyard annexe, somebody's
hilltop field walled round, a place
like the vegetable garden of an old asylum,

lowered from the drizzle in the hour between
service and wake, inventions that made life
stand up on end and shake. The church

cleared for the People Show's
deepest dignities, *Kaddish*
by Bernard Stone, alternate
cries striking the nave in brass –

Nuttall from the floor, from the rafters
Miles Davis. Your house filled up fast with stricken
friends muttering mischiefs up the stair

to the room where latterly
you'd lived mostly by the windows,

looking out, letting in, surrounded
by what used to be the bookshop stock,
priced up safe against buyers: *I can't have
anyone taking my good friends away from me.*

Afloat on the mood all day, Judi
doing your looking out for you
for a spell. From the middle of the room
to the window and through it, steadily
up towards Bell House Moor. Downstairs,

barrelhouse music and booze. On. Everybody
freed to be with you in your house again, the clocks
seriously unhitched. And visible in the crush
through the dark afternoon, Ken Smith, suit
worn at a rakish angle, the face worn
lightly if at all. And on we go.

The stone's as you asked for it:

FOOLISH ENOUGH TO HAVE BEEN A POET,
                                          Asa,

your hat's in the bathroom.

You Should Have Been There
(for Peter Riley)

You should have been there
mornings in '58 in Walsall

the side-street café
round from the foot of the market

modern, worn, built
as if ready sandbagged, swing door
at bevelled corner, windows of frost
or vapour set above head-height
in walls bottomed with blond veneer
spilt on and singed
                    — these steams
        these broths, this laundry food
        in filtered sun, these coats
        these faces set all about
        coming and going

                    Peter,
you should have been there
to make two of our sort

too many for the territory

I'd split the shift with you
walking out through the square
rising as if on marble
                    into the Gaumont
up the broad staircase of empty scents
to the hollow of the restaurant
its few unhooked people
                    even the first
sip of coffee arrested, thoughts, of a kind,
sliding from under the arrest
                    while the broad-
bodied waitress in black with the ominous eye
stalks by

Songs from the Camel's Coffin

(for Gael Turnbull)

1

And it's all coming together
at last, quiet in the eye.

I've come apart.

Falling what's left of me together
to take to myself what's at last
coming in – whatever's
left of that, not already
fallen away on approach. Lost

lives, lost voices, blanked–out
patches of myself now all
of a kind together. Echo.

They are all gone into the world.

2

This hard world.
Difficult world.
Insoluble world. This stone-
hard, heartless
world –

Fine word, world.

3

Born in the middle of the island and never leaving it
in fifty years, then startled
on stepping down to the battered tarmac of O'Hare
to discover that the air above it,
the entire medium of elsewhere,
wasn't as I'd guessed it would have to be, a heavy
yellowish fluid tending towards glass,
towards mica. Why in all that time
had nobody said?
I'll never be sure, that's for certain.

Homage to Edwin Morgan

When Scotland shall secede, and lift itself
clear of the yelping South, let the boundary
be drawn again with tact. There must be room
for the lately abandoned counties of England
and the defectors drifting north.
So have the southernmost frontier post
set at the bridge by Derby
where the '45 petered out. My house sits
forty miles to the north, so I can show
ways through Derby by back roads in darkness. Pay me
with sure asylum and a strong border;
don't let me go to London any more.
I know of *real* Scots Fishers; my first name
comes from the Gaelic. I'll learn to spell it.

And I invoke your gods. First, in his knobbly bowler,
the Burry Man at South Queensferry, then,
at the South Queen Mary Ferry – Burns!
The Merry Queen; the Whittrick (where
in Hell did *that* come in from?) – Hey! Suddenly
there's a man at the Queen's south fur...

O furry Queen of Scots! McGonagall
should bring anew your softness to the breasts of Englishmen,
and respectfully remind you how our Buxton waters, gently mineral,
used to help your arthritis considerably, now and again.

Processional

(for Lee Harwood)

the pavilion comes too

lama-hatted

fireplace clanking softly

there's nobody now living
remembers the paintwork
as it was

its colour
whether bright or dull

pea-green is guessed

a group of small horned cattle
moving in front
rich blood-brown
streaked and spotted randomly
with marl-grey
across their flanks
isolating a leg
spotting guilt over stubborn faces

their tilted stony pasture
sour and snug
comes along with them

happiness in the polluted village
left in the crook of the road
between the town's two
separated ends

where wires stretch across
at the coal yard
and by the laundry
some of the town gods stand once again
on the pavement
on the cinders
their lifted radiant faces immobile

the god that dances
dances in a corner

Emblem

(for Basil Bunting)

Wing
      torn out of stone
like a paper fan

hung in a sky
            so hard
the stone seems paper

bare stems of ivy
            silver themselves
into the stones

and hold up the wall
            like an armature
till they force it apart

Every Man His Own Eyebright

(for Tony Baker)

two-lipped, open-mouthed/
in general/
small, erect, slender or
robust annual/

variable low/ short
often bronze-green semi-parasitic/
late twentieth-
century English poet/ often described
as belonging to an aggregate
species/ hairy
annual/ one good reason for not
describing the species individually/

common on heaths and
dry fields/ for roy
fisher/ the lower lip three-lobed/
in very specialised

habitats/ purple lines on the lower
lip/a generalised description
would suit most of them/ quite
definite distributions/ unstalked
with a two-lipped corolla

characteristically marked with
a yellow spot/ derelict
industrial areas/ very
complex group/ favourite words:
or, if / under
the two-lobed upper lip/
flowers, white, often tinged

with purple veins on a
yellow spot/ little
discernible forward movement
in the axils of the upper leaves/ the upper
lip with two reflexed lobes

and the lower lip with three
lobes/ favourite colours:
silver, grey, whitish / often
no more than six inches
high/ with white hairs on the stem/
as often as not in prose/

split up into a large
number of species difficult
to distinguish/ often well-
branched/ more or less oval,

deeply toothed, the upper sometimes
alternate/ perceptual scepticism/
with broad toothed bracts/

many species described would be unlikely
to be the one found by any one
person/ blue, violet
or white, and two-lipped/ further
complicated by the fact
that they often hybridise freely/
rust / all look much alik/ fruit hairy

Staffordshire Red

(for Geoffrey Hill)

There are still clefts cut in the earth
to receive us living:

the turn in the road, sheer through
the sandstone at Offley
caught me unawares,
and drew me, car and all,
down in the rock

closed overhead with trees
that arched from the walls,
their watery green
lighting ferns and moss-shags.

I had not been looking for the passage,
only for the way;

but being suddenly in
was drawn through slowly

– altering by an age,
altering again –

and then the road dropped me
out into a small, well-wooded
valley in vacancy.
Behind me.
was a nondescript cleft in the trees.
It was still the same sunless afternoon,
no north or south anywhere in the sky.
By side roads
I made my way out and round again
across the mildnesses of Staffordshire
where the world changes with every mile
and never says so.

When I came face to face with the entry
I passed myself through it a second time,
to see how it was.

It was as it had been.

The savage cut in the red ridge,
the turn in the traveller's bowels,
by design ancient or not;
the brush-flick of energy
between earth and belly;
the evenness of it. How hard
is understanding? Some things
are lying in wait in the world,
walking about in the world,
happening when touched, as they must.

Rules and Ranges for Ian Tyson

Horizons release skies.

A huge wall has a man's shoulder. In the only representation we have it is mottled with a rash and distorted overall, seen through gelatine.

The Thames with its waterfronts; a fabric with a Japanese Anemone design. They intersect at Chaos.

The force of darkness is hard, rigid, incapable of motion either within its own form or by way of evasion. All the same, it is very difficult to find.

The experience of a wind, as if it were a photogravure made of dots. To be vastly magnified.

To walk along two adjacent sides of a building at once, as of right.

After a fair number of years the distasteful aspects of the whole business become inescapable. Our frustrations will die with us, their particular qualities unsuspected. Or we can make the concrete we're staring at start talking back.

Watch the intelligence as it swallows appearances. Half the left side, a set of tones, a dimension or two. Never the whole thing at once. But we shouldn't need to comfort ourselves with thoughts like this.

Under the new system some bricks will still be made without radio receivers or photo-electric elements. No potential for colour-change, light-emission, variation of density – just pure, solid bricks. They'll be special.

A terror ruffling the grass far off, and passing without coming near. Between that place and this the grass is a continuous stretch with no intervening features.

Under the new football rules the goals will be set, not facing each other down a rectangle but at the centres of adjoining sides of a square pitch, and the teams will be arranged for attack and defence accordingly. Some minor changes in rules are bound to be necessary, but there will also be rich variations in styles of play.

Darkness fell, surrounding and separating the hollow breves. They howled and shone all night.

Poem Beginning with a Line by Josephine Clare

The sun falls in sharp wedges inside
the room.
        ('Morning')

The sun falls in sharp wedges inside
the night. When knowledge of darkness
and knowledge of day start moving
undeniably on separate
axles and slowly shake themselves
to bits that tumble back together,
new companies.

                Time
hauling the time away,
fingernails windows of the spirit.

Within this ragged memory
I'm running the truth.

Drop on Drop
(for Jeremy Hooker)

Walking
under the dark

with the dark under
walking

bone
or horn underfoot
night weathering the wood

and again in each glass dish
on the curdled milk
a blood comma

The Ticket-of-Leave Man
(for Jonathan Williams)

Jonathan, I dreamed last night of Basil Bunting,
four years dead but seeming
no worse than a bit drunk. It was for a pub lunch
in somebody's house he'd come back for an hour,
and to tell us about the play he'd been writing,
based, so he said, on a 'fragment of Chaucer – a *terzel*'
he'd doubtless made up himself. At a guess,
they'd been keeping him very short of people
he could talk to. One of us, a big fellow,
put an arm round the old man's shoulder. 'Nobody
would ever have tried *that* on
while he was alive,' I thought.

Style

(for Michael Hamburger)

Style? I couldn't begin.
That marriage (like a supple glove
that won't suffer me to breathe)
to the language of one's time
and class. The languages
of my times and classes.

Those intricacies
of self and sign. The power to mimic
and be myself. I couldn't.

I'd rather reach the air
as a version by my friend Michael.
He knows good Englishes.
And he knows the language
language gets my poems out of.

The Toy
(for Robert Graves at Ninety)

Low arch, its marble overlip
by passage through
polished and moulded back
to a tallow sheen
touched by captive
daylights, their patterns to and fro
tugged in a membrane
that answers to leaf-shutters restless
on constrained branches at an aperture
or to captive water
set rocking in a cistern
within this wholly enclosed
fragmentary labyrinth
whose low arch glances
down to the inner floor below
and nothing more;
haunting is artifice, and a spy's view.

To be shut in
not with a disquieting
spirit that makes or
motions with the lights
but with the certain power of shaking
the whole of the place by taking thought
and the compulsion
not to resist the thinking of it,

the craning to perceive
sidelong, by moving sidelong
on a tilt, any way that it would,
and still to be shut in;
captive desire, set rocking
about an axis that locates itself
back, to one side and far above
in darkness.
    Shut
in, but perceiving in a glimpse
without grip, focus or tenure
the first of the concealed
spaces: nothing continuous with the marble
or its limited vista; but night air

all around and the rim of an old
galvanised bucket to touch; a jacket
thrown down but seeming
familiar; a sunk garden
thick with growth; moonlight
strong enough to imagine colours by.

Epitaph
(for Lorine Niedecker)

Certain trees
came separately from the wood

and with no special
thought of returning

News for the Ear

On a kitchen chair
in the grass at Stifford's Bridge,
the cataracts
still on his eyes,
the poet Bunting
dozed in the afternoon,

bored with the talk
of the state of literature that year,
sinking away under it
to his preferred parish
among old names, long reckonings;

but roused at the sound of good news
and surfacing with a rush,
a grunt of delight
from centuries down: 'What?
Has the novel blown over at last, then?'

Don't Ask

(for Edwin Morgan)

In the dream, the message
comes clear: *Hugh*
Charnia has married Skellatis,
the Mari Moo.
          Beyond that,
nothing. Just waking questions,
the dream draining
quietly away to leave
only an impression
of bony islands.

          Who are they?
Is Charnia the adventurer his
name suggests – look of a round-
faced surgeon or auctioneer,
blue eyes, grey flannel?
what's in it for him? Was he drunk?
Is he after his death, then, or his
coming-to-grief, that he
tackles the Marrying Maiden?

    Undertakings bring misfortune.
    Nothing that will further –

Skellatis with downcast
inward-turned eye
and long, sallow
crossed-over thighs –

          Is it
unknown energies by mystical means
he's after? What
business has failed him?
What title to what? *Could* she have
declined? does she possess
language to decline with? Does she at all
possess mind, as we know it?
Has he married above himself, then,
commoner of the same society where
she's the nobility? Or is he out of
a fatter one that overrides? Might she be

211

just an artist, whose pleasure it is
to be married mad? Or is she fly, and wiser
than he, and he an infatuate,
a colonist?

              If
she has the measure of Hugh Charnia,
have I, though? Was the wedding
really a wake
for one or the other? And
what *was* the toast?

When I'm Sixty-four

(for Eric Mottram)

– which is tomorrow what with thin
mauve cloud cigars filling the receptacles
I'll set myself to
reverence and to even senior poets
considering I may be past it this
writing thing what with
growing old enough to lend my
falser names to causes; and to the
question 'Are you yet capable
of gavelling all these bushes?'
my answer will simply be 'Here!'

Appearing in the dead of winter on a day
when 'Bromo' Sulser's Iowa Collegians
played the Garden Theatre in Davenport
but not a single jazz musician of importance
anywhere recorded a note
lest your first cries be impeded
on their journey towards us through the years
by the company of anything
canonical – how you've fed us! And how well you've
misunderstood us at those
moments when a good
misunderstanding's what we've
most been needing!

(10 June 1994)

The Fisher Syndrome Explained
with
How to Stay Succumbed

(for R.F. Langley)

1. To facilitate free passage, position yourself centrally in your poem.

2. In case of accident, carry this card with you at all times during your poem:

> *Verses that to themselves suffice*
> *Puff up their practice at a price:*
> *A modest style cuts twice as keen –*
> *For poems need not be but mean –*
> *And language hands each poem a bin*
> *To keep its explication in.*

And on That Note:
Six Jazz Elegies

Wellstood, for forty-odd years,
guessed what there was to do next
and did it. Tipped
the history of the art half over
and went in where it suited;
and understanding that music's
more about movement than structure
proceeded to lurch, stamp,
splash, caper, grumble, sprint,
bump and trudge – mostly
on the piano – then sat down
in his hotel room before dinner
and, too soon, stopped.

Strange channels for new noises. That steely-eyed
old man, dapper,
sugar-coated in famous vanity
and endless glad-handing,
carried always somewhere about him
what he'd come upon early, a monstrous,
husky, thoroughly dangerous saxophone sound
never before heard on earth;
and on a bandstand if you put your foot
behind him hard enough,
out it would still come honking
with no manners at all.

Three piano-players
taking turns on the portable
stool. The first
tucks it close in
and perches like a hamster, as he must.
Second, I slide it back
to make good room to slouch
as I permit myself. Finally,
gaunt and purposeful, he drags it
to the extreme: Glenn Gould
plays Crazy Horse in crimson suede
pointed boots; extensible arms
reaching for distant keys, spine curved,
navel in phobic flight from the piano. The music,
after a moment's meditation, comes streaking out
in elasticated pulses: wild, dramatic,
timeless East European Stride

Taking care never to learn
the ways of the world till the moment
the alto would assume its insinuating angle and get
blown straight into life. Seeing a waiting audience, then
blinking awake mildly, leaning down to whisper
surprise news to the pianist: 'Trouble is,
I just can't seem to remember the names of
any tunes at all. Serious problem there.' Prolonged
pause, prolonged. Again, after some painful night:
'How can those people go on playing
for twenty or thirty years and never even
start to want to learn their instruments?'
Serious question there.

Ears up, neck solid,
punching pretty tunes off centre
through a stubby *cornett*: 'The way I figure it,
the sound comes out
that much closer to my face, and
that's where I want it.' Lovely old
American tunes, and talking: 'I guess you people
must all be thinking I'm just another American
loudmouth!' Talking: 'What key?
THIS key!' 'What tempo?
It's a BALLAD, for Christ's sake!' On a sofa
at a party in his honour, persuaded
to toot gently and graciously for his supper,
looses off at full volume and quells
New York Town Hall, with nothing
in pursuit but my quite small piano.

Whistling in the dark,
wobbling a pallid flame down
to the bottom of the bottle:
owl-sounds, muffled
squawks. Nothing
better to do but whistle
when there's so much dark.

VI

Poem

The small
poem
the unit of feeling

Pretty red mouth
blotted and
asking why

Here is your photograph
It is a square
view of the air of things
one certain hour –

when just in the background
a green engine goes mad in a tree
to the end of time, pretty mouth.

Commuter

Shallow, dangerous, but without sensation:
sun beats in the rear view mirror
with cars squatting in the glare
and coming on. This continues.
Gasholders flicker along the horizon.

Out in all weathers on the test rig
that simulates distance by substituting
a noise drawn between two points;
shallow, my face printed on the windscreen,
profile on the side glass; shallow –

Either I have no secrets
or the whole thing's a secret
I've forgotten to tell myself:
something to make time for on the night run south,
when the dazzle turns to clear black
and I can stare out over the wheel
straight at Orion, printed on the windscreen.

For Realism

For 'realism':
the sight of Lucas's
lamp factory on a summer night;
a shift coming off about nine,
pale light, dispersing,
runnels of people chased,
by pavements drying off
quickly after them,
away among the wrinkled brown houses
where there are cracks for them to go;
sometimes, at the corner of Farm and Wheeler Streets,
standing in that stained, half-deserted place

– pale light for staring up
four floors high
through the blind window walls
of a hall of engines,
shady humps left alone,
no lights on in there
except the sky –

there presses in
– and not as conscience –
what concentrates down in the warm hollow:

plenty of life there still,
the foodshops open late, and people
going about constantly, but not far;

there's a man in a blue suit
facing into a corner,
straddling to keep his shoes dry;
women step, talking, over the stream,
and when the men going by call out, he answers.

Above, dignity. A new precinct
comes over the scraped hill,
flats on the ridge get the last light.

Down Wheeler Street, the lamps
already gone, the windows have
lake stretches of silver
gashed out of tea green shadows,
the after-images of brickwork.

220

A conscience
builds, late, on the ridge. A realism
tries to record, before they're gone,
what silver filth these drains have run.

It is Writing

Because it could do it well
the poem wants to glorify suffering.
I mistrust it.

I mistrust the poem in its hour of success,
a thing capable of being
tempted by ethics into the wonderful.

The Hospital in Winter

A dark bell leadens the hour,
        the three-o'-clock
light falls amber across a tower.

Below, green-railed within a wall
        of coral brick,
stretches the borough hospital

monstrous with smells that cover death,
        white gauze tongues,
cold-water-pipes of pain, glass breath,

porcelain, blood, black rubber tyres;
        and in the yards
plane trees and slant telephone wires.

On benches squat the afraid and cold
        hour after hour.
Chains of windows snarl with gold.

Far off, beyond the engine-sheds,
        motionless trucks
grow ponderous, their rotting reds

deepening towards night; from windows
        bathrobed men
watch the horizon flare as the light goes.

Smoke whispers across the town,
        high panes are bleak;
pink of coral sinks to brown;
a dark bell brings the dark down.

Wish

That, once sighted,
it should move of its own accord,

right out of view most likely;
and if it does that
a more primitive state altogether
gets revealed:
              a hardened
paste–patch
of rhubarb and mud-green.

– here comes morning again,
sunshine out of an egg –

and where the first sight
was all design
              what's left
shows its behind,
stamps and wiggles,
resists transference,
won't be anybody's currency;
doesn't aim to please
and for the most part doesn't.

From the *Town Guide*

Out in the air, the statue
gets cold. It needs a coat.

The coat must have a face on top
to squint for dandruff on the shoulder.

It always did have trousers,
remember? And a wife.

– She was a raver, great big
wardroby body. Insatiable. Still is.

She drives a car like that one
by the Conveniences. His epitaph

stands all about. But on his plinth
read simply: 'The Unknown Alderman'

The Sign

First I saw it in colour, then I killed it.
What was still moving, I froze.
That came away. The colour all went
to somebody else's heaven, may they
live on in blessedness. What
came to my hand was fragile, beautiful
and grey, a photograph twilight;
so little to decay there, yet it would
be going down, slowly, be
going down.

Necessaries

A spread hand of black trees,
long commands of shade,
old people's polished knuckles
and centuries of timber, thick, lead-veined;

smoke, rolled years of sound
furred into distance; open mouths,
lazy eyes and silver
envelopes of afternoon;

skirted trees and towers
talking like cattle, lengthily.
Gold bells of surrounding days;
stars wheeled into position
while the light lasts, pale.

We need them, you and I; while after dusk
the vans come trundling in, dusting the leaves.

Still our conversation travels
up and down the window panes,
up and down, variously,
while a thin rain film blabs and blears our faces.

Artists, Providers, Places to Go

The little figures in the architect's drawing
the sleep of reason begets
little figures.

Nose the car up through the ramps
into a bay, and leave it,
keys in the dash by regulation –
cost-effective:
come back and find it gone,
you got free parking.

The concrete multi-tiers
on the high-rise estate
hold everybody's wagon.

Only they don't. What's left there
their kids tear apart, Monkeyville –
anybody in their right mind would have known it.

Next, the Adventure Playground.

Next, celibate adult males
shipped in from the Homelands for work
sleep on long shelves of concrete,
Unity of Habitation. No damp.

– for that drawing, reduce
Sleepers in the Underground to cosiness,
consider the blanket concession.

And there'll always be a taker
for a forgotten corner out of Brueghel
suitable for a bare-buttocked, incontinent,
sunken-cheeked ending. Little figure
settled in there.

Upright

Narrow free-standing spire
dropping the whole way
from lifted kangaroo-head, its own
apex of intent,

to squat lightly into the earth,
an air machine,
pale stone chambers smelling
softly of law, puckers

that carry vibrations,
vulcanite to polished bone.
It need not obey
darkness, depth. It seeps

only evaporations,
needs no drain. A dream of
splendour designed it against us
before our time. It is all

given. A woman with rows of teeth,
lanky, sick, lonelier than mothers,
would call the children, make them take
presents they had to hide.

Colour Supplement Pages

Two dimensions. Diptych divided by a house wall seen end-on.

To the right, the street, travelling rapidly towards you and away, folding itself
        into and out of itself and crouching as low as it can get,
a street with concrete slabs, stuck leaves from lime trees beside the river,
small billboards screening a lorry park, puddles in asphalt, punch-marks of
        heel and ferrule, people with pink wrinkles, plimsolls and moist jaws,
a barrow with cream wheels, a crushproofed old woman, a showerproofed
        detective, a sunblown blonde;
pale strides, advancing smiles, men crumpled together, blue shadows on
        working shirts, wet baby mouths and scaffolding.

Through the wall, raised a little and remaining still, the room,
where a woman, tall and rich-bodied, with thick dusky skin and matt black
        hair falling to the pants that are all she wears,
stands glaring vaguely at a television screen:
a brown longhaired dachshund
raises its head from dribbling on a cushion, and watches her for a while.

– Frame it in glitter, or dirty reseda.

In Touch

I took down *Pictures from Brueghel*
          to see what ways Doc
Williams had of taking off
          into a poem

          a strong
          odour of currants
rose from the pages –

well that was one way.

3rd November 1976

Maybe twenty of us in the late afternoon
are still in discussion. We're talking
about the Arts Council of Great Britain
and its beliefs about itself. We're baffled.

We're in a hired pale clubroom
high over the County Cricket Ground
and we're a set of darkening heads,
turning and talking and hanging down;

beyond the plate glass, in another system, silent,
the green pitch rears up, all colour,
and differently processed. Across it in olive overalls
three performance artists persistently move
with rakes and rods. The cold sky steepens.
Twilight catches the flats rising out of the trees.

One of our number is abducted
into the picture. A sculptor innocent of bureaucracy
raises his fine head to speak out;
and the window and its world frame him.
He is made clear.

The Whale Knot

Sea-beast for sky-worshippers, the whale
easily absorbs all others.
Colours, languages, creatures, forms. Read
the whale in all the ways clouds
are read. The clouds out of sight
are patterned and inscrutable: chaos
from simple constituents,
form out of simple chaos.

A long-drawn complicity with us all
in the sperm-whale's little eye;
among its cells, somewhere,
land-knowledge, the diverse, our condition.

Decamped into boundless viscosity,
our Absolute,
the whale seems simpler than it is:
as easy water-to-land knot
in the museum sperm-whale's bared
head-bone, alive

as the megaliths are alive, all
the force-lines crossing
within their singular undemanding
forms. Lifted from the whale-head,
a disused quarry
swims, borne on the earth;
its cliffs a moon-cradle,
its waters part of the sky.

The Host

This memory, never mind what it is,
breaks in from nowhere with senses charged

and orders me to move over. Over
me it takes precedence. It's in flood.

Nobody but me has this memory. This
memory has nobody but me.

And for thirty-eight years eight months,
not subject, as I've been, to ageing,

it has lodged in me without ever
communicating with me in any way

I've recognised. There's nobody else
it can have been in touch with in all that while

except through me; and I know it's never tried.
Vampire memory, quietly feeding off me.

A Poem Not a Picture

On a ground remarkable for lack of character, sweeps of direction form.

It's not possible to determine whether they rise from the ground's qualities or
are marked on to it. Or whether, if the first, the lines suck the ground's force
up, or are its delegates; or if the second, whether the imposed marks mobilise
or defeat it; or both, in all cases.

Out of a scratch ontology the sweeps of direction form, and, as if having direction,
produce, at wide intervals, the events.

These are wiry nodes made of small intersecting planes as if rendered by
hatching, and having a vapid, played-out look. But they are the nearest the
field has to intense features. Each has a little patch of red.

Chirico

What I listen to is worthless. There is no mystery in music.
GIORGIO DE CHIRICO

Let the flute
be silenced
and the breath
drawn back and photographed
a word.

And the stone
wagons
at rest on my ears
to quieten. My ears know
how to read.

My eyes
know how to
count each other
sleep or wake. Let the flute
be entered.

Be spoken
be used
imprinted
in a man's spine or a roof
or cloud.

Let the flute
be no flute
and the mouth
drawn back to talk
about teeth.

There are stairs
in cylinder
and for notes
posters of insurrection
print ebony.

And the clock
contends
even with masonry. Through
stone I hear it emptying
like a washbowl.

When time
is a hole
the musician loses
his notes through cracks between
the paving stones.

Let each one
be deaf
and the tone
damped under the slab. I read
a typewriter of stone.

Mouth-talk

Mouth of artifice
fashioned to make
mouth-talk.

Not formal. Familiar.

The tablecloth
            falls,
                        legs
rest on the floor;
            draperies of the design
everywhere of the most temporary:

it is made

It has motion:
            the floor a wind
propelled by the thought of a fan –

            (happy the world so made
            as to be
            blessed by the modes of art)

driven by fan blades
and their dark eddies,
            wave-patterns that convert
into mouth-talk.

A Debt for Tomorrow

I should sleep now.
    I do not wish it:

even in this pearl silence
the day is not composed to rest as I am.

What is it like, this day
    that I must kill, remorsefully?

A friend. I love him for
his deep simplicity, his understanding
of all I desire or do;
his humour.
        Though hour by hour
steadily his coarseness jostles,
his heavy beauty disappoints and drags
    like a full meal, sleepily;
so now what does he ask for,
of what does he complain? He says
my friendship made a life in him; and now
I'll not stay by to live it out. Surely
if there's a life it's his, his to keep?
How weak it makes him seem, to offer it me!

Without Location

A life without location –
just the two of us
maybe, or a few –

keeping in closeup:
and the colours –
and just the colours

coming from the common source
one after the other
on a pulse;

and passing around us,
turning about and
flaking to form a world,

patterning on the need for a world
made on a pulse.
That way we keep the colours,

till they break and go
and leave no trace; nothing
that could hold an association.

A Song

A song wiser than its words
cuts a wall out of nothing
with a jagged blade. Cuts it
clean, the jagged wall
to sit against, head lifted,
the song a glossary away, the voice
a substitute for smoking.

Not many sing
so narrow,
so wavering,
to the tune of a saw-cut.

Three Stone Lintels at Eleven Steps

Low down in the tall
chimney-breast, sandstone-faced
with flakes taken up from the field
and cemented into a spread of kitsch,
a single working stone,
bridging the fire-hole as if it held
the house up free of the flames;
by way of work it also
decorates the blaze with a law and looks
almost as old as fire, the spare smoke
buffeting across it with a sooty stain.

Sign of a passage
through the field-wall that keeps
the sheep out of the garden; a long
ponderous dressed stone set level
just high enough for a man or a sheep
to crawl under it and out
through the opening, if there were one.
There's none. Nor has there ever been. Just
solid courses, below as above. The lintel lies
supported and easy, doing little
beyond directing the mind
strongly towards what is not.

The patch marked off as garden, finally
running down into disorder and peat-bog,
ends with a dry-stone wall, then
the moor carries on. Midway
in the wall sits a focus of all
the downwardness, gathering
as seeped waters intimate
in a knot of nettle and dock
that filters a cracked flood-drain and the ceaseless
trickle of the household, odourless after its
slow passage down through the tanks.
The puddle fills and flows over
through a roofed slot in the bottom of the wall
then straight out into the moor.
With the sun striking the stone and the lapwings
everywhere in the air above, an acrid
whiff blows back off the marsh
and across the wall and the lintel

that sits in its nettles,
taking the morning light like the cover
of a pure spring, but facing uphill.

Dark on Dark

Dark on dark –
they never merge:

the eye imagines to separate them,
imagines to make them one:

imagines the notion of impossibility
for eyes.

The Lesson in Composition

Often it will start without me and come soon to where I once was
whereupon I am able for a while to speak freely
of what I have seen, imagined,
suspected, smelled, heard. I have never chosen
to speak about what I have
myself said, seldom of what I have done.
Though these things are my life
they have not the character of truth I require.

What I have been doing in the world as long as I can remember
is to witness and make conclusions. These are things
you cannot learn unless you dissemble, especially
if you start young. Like those of a spy
my words and actions have leaned to the oblique, my troubles
to the vague and hard-to-help. Likewise
I have been a teacher, I have been an accompanist.

Often it will start without me. More truthfully
other than without me it wouldn't, I have to be away:
for a while I must seem to be away, yet after so many years
I still can't pretend to pretend; taking that walk is compulsory, for
there's something about me
I don't want around at such moments – maybe
my habit of not composing. I could feel slighted,
knowing my own work hardly ever mentions me, except
by way of some stiff joke like this one.

– Tedium of talking again,
or at last, about composition and art, while I have one
eye on a thrash of clouds breaking around the guileless
blue of this December noon and the other
on the notion that there's no other topic to be had.
Whatever I start from
I go for the laws of its evolution,
de-socialising art, diffusing it
through the rest till there's no escaping it. Art talks

of its own processes, or talks about the rest
in terms of the processes of art; or stunts itself
to talk about the rest in the rest's own terms
of crisis and false report – entertainment,
that worldliness that sticks to me
so much I get sent outside
when the work wants to start.

I'm old enough to want to be prosaic;
I shall have my way.

Of the Empirical Self and for Me

(for M.E.)

In my poems there's seldom
any *I* or *you* –

    you know me, Mary;
    you wouldn't expect it of me –

The night here is humid:
there are two of us sitting out
on the bench under the window;

    two invisible ghosts
    lift glasses of white milk
    and drink
          and the lamplight
stiffens the white fence opposite.

A tall man passes
with what looks like a black dog.
He stares at the milk, and says
    It's nice to be able
    to drink a cup of
    coffee outside at night...

and vanishes. So –
What kind of a world? Even
love's not often a poem. The night
has to move quickly. Sudden rain.
Thunder bursts across the mountain;
the village goes dark with blown fuses,
and lightning-strokes repeatedly
bang out their own reality-prints
of the same white houses
staring an instant out of the dark.

The Home Pianist's Companion

Clanging along in A-flat
correcting faults,

minding the fifths
and fourths in both hands
and for once
letting the tenths look out
for their own chances,

thinking of Mary Lou,
a lesson to us all,

how she will trench and
trench into the firmness of the music
modestly;

thinking,
in my disorder of twofold sense,
or finding rather
an order thinking for me as I play,
of the look of lean-spoked
railway wagon wheels
clanging on a girder bridge,
chopping the daylight, black
wheel across wheel, spoke

over rim, in behind girder and out
revealing the light, withholding it,
inexorable flickers
of segments in overlap
moving in mean elongate
proportions, the consecutive
fourths of appearances,
harsh gaps, small strong
leverages, never still.

The sour face
on that kind of wheel:
I've known that
ever since I first knew anything;
a primary fact of feeling,
of knowing how
best to look after yourself.

Clanging along in A-flat, and
here they come,
the apports, the arrivals:
fourths, wheel-spokes,
and rapidly the eternal
mask of a narrow-faced cat,
its cornered, cringing intensity
moving me to distraction again.

But into the calm
of a time just after infancy
when most things were still
acceptable

this backward image-trail
projects further
on a straight alignment
across what looked to be emptiness,
checked as void

and suddenly locates the dead,
the utterly forgotten:

primal figure of the line,
primitively remembered,
just a posture of her, an apron,
a gait. Vestigial figure,
neighbouring old woman
gaunt, narrow-faced, closed-in,
acceptable,
soon dead.

Still in the air
haunting the fourths
of A-flat major
with wheels and a glinting cat-face;

reminding me
what it was like to be sure,
before language ever
taught me they were different,
of how some things were the same.

In the Black Country

Dudley from the Castle keep
looks like a town by Kokoschka,

one town excited
by plural perspectives

into four or five
landscapes of opportunity

each one on offer
under a selection of skies,

and it wheels, dips,
shoulders up, opens away

with clarity and confusion –
Art's marvellous.

A Working Devil for the Birthday of Coleman Hawkins

Night cities
rotating slowly,
nothing under them,
or above, or between.

Pillars
of darkness erect
cities laced with lights.
Dark tongues push down.

Head for where lights grow
in strings, in thickets;
feel for a pavement.

Not
unnatural: territory animal
slopes through the stacked
pens it constructs;
feeds from a factory district, drinks
from the still. Goes to bed
on floors of silver-fish.

Music built like a street,
tunnel of town breath
shifting with traffic. Heaviest
sounds leach out, slip down,
swill on the car floor,
booting back up through the seats and
into what weights them.

Plaited
in the music, in the long
twist of its slippery inner fold,
the agitation of pleasure, hard-working
stairway devil. All
the split-skirt, white-gartered
clan regalia: satin,
spray-on skin-tangs, more
than enough perfume to sweat into;
trembling, charged,
helpless with self.

Never far off, black mood
at how things ought to be: rough
freedom-guesses, mind-scours,
bodily energy
knocking itself out for folks
to marvel at, take heart from
and duck. Pleasure
a brush fire, feeding
on who's around, crackle of
static in scented hair. Wonderful
dangerous glitter; heavy self
gets sacrificed for the show,
hacks on, an urgent phone; overpass,
underpass, ringroad.

Steady. A roadhouse bar's a town
so long as the staff have
a jacket between them and nobody
comes by tractor. Shut out
the empty world. Settle. The spirit's
urban, right to the toecaps.

Hulk city. Streetlamp giants
stare in through tall dull windows,
shadowing a floor mattress
on or near whose corner
the kittens learn how to piss. Tough
sleep. Anyone can do this much.

Morning an uncleared head and a runway
ninety miles long to the next place,
with wagons, a built-in gale, grit.

Liberal inclinations
plaited into the music's leather
that's strong enough
to protect sprawls,
lurches, scratches, all
knees and whisky. Not every self
can help itself. Once more, let fly.

Quarry Hills

Tail lights turn off the quarry road
into comfort
from desolation there
to new houses of cinder brick
with cemetery gardens.

Nothing much moves.

Only a feeling that strokes of shadow
flicker down the hill
walking,
as strokes of rain fall on a field,
down across the gutters
constantly through the shallow dark.

Hawthorns thick with lorry dust,
trackways slimed with it;
in forecourts
scents of hot engines die away.

Strawberry lampshades.

All the machinery
rickety and ageing;
the hills dwarfish,
almost eaten through with roads.

Barnardine's Reply

Barnardine, given his life back,
is silent.

          With such conditions
what can he say?

            The talk
is all about mad arrangements, the owners
counting on their fingers,
calling it discourse, cheating,
so long as the light increases,
the prisms divide and subdivide,
the caverns crystallise out into day.

Barnardine,
whose sole insight into time
is that the right day for being hanged on
doesn't exist,
          is given
the future to understand.

It comes
as a free sample from the patentholders;
it keeps him quiet for a while.

It's not the reprieve in itself
that baffles him:
he smelt that coming
well before justice devised it −
                  lords
who accept the warrant,
put on a clean shirt,
walk to the scaffold,
shake hands all round,
forgive the headsman,
kneel down and say, distinctly, 'Now!' attract
pickpockets of the mind −

But he's led away
not into the black vomit pit
he came out of
but into a dawn world
of images without words
where armed men, shadows in pewter,

ride out of the air and vanish,
and never once stop to say what they mean:

— thumb with a broken nail
starts at the ear lobe,
traces the artery down,
crosses the clavicle, circles
the veined breast with its risen nipple,
goes down under the slope of the belly,
stretching the skin after it —

butchered just for his stink,
and for the look in his eye —

In the grey light of a deserted barn
the Venus, bending to grip the stone sill,
puts up no case for what she's after,
not even a sigh,
but flexes her back.
                    No choice for the Adonis
but to mount her wordlessly, like a hunting dog —
    just for her scent
    and for the look in her eye.

Somebody draws
a Justice
on the jail wall;

gagged with its blindfold
and wild about the eyes.

Just Where to Draw the Line

A comment on Saul Bellow: 'It's marvellous —
I mean, just the little incidental descriptions
are better than most poetry. And they
just keep coming.'

— those Quattrocento paintings
with a tiny peacable city
on every hilltop in the distance
bobbing on the skyline in a rich
luminous watery twilight. While
near at hand huge imaginary personages
slug out needless religious nastiness
and mess up the view.

Simple Location

In simple location
the sticks take fire:

they cross and tangle
with smoke-spurts

breaking into the sunlight
as it strikes the ground,

coming in from a fog-rim
through the bleached grasses;

and if a golden drop escapes
anywhere on the skin

of a boy I've seen starting to sweat
in my dream

it has its place –
or if it should leave his eye

by way of the honey-crust there
and slowly trickle

down by the corner of his mouth
to undo everything.

If the sense of charged confinement
should come again

it seizes on a breath
caught in its place in the body,

held there a moment; still
filled with the fire-scents.

If I Didn't

If I didn't dislike
mentioning works of art

I could say
the poem has always
already started, the parapet
snaking away, its grey line guarding
the football field and the sea

– the parapet
has always already started
snaking away, its grey line
guarding the football field and the sea

and under whatever progression
takes things forward

there's always
the looking down
between the moving frames

into those other movements
made long ago or in some
irrecoverable scale
but in the same alignment
and close to recall.

Some I don't recognise,
but I believe them –

one system of crimson scaffolding,
another, of flanges –

All of them must be mine,
the way I move on:

and there I am,
half my lifetime back,
on Goodrington sands
one winter Saturday,

troubled in mind: troubled
only by Goodrington beach
under the gloom, the look of it
against its hinterland

and to be walking
acres of sandy wrack,
sodden and unstable
from one end to the other.

From an English Sensibility

There's enough wind
to rock the flower-heads
enough sun
to print their shadows
on the creosoted rail.

Already
this light shaking-up
rouses the traffic noise
out of a slurred riverbed
and lifts voices
as of battered aluminium cowls
toppling up;
black
drive chains racking the hot tiles.

Out in the cokehouse
cobweb
a dark mat
draped on the rubble in a corner
muffled
with a fog of glittering dust
that shakes
captive
in the sunlight
over pitted silver-grey
ghost shapes that shine through.

The Red and the Black

Most of the houses were brick
and soft by night. But these were all done

with timber painted
gloss black across white plaster. Big, they were

stepping down
both sides of the steep street

towards the skyline out there
and the moon coming up. Yes,

there were crimson curtains all right,
and cushions of the same. After

the war. Coming up to the next war.
Between the wars. Between times.

The park lake in the suburb has been
honoured up into art, flat

on the back of a playing card.
The poplars in silhouette are climbing

nearly to the gold moon that floats
in scarlet. The houses,

dense black, with gold and scarlet windows,
have reared high into the poplars;

a thin rendering of *Clair de Lune* gets
drawn acrosss the night as it is condemned to be.

Don't think I'm being patronising.
The women's wiry hairs

are real enough, moist in the dark,
shifting on painted benches

among the graves, lipping and tugging
at the fingers' ends. The day

you're patronising to a woman's cunt
you're faded, you're a kidney

dropped in the gutter, you're a dried
bag. That's the faith of it, at least.

A faith against what odds? Deciding
she needed glasses she'd appear

glimmering with finish, staring
brightly through the black frames,

hair cut to a knife of ink,
neat lips of crimson; but bringing

the same good-natured
perfumed crotch, that was

tangy, commercial, ambitious,
epithet-hungry, effective, timeless,

whatever Lawrentian strictures
came bubbling from her head.

Albion the cinema had a garden
where the orchestra used to be.

And it was always there in the dark
under the guns, or the light

from the transparent ruched curtain
that held floods of colour

or from huge white faces
flapping over its canvas arches.

It had low walls, and something
like a fountain.

and it was modest,
with hand-built hollyhocks.

Between shows they used to play a blue
moonlight over its pastel stones.

A hill of galantine
waits for me in its frame.

In a black and gilt photo frame
it's with me always, in colour:

steep, a flat-topped tumulus,
God's Grave,

a mound that might sit with authority
on a low hill among tall hills

green under a rolling sky
and seeming to offer the promise.

of being put to the breast
every day of a long life.

If it were earth, that's how it would be.
But this is meat

shining in parsley-green and white
and part sliced away.

Solid right through, rich pink
shading to red, cream-veined,

filling the black rectangle
behind the glass, it feels

dense with its energies,
and the fork

stuck in its crown
must never once have quivered.

The green and white,
the meat, the frame,

vehement, inert,
endure. I was meant to

glance at it all just
once and move on

but I wouldn't. I fixed it.
It tried to fix me. The mound

goes rising into the sky backwards,
bitter in its green crust;

into the stormy sky of woodstain
shot with petal flares

and as it lifts obscures the mimic
shape of its own cut section

rises oblique across it and faster,
satellite, or utter independent,

marbled with rose –
pink and terracotta gases,

advancing over or voyaging into
that which is not itself,

limpid element,
shattered wherever the bow wave,

ghosting forward, strikes it,
into a sudden precipitate

of opposite green particles
heaped so that it has to

push through and leave a widening
tail as the event passes over.

Item

A bookend. Consider it well
if that's the way your mind
runs. One-handed

this year at least, and lame,
unable to shift it somewhere better
than where it unbalances

one of the unsafe heaps that
make up my workroom, even I
get driven to consider it,

putting myself at risk of unaccustomed
irony, metaphor, moral.
It's one of a couple. The other's long

lost in the house and has turned to pure
thought. This one's material,
cut from three-quarter-inch softwood,

deep-stained as oak and varnished
heavily; a few scratches. Made up
of three pieces. The face,

five inches across by four-and-three-quarters,
with the corners cut in at forty-five
degrees from three inches up; two

nails struck through to the base,
same shape, but three by three-and-a-half,
hollowed and plugged with lead. A buttress

effective as a brick would be
but with less style. No trace
of commercial fancy anywhere on it.

When my life's props come to suffer dispersal
this piece gets dumped, if I've not
done it myself first. Should it get to a junk-stall

there'd be nothing to know but these
its observable properties. All the same
it does have unshakeable provenance – unless I

choose to suppress it. I don't.
I've certain knowledge the thing is fifty-two
years old, manufactured in 1944

at the enormous works of the Birmingham
Railway Carriage and Wagon Company,
the neighbourhood's mother-ship and provider,

her main East entrance
sunk in the bend of the street I lived in.
Set up to build saloons for the world's

railways. Then Churchill tanks. Then latterly
by day and night, huge helpless plywood-skinned
troop-carrier gliders that were crawled out

wingless and blind between the houses,
lacking engines, armour or arms. Lacking
bookends. The bookend maker was a foreman

coachbuilder from the top of the
street, a man of some status, genial; Mikhail
Gorbachev would be good casting if unemployed

when this poem's filmed. My bookends
formed part of a short, non-commercial,
privately produced domestic series

using materials, tools and time stolen
from the Ministry of Aircraft Production
and its contract, and designed as family gifts

for the Friday firewatch team, four veterans
of the Great War who gathered as ordered
by law and played cards in an empty house all night,

never looking outdoors. Against
regulations, but less culpable
than the woodworking: it was forbidden

ever to reveal the sources of one's secret bookends.
The same foreman had an only daughter.
Well-provided: plenty of body, a job

in the factory office, a husband stationed
not far away, a home with her parents. Tapping
into a quiet custom of the time,

257

she worked out the date of her army call-up,
got pregnant, got herself certified so. Aborted
the foetus at home while the debris

was still small enough for the closet in the yard
to flush it; kept quiet, played for time;
won. Another little knot of illegalities.

As to this bookend, to say that the first
load it supported was a crimson-backed set of miniature
home enyclopaedias, forced into the house

in the newspaper wars of the Thirties by the agents
of Beaverbrook, later Minister of Aircraft Production
would be artistic, ironic, and, just possibly, untrue.

VII

Interiors with Various Figures

1 *Experimenting*

Experimenting, experimenting,
      with long damp fingers twisting all the time and in the dusk
white like unlit electric bulbs she said
'This green goes with this purple,' the hands going,
the question pleased: 'Agree?'

Squatting beside a dark brown armchair just round from the fireplace, one
      hand on a coalscuttle the other prickling across the butchered remains
      of my hair,
I listen to the nylon snuffle in her poking hands,
experimenting, experimenting.
'Old sexy-eyes,' is all I say.

So I have to put my face into her voice, a shiny baize-lined canister that says
      all round me, staring in:
'I've tried tonight. This place!' Experimenting. And I:
'The wind off the wallpaper blows your hair bigger.'

Growing annoyed, I think, she clouds over, reminds me she's a guest, first
      time here, a comparative stranger, however close; 'Doesn't *welcome* me.'
      She's not young, of course;
trying it on, though, going on about the milk bottle, tableleg,
the little things. Oh, a laugh somewhere. More words.
She knows I don't *live* here.

Only a little twilight is left washing around outside, her unease interfering
      with it as I watch.
Silence. Maybe some conversation. I begin:
'Perhaps you've had a child secretly sometime?'

'Hm?' she says, closed up. The fingers start again, exploring up and down
      and prodding, smoothing. Carefully
she asks 'At least – why can't you have more walls?'
Really scared. I see she means it.

To comfort her I say how there's one wall each, they can't outnumber us,
      walls, lucky to have the one with the lightswitch, our situation's
      better than beyond the backyard, where indeed the earth seems to
      stop pretty abruptly and not restart;
then she says, very finely:
'I can't look,' and 'Don't remind me,' and 'That blue gulf'.

So I ask her to let her fingers do the white things again and let her eyes look
      and her hair blow bigger, all in the dusk deeper and the coloured
      stuffs audible and odorous;
but she shuts her eyes big and mutters:
            'And when the moon with horror –
            And when the moon with horror –
            And when the moon with horror –'
So I say 'Comes blundering blind up the side tonight'.
She: 'We hear it bump and scrape'.
I: 'We hear it giggle'. Looks at me,
'And when the moon with horror,' she says.

Squatting beside a dark brown armchair just round from the fireplace, one
      hand on a coalscuttle the other prickling across the butchered remains
      of my hair,
'What have you been reading, then?' I ask her,
experimenting, experimenting.

2 *The Small Room*

Why should I let him shave the hairs from me? I hardly know him.

Of all the rooms, this is a very small room.

I cannot tell if it was he who painted the doors this colour; himself who lit the
      fire just before I arrived.

That bulb again. It has travelled even here.

In the corner, a cupboard where evidently a dog sleeps. The preparations are
      slow.

He is allowed to buy the same sort of electricity as everybody else, but his
      shirt, his milk bottle, his electricity resemble one another more than
      they resemble others of their kind. A transformation at his door, at
      his voice, under his eye.

This will include me too; yet I hardly know him. Not well enough to be sure
      which excuses would make him let me go, now, at once.

Shave the hairs from my body. Which of us thought of this thing?

3 *The Lampshade*

It is globed
    and like white wax.
Someone left it
    on the table corner
under the lamp-holder with the stiff ring.

Across its curve
    a few red strands stick.
Just now she wrapped her hair around
to stage an interview with it
inside the hair.

Now, beside the cupboard,
    skirt pulled down,
she sits on the floor
watching me
    through brass eyes.

Thinking what she told the lampshade,
    what it volunteered,
the moist globe in her hair.

Soon she'll stand up.
She helps me make the bed and gets us
brownish wet food about this time.

The white globe stays with us
at mealtimes.

4 *The Steam Crane*

Before breakfast you drew down the blind.

Soon it will be afternoon outside. Hear the steam crane start up again

deep in the world.

You sprawl with no shoes, wet with something from the floor you didn't see
    in the dark.

Black skirt. Black hair. Nothing troubles you, you big shadow. Much time
    has fallen away.

Wearing a blanket I sit in a hard armchair, a jug at my feet.

There's nothing I can give you as beautiful as the flowers on the wallpaper.

Under the wallpaper, plaster, bonded with black hairs.

5 *The Wrestler*

Stripped more or less, they wrestle among the furniture on his harsh green
    carpet.

This is their habit, the three of them, these winter mornings.

And this is my time for being with him afterwards. When I hear the others
    go downstairs I come to him,

finding him spread squarely across a sofa, shirt and tie and brown suit pulled
    straight on again over his sweat.

He needs me there. Alone, he might drop the bottle and be upset; he might go
    down to thresh on the carpet again. I think this could happen.

But now he's still, only his fingers working through his stubble hair, suddenly
    across the face, down the bent nose:

the colours in his eyes have run together, and he stares up at the unlit bulb
    that keeps constant distance from him as he floats backwards to the ice.

He says nothing, though his mouth is open. Whisky is a fluid squeezed out of
    damp ropes, wrung out of short sweaty hair.

He's glad to have me just sitting.

She has left an empty glass, a cigarette butt in the fireplace and a tissue here
    in the wastebasket;

the man an empty glass and the present of a cigar for him to smoke after
    lunch, when the television sports shows start.

Those two always choose the morning: a time when he's barely civil.

The carpet straightens its pressed patches. Drifting back where he sits he
    travels it like a cloud shadow, breathing more gently.

The bull's eye in its jar of formalin, usually on the mantelpiece, still sits out
    of harm's way on the cupboard-top.

6 *The Foyer*

The foyer's revolving doors are fixed open to let the dull heat come and go;
this afternoon, old woman, the hotel extends a long way through the streets
    outside: further than you've just been, further than you can get.

Collapsed long-legged on a public armchair beside the doorway under the
    lamp whose straight petals of orange glass hide its bulbs,
you can't see the indoor buildings along the street;

You can see only me, roofed in with lassitude in the armchair opposite,
against the brown panelling, under the criss-crossed baize letter board.

And not even that do you see, one hand spread like a handkerchief over the
    middle of your face –
my hand feels cautiously across my summer haircut; my suit's too big.

Your dress and cardigan, flowery and crisp, stand away from your brown
    collapse and resignation like a borrowed hospital bathrobe.

The heat flushes you in patches, the confinement takes your breath;

so many things are ochre and mahogany: the days, the flowers, an attempt to
    look a dog in the eye;

this seems to be the place where they wrap us in paper and tie us with string.

Though the windows are square and dingy here they're too big for you, the
    ceilings too high to think about,

the doorway too lofty.

To cut any sort of figure going out, you'd have to let me carry you through
    on my shoulders.

7 *The Wrong Time*

It's the wrong time; that makes it the wrong room:
I'm here, he's not; he was here, he will be.

Meanwhile, please use the place. It can use you,
your scent, silk, clean lines, mouthwash conversation.
With him away it's sour and frowsty. You have
to swell your light to absorb the faint bulb, scuffed greenish walls,
    breakfast wreckage,

till the silk stitches hurt. You win. But the place contains me.
I'm not what you want. You're not what I want. What do you do with me?
Do you take me in, with the milk in the bottom of the bottle; dazzle me,
     with the grease spots, out of reckoning?

Or do you see round me, a man-shaped hole in the world?

Looking at you, I can't tell. You don't seem to find it hard, either way.

8 *Truants*

That huge stale smile you give –
was it ever fresh?

Ancient sunlit afternoon
on a ground floor below street level.
The back window,
curtained with dark chenille,
          spinach-coloured,
gives on to a brick wall.

Poor quarters for you, old carcass,
But the cushions are fat over the springs;

You had plenty in that bottle, too.

For me, this is a truancy,
five minutes' tram ride out of town
in the wrong direction:
I could feel trapped.

          You're different,
truant entirely, inside your smile.

Two grown-up people.

9 *The Arrival*

You have entered, you have turned and closed the door, you have laid down
     a package wrapped in cloth as dull as your clothes and skin.

You have not looked at me, you have not looked for me, you have not
     expected me.

You busy yourself with the package, bending over it, your scuffed backside
    towards me.

You remain in the dirty shadow that edges the room, filtered through the
    fringed green lampshade; only here, just in front of me, does the light
    fall on the carpet.

You would think the light had eaten it away down to the threads.

You, being you, would expect the light to do a thing like that.

You wouldn't notice.

You might expect the faint smell of gas in here to have materialised into
    something like me. I want to go out.

You might notice my leaving. I shouldn't like that.

10 *The Billiard Table*

Morning. Eleven. The billiard table has been slept on.
A mess of sheets on the green baize.
suggests a surgery without blood.

Starting the day shakily, you keep glancing at it
till the tangle looks like abandoned grave-clothes.

And watching it from where I sit
I see it's the actual corpse, the patient dead under the anaesthetic,
a third party playing gooseberry, a pure stooge, the ghost of a paper bag;
something that stopped in the night.

Have you ever felt
we've just been issued with each other
like regulation lockers
and left to get on with it?

Nobody would expect
we'd fetch up in a place like this
making unscheduled things like what's on the table.

No longer part of us, it's still ours.

Bring the milk jug, and let's christen it.

Seven Attempted Moves

If the night were not so dark
       this would be seen
deep red,
       the last red before black.
Beside the soft earth steps
       a wall of heaped stones
breathes and
       flowers
and breathes.

       *

A cast concrete basin
       with a hole in the bottom
empty but for
       a drift of black grit
some feathers some hair
       some grey paper.
Nothing else for the puzzled face to see.

       *

Crisis –
       a man should be able
to hope for a well made crisis,
something to brace against.

But see it come in rapidly and mean
       along some corridor
in a pauperous civic Office.

       *

Under the portico
huge-winged shadows
       hang
brown, with a scent
       of powdered leather.
Up the steps
       into this
depth. Recession.
Promise of star-scratched dark.

Then put your ear to the door;
       listen

as in a shell
            to the traffic
slithering along behind it.

                    *

Here are the schoolroom chairs on which
            the ministers, in the playground,
sat to be shot.
            Four chairs; the property
of the Department of Education;
stolen
            the same night
by this souvenir hunter
            with his respect for neither side –
just for things happening;
            then sought in vain
and after a long while
            written off the books
of the Department of Education.

                    *

Bright birchleaves, luminous and orange,
stick after six months to the street,
            trodden down;
now, as at every minute, perfect.

                    *

It is a shame. There is
            nowhere to go.
Doors into further in
            lead out already
to new gardens
small enough for pets' droppings
            quickly to cover:
Ceilings
            too soon, steps curtailed;
the minibed; minibath;
            and jammed close
            the minican.

Confinement,
            shortness of breath.
Only a state of mind.
            And
statues of it built everywhere.

Handsworth Liberties

1

Open –
and away

in all directions:
room at last for the sky
and a horizon;

for pale new towers in the north
right on the line.
It all
radiates outwards
in a lightheaded air
without image;

there is a world.
It has been made
out of the tracks of waves
broken against the rim
and coming back awry; at the final
flicker they are old grass and fences.
With special intensity
they gather and break out
through birch-bark knuckles.

2

Lazily into the curve,
two roads of similar importance
but different ages, join,

doubling the daylight
where the traffic doubles,
the spaces
where the new cut through
cleared the old buildings back
remaining clear
even when built on.

3

A thin smoke
in the air as dusk approaches;
unpointed brickwork

lightly soiled,
not new, not old;

papery pink roses
in the smoke.

The place is full of people.
It is thin. They are moving.
The windows.
hold up the twilight.
It will be dark, but never deep.

4

Something has to happen here.
There must be change.
It's the place
from which the old world fell away
leaning in its dark hollow.

We can go there
into the seepage,
the cottage garden with hostas
in a chimneypot

or somewhere here
in the crowd of exchanges
we can change.

5

From here to there –
a trip between two locations
ill-conceived, raw, surreal
outgrowths of common sense, almost
merging one into the other

except for the turn
where here and there
change places, the moment
always a surprise:

on an ordinary day a brief
lightness, charm between realities;

on a good day, a break
life can flood in and fill.

6

Tranquility a manner;
peace, a quality.

With not even a whiff of peace
tranquilities ride the dusk
rank upon rank,
the light catching their edges.

Take masonry
and vegetation.
Witness composition
repeatedly.

7

The tall place
the top to it
the arena with a crowd.

They do things by the roadside
they could have done in rooms,
but think this better,

settling amid the traffic
on the central reservation turf,
the heart of everything
between the trees.

And with style: they bring
midnight and its trappings out
into the sun shadows.

8

At the end of the familiar,
throwing away the end
of the first energy, regardless;
nothing for getting home with –

if there's more
it rises from under the first
step into the strange
and under the next and goes on
lifting up all the way;

nothing has a history. The most
gnarled things are all new,

mercurial tongues
dart in at the mouth,
in at the ears;

they lick at the joints. It is new,
this moon-sweat; or by day
this walking through groundsel
among cracked concrete foundations
with devil-dung
in the corners.

Newest of all
the loading platform
of a wrecked dairy,
departure point
for a further journey
into the strangest yet –

Getting home – getting home somehow,
late, late and small.

9

Riding out of the built-up
valley without a view
on to the built-up crest
where a nondescript murky evening
comes into its own
while everybody gets home
and in under the roofs.

A place for the boys,
for the cyclists,
the strong.

10

A mild blight, a sterility,
the comfort of others'
homecoming
by way of the paved strip
down one side of the lane;

the separate streetlamps lead
through to the new houses,
which is a clear way

flanked silently
by a laundry –
brick, laurels, a cokeheap
across from the cemetery gate –
a printing works and a small
cycle tactory; hard tennis courts.

The cemetery's a valley
of long grass set with marble,
separate as a sea;

apart from the pavement
asphalt and grit are spread
for floors; there are railings,
tarred. It is all
unfinished and still.

11

Hit the bottom and spread out
among towering structures
and total dirt.

The din compelling
but irrelevant
has the effect of a silence

that drowns out spirit noise
from the sunlit cumulus ranges
over the roofs.

On the way to anywhere
stop off at the old furnace –
maybe for good.

12

Travesties of the world
come out of the fog
and rest at the boundary.

They never come in:
strange vehicles,
forms of outlandish factories
carried by sound through the air,
they stop at the border,
which is no sort of place;
then they go back

Why do they manifest themselves?
What good does watching for them do?
They come
out of a lesser world.

I shall go with them sometimes
till the journey dissolves under me.

13
Shines coldly away
down into distance
and fades
on the next rise to the mist.

If you live on a slope, the first
fact is that all
talls before anything rises.

and that can be too far away
for what it's worth. I

never went there.

Somebody else did, and
I went with them;
I didn't know why. I remember
coming a long way back
out of the hollow

where there was nothing to see
but immediacy, a long wall.

14

A falling away
   and a rejoicing
 soon after the arrivals –
 small, bright, suspicious –
were complete:
   strangers
sizing one another up
in front of the shade.

With the falling away
    the tale finishes.

Before, nobody knew them,
after, there was nothing to know.
They were swept down into the sky
or let to drift along edges
that reached out, finite,
balking the advance, delaying
their disappearance out
into the clear.

15

No dark in the body
deep as this
   even though the sun
hardens the upper world.

      A ladder
climbs down under the side
in the shadow of the tank
and crosses tarry pools.
     There are
metals that burn the air;
a deathly blue stain
in the cinder ballast,
and out there past the shade
sunlit rust hangs on the still water.

Deep as we go
into the stink
this is not the base,
not the ground. This
is the entertainment.

16

This is where the game gets dirty.
It plays
the illusion
of insecurity.

Shops
give way to hoardings,
the ground rumbles,
the street turns to a bridge –
flare and glitter of a roadway
all wheels and feet.

There's no substance;
but inside all this
there's a summer afternoon
shining in a tired room
with a cast-iron radiator,
pipes for a gas fire:
no carpet. No motion.
No security.

Matrix

1

So, the water gate
starts out of the lake
or inlet

and petrol-blue
around its pier-timbers
the waters, after sundown,
draw their lymphatic currents by,

circling the clutch of islands,
or segmented Isle;
brimming on the shores.

Alone, it could be a house,
chin on the water,
hat-roofed,
but rising behind it
there is more.

So it gives footing
first on to rock

where channels cut shadow:
or was it the last thing built
of all the provisions
in the pattern –
the one lacking purchase
and pushed on to the waves?

Domestic-secretive:
secretive-institutional.

One of the smallest.

2

Eight or nine yards
of offered crossing:
outcrop, with pushed-up strata.

Levelled, the chasms filled,
pinnacles snagged off,
skimmed with a surfacing
that cakes into a path;

not altogether closing
over patches of rock-knuckle
and the backs of waterpipes.

3

There is a place of cypress fingers
thrusting from cypress mounds.

Low walls
built with old money.
Turf and aubrietia
painted around the stones.

This is where the dead
are still supposed to make
their disappearance:

but always the same dead
seem to be walking.

Spectres of respect.

The slopes that overlook the island,
or nest of islets,
light up with coloured squares
in among the elms:

separate plots of twilight
running the same destiny:
the boat, with muffled oars,
the hooded figure, BD,
its hand upraised,

a small classical temple
of the Lutheran cast
off to one side of the walk
on a knoll;

the mountains of the cypresses
are the real dark of the path,
humping their way higher;

always a dark like that,
set off by some artifice,

growing

4

In long shapes over the channel's
fading blue,
footbridge slats,

with slatted sounds of crossing:
the shadows rattle on the blue
trough-water in the rock

where nobody lies,
nobody rests, at present.

5

Sugar flowers
on a windowsill
in the dark,
Saintpaulias in sugar,

pink, and flock violet:
everything eclectic,
building in deeper.

Spiralling from the shore
in blocked paths and on dropped
or jutting levels,
the stations of the thing
face over one another,

inseparable, interfolded,
wall-face into roof-angle,
catwalks over the garden-clefts
hung with valerian:

variants on cochlea,
invisibly thin
stone ear in the sky;

on how to get down
in through the horn
of the gold snail-shell
and not grow small.

One way and another
inward from the shore,
the narrow ground repeats itself:

trenches of silver water pierce
the island-cluster
or do no such thing:

it is all or nothing there.

6

Religious garden
dropping between two gables
ravine of black silk
twined with a cataract
and bearded flowers
their padded scents
coming as if through gauzes
printed with petals
in a draper's.

7

Ocean-lights go flashing
over the skeined roof of the sea:

miles of deep water,
northerly, heard in the dark
island-hole;

surface that races
under the wind;

that will not break;

whose lights sink,
distort, endlessly turn again
to the wave-glass,
glittering up out of the weight,

Fabergé medulla.

quartz-fires
in the under-vault,
scattered through softer globes,
their spiral trails
chasing and merging,

to form an uneasy field,
its charges drawing
the dwindling emerald waters
densely in,

as if, past all extension,
to the devouring drop.

8

Blood-red and blue glass
stain the air thinly
on a deep turn:

maybe it is approach –

maybe *kitsch*,
like so many orchids, or

the Night-Blowing Cereus,
by God, not Reinagle:

If it is approach,
it has come already;

if *kitsch* –
it turns to approach.

9

Doctor Menière –
the cabin has to tilt
here most of all
planted on earth
with clematis at the window,

close under which the corner,
with moonlit carpet, drops
like drawers,
and goes on down;

the floorboards opposite
heave up, keep coming,
silent dog attack –
spreadeagle as the floor
becomes a roof
to slide off –
the whole room
falling betrayals
always the same way,
insatiable axis.

Afterwards
when the head turns
his liquid contents follow,
heavily drifting;
slow to a near-stop.

Somewhere in all the whirl,
exposure,

visions of the rock, Doctor,
bare and brown

thrusting a back up
with elephant-hide fissures;

dispensing
with sheets of grass and sky.

10

There's a time, finally,
when it doesn't matter
that the rings of the eye
slacken, and won't mark
so many differences:

whether the water-lilies
are blue, or the water,
or the sky in the water,

or the ocean-levels
through the confused floor
of the garden channel;

long white and green
ravels in the blue
tensioned over the shimmering
chalky surface;

net of fine hairs,
some grizzle, or black,
the weave on flank and belly,
delicate envelope,
whole surface on the move

filtering currents

tangled with trailers
of sky, and maybe lilies.

Texts for a Film

1 *Talking to Cameras*

Birmingham's what I think with.

It's not made for that sort of job,
but it's what they gave me.

As a means of thinking, it's a Brummagem
screwdriver. What that is,
is a medium-weight claw hammer
or something of the sort, employed
to drive a tapered woodscrew home
as if it were a nail.
                              It's done
for lack of a nail, a screwdriver, a drill,
a bradawl, or the will to go looking.

The results come out mixed. It blunts
the screw-point, strains the shank,
bashes the head-slot flat. But
forced straight into the splitting wood,
it won't wind loose, and it can't
be twisted back out, even
if there's enough slot left for the bit.

It's instant, and it's obstinate,
and it's nobody else's future.
The screw dies in the attempt.
But you can be sure, if it's Birmingham,
that everything'll be altered
by the time you'd have wanted it again.
This isn't Yorkshire, or Paris.

– Eyes down, always down,
looking for the truth of it

fallen out of the air, out of
the vents of animals,

flaked from the skin of us all,
our pockets, the underparts of cars;

landlocked creeks
of dead ground, waste oil
with no dead river to float on.

Eyes down
for our own tracks, pressures of feet
that pack the soil down and mummify it:

lifeless trail, confirmed in
tarmac, concrete, crumbled and patched
causeways; innocence and habit

perpetually breaking the ways
across the earth, breaking the earth.

A zone of the air, ankle-high,
where dead stuff drops or hovers
in the taboo.

Dog zone,
shoe zone. Don't sit. Avoid
falling. Don't eat what's been dropped.

Disinfect dirty money if you find it.
Eyes down. Watch your step.

If you get systematic,
and follow power around, you arrive
at a bedrock out of a book. Sandstone
by Keuper, soft, so friable
it rubs back into sand under your thumb.

Exposed when the slopes need carving, it looks
imported, some sterile by-product
stuffed into the hills to swell them up.

The bald cliff of it that props the Jewellery Quarter
over the grandees' tombs gets concrete sheeting
to save it from the rain. Some bedrock.

Believe the Book of Bedrocks,
as, in the end, you must,
and you evolve Book City, just
as it evolved itself: rock, water,
forest, settlers, trade. Then
property, sewage, architects, poets.

Interesting. But what is it
when you're first set loose in it, with only
your nostrils, fingertips, ears, eyes
to teach you appetite and danger?

Is it the primal ocean, condemned
and petrified? Is it a giant
lagoon in Tartarus, petrified,
redeemed, made habitable?

There's one thing certain: this is
the centre of the universe.

The universe, we define
as that which is capable of having
a place like this for its centre.

There's no shame
in letting the world pivot
on your own patch. That's all a centre's for.

Anything else is politics: how far
West Bromwich is from London,
Handsworth from Rome, Sun
from his galactic vortex; Earl
Sterndale from Oxford; how far Clare
needed to walk
from High Beech back to Helpston.

Close by Apollo's
abandoned incinerator-house at Delphi,
its columns giving the air of a ruined
ironworks in the mountains,
I've held my hands to the displaced
Omphalos-stone, the single centre,

not of the planet, but of the earth's shifting
surface, the live map. To touch
the centre keeps everything round it
fluid, just as it did
when I still lived at ground level
and centred the universe
just beyond the mid-point of the garden path
of Seventy-Four Kentish Road, Handsworth.

This pair of big split pebbles set in the path
governed. Two, to be on the safe side –
I've always been a two-moon man. Keeping
a check on each other, rounded, odd-sized,
needing the company,
maybe they were the world's
testicles, or its nipples, or
its mismatched eyes, like mine; maybe its little
buttocks, or big toes. Playing safe,
and liking to feel at home wherever I live,
I keep them with me.

Again. What can it be?
A mountain with the wind knocked out of it,
fallen flat into its spread, wrinkled
skin, a wreckage in Nature,
with all its creatures forever
struggling out from under.

It's an artefact. A sculpture
a dozen and more miles across. Everything
that stands in it now
the work of one protracted
moment, an impulse to make;
a long century, the sort of time
it took to envisage and carry out
an unsigned medieval cathedral.

If a certain mind
could conceive that, and get it done,
the same goes for this work of art. It houses
a spirit that talks in ribbons
of tarmac and brickwork, puzzle-spaces for the people
to clamber on and spill through.

Either you run, or you face it. Compress
a shallow history to an act. Enquire who's there,
not signing. Inspect the signs. Eyes
down, for any lost clue.

What hand, what eye. Indeed. To have made
a work of art that's at the same time
the by-product of a spastic purpose,
oozing as miraculous drops
from a sort of spirit into a sort of matter,
gathering in pools, trickling to fill

wrinkles, indentations, then congealing as
masonry: factories, floods of houses,
shallowing as they spread, converted
again to spirit in the understanding. Spirit
filtered through brickwork. Counter-Nature,
caught into the sculpture and leased out
like the Nature that drips all down
the front of La Sagrada Familia.

The artist of the place
left plenty to chance, and time
and again got well served out. Who plays
in and out the tunnels? Who hangs in?

Seven hundred years ago
an earlier model of the idea, set up
on land above the Bull Ring by the proprietors,
did business as an Enterprise Park
for freed serfs. Similar rules apply.

And it stays centred
on the same spot, ignoring superseded
layouts and the quick turnover of the people; it holds
the inertia of an authoritative will.

The artwork's the figure of authority. Swung
on a green rail somewhere, with a low brick wall
under your feet, you hear
a moment in your life tell you that.

Ignore it; or go looking for it
behind all its names. Never
in the centre. Not the old centre,
nor any of the new ones. Suspect
repeated shifts of centre. The pace gets quicker.

The Forum of Augustus, sitting firm and new,
drawing centrality to itself,
had to have its back to a massive
curtain wall, set there to mask
slum tenements behind. That sort of place.

2 *Birmingham River*

Where's Birmingham river? Sunk.
Which river was it? Two. More or less.

History: we're on our tribal ground. When they
moved in from the Trent, the first English

entered the holdings and the bodies of the people
who called the waters that kept them alive

Tame, *the Dark River*; these English spread their works
southward then westward, then all ways

for thirty-odd miles, up to the damp tips of the thirty-odd
weak headwaters of the Tame. By all of the Tame

they settled, and sat, named themselves after it:
Tomsaetan. And back down at Tamworth, where the river

almost began to amount to something,
the Mercian kings kept their state. Dark

because there's hardly a still expanse of it
wide enough to catch the sky, the Dark River

mothered the Black Country and all but
vanished underneath it, seeping out from the low hills

by Dudley, by Upper Gornal, by Sedgley, by
Wolverhampton, by Bloxwich, dropping morosely

without a shelf or a race or a dip,
no more than a few feet every mile, fattened

a little from mean streams that join at
Tipton, Bilston, Willenhall, Darlaston,

Oldbury, Wednesbury. From Bescot
she oozes a border round Handsworth

where I was born, snakes through the flat
meadows that turned into Perry Barr,

passes through Witton, heading for the city
but never getting there. A couple of miles out

she catches the timeless, suspended
scent of Nechells and Saltley – coal gas,

sewage, smoke – turns and makes off
for Tamworth, caught on the right shoulder

by the wash that's run under Birmingham,
a slow, petty river with no memory of an ancient

name; a river called Rea, meaning river,
and misspelt at that. Before they merge

they're both steered straight, in channels
that force them clear of the gasworks. And the Tame

gets marched out of town in the policed calm
that hangs under the long legs of the M6.

These living rivers
turgidly watered the fields, gave

drink; drove low-powered mills, shoved
the Soho Works into motion, collected waste

and foul waters. Gave way to steam,
collected sewage, factory poisons. Gave way

to clean Welsh water, kept on collecting
typhoid. Sank out of sight

under streets, highways, the back walls of workshops;
collected metals, chemicals, aquicides. Ceased

to draw lines that weren't cancelled or unwanted; became
drains, with no part in anybody's plan.

3 *Town World*

Buckled and tilted a few degrees
this way and that, a plane

that runs always
to a horizon of roofs;

tarmac tracks
stamped through roof-slates;

tree-heads, ornate school chimneys
pushed high enough up to imagine over

to the next hard skyline,
border to another brick dish

with another covered river;
then over again to almost the same valley,

and past that to places that might look
the same but where *you'd*

be different; places where rumours start up
then crawl here on names without images; alien

factory-odours drawn up by the sun
and slid our way. Districts

with ancient buses; black air;
roadways of girders; concrete

visions in sunset dust. You'd never get home.

4 *In the Repair Shop*

The piano's a machine
hidden in a heavy piece of furniture.

As a machine, it's devised
to spill out infinities of notions

as a piece of furniture
it's a wardrobe, a cupboard, a house,

an hotel big enough
to hide every possible music

among corridors of blond wood,
passageways, staircases, all

ordained from the beginning, the sounds
buried like the veins in rock.

To play is to go searching in the keyboard;
to make music's to recognise what's found.

5 *First Terms*

Low
over infinite city
one urban sky that all its horizons share.

They'll tell you the place developed
like a coral-reef,
by millions of little responses and a few
major ones, cleansing its errors by the day.
The idea of a city. The ethical body. But
the empirical body's a unity: brittle,
slaggy lacework of roads, bastions,
breeding-cubicles, draped
on a thin armature of sewers
threaded with cabling and gas-mains.

Under that frame, nothing
you can sense, not even empty space.
Earth plots variously cut
in the floor: pitches, dog-walks machined
in tough grass: social soil.

Country's nothing but a single island
lapped in City, a benign
fistula where it all pulls open
by a few miles in every direction.

There, under different laws, a local Nature
hangs on, not even old,
just separate; its crumbling
dark brick barns and pitbanks,
looked down on from the sides
by cooling towers, an orphanage,
a fringe of houses. Deep
in that separateness, a ploughed field
makes heavy going to be with; equates itself
with an asphalt playground.
Hard court,
grass court; same game.

6 *Abstracted Water*

Abstracted water, captive for a while,
becomes abstract, a proposition in hydraulics,

slops through lock-machines, goes level,
carries coal, parties, makes money,

slides back into Nature, used. If it hadn't come
leaking out of the hills to be cornered

you could synthesise it: a float-medium,
liquid vermiculite, a thin gel

flavoured with diesel,
rust, warm discharges.

The Cut's a notion, an idea cleaner than a river,
and closed at both ends. It's venture-water.

The design depth doesn't allow for motor-bikes, or
layers of sunken gondolas from supermarkets;

Garbage In, Garbage Out. The boat called 'Heritage'
comes dredging. Nothing much fronts

the canal. Where buildings on a street
stare you out, here it's you who do the looking,

left in your peace a little way
from the backside of it all, among

blank, patched-up walls with huge
secrets that stink and flare,

piss out coloured suds. Secrets
half-guarded, absorbed; secrets forgotten,

left to decay, bursting apart,
letting the dead stuff spill out. Sunlight

under bridges stays enclosed,
lattices to and fro. There's a law

dirt grows out of.

Glenthorne Poems

(for Ursula and Ben Halliday)

1

Straight into the sea fog
the descent
drops
red track
with sudden angles
turn below turn
into the white

Face
over the drop
the car blank
face of the descent

From the moor road
red track seaward
skirting a crater rim
charred bracken black
brimming the fog

Falls from the world
doubles down
into white

At sudden turns to meet
treetops below
hillsides of rhododendron
drifting
higher into the white

A different depth
opening
past savage gateposts

the hills' cleft
narrowing to a floor

Towers in the woods
and over the last pines
the sky wrinkled
call it sea

A different depth
with light soft
on roof leads

No sound but breakers
under the cliff
the hills deep
the sea standing
into the cloud

2

I have slept shallow a long while
living where car park lamps
neutralise the night
to a damping of action circuits

rooms to street annexes

and sleep to readiness

3

Gone down
from the upper air

Sunk under the hill
as in my own
sleeping body

Possessing nothing
warming the spring
with paraffin and pear wood

After midnight
when the generator cuts out
listening to the trees

4

Real things move
as if they were free

Pillars of smoke
rose coloured
white
smoke fans

flat like burner flames
suddenly displayed
on silver squares

All that
is Glamorgan

Celestial Aberthaw
breaking above the haze
a dozen miles across channel

Clear day
lighting the woods
here on the headlands

And as if they were free
patterns the breeze inshore
makes on the blue

far below
move under the trunk of a pine
down on the cliff edge

Eastward in the sea
Steep Holm
Flat Holm
islands towards Severn
keep their distance

Then dulling of the sky
darkens the Welsh coast
to what it is

As if free
it pushes closer

5

At sunset over the water
the nondescript cloud
builds up and breaks
in dirty dramas across the sky

With colours from clinker beds
brilliant in paradise rims
or washed wide

Sun dazzles along the waves
and slaty shoals of low water

Strikes up the cliff
in under the dark of the bushes
with tangles of burning wire

To chance on a gold thrush

6

The hills lie thick
under a three-quarter moon

The bank falls steeply
from the big oak

The oak's bare branches
fill the sky

There are stars in it
and other lights

In red stacks and white lines
mark out the sea horizon

7

Freedoms
out of contrivance

A stillness
breaking at the edges
to paradigms of freedom

This stillness I contrive
branches low under the mass
and runs for the dark

Weight to be shifted

I have
a worn black pebble

hangar-shaped
and traced over with veins
that stand to the touch

Once
I watched it ingest
a violin concerto
of Bartók entire

8

A steep turn down
to a water butt

A wall
of Mexican Orange Blossom
its shiny three-lobed leaves
scenting the hollow

An iron roof
cinnamon with rust

Beyond it and the long
wall of the garden
the cold sea runs

9

Walking at dusk often
twelve years back

On pavements of the hill
where we were neighbours

worn volcanic knob
over the Teign valley
planted with roofs
and a few pines

I'd hear the pumps
chuck and clink
out in the clay workings
weed islands
on white
lakes of slurry
over to marsh meadows
where the single railway track
ran past plantation belts
up into the foothills of the moor
where there were shadows
darkening red

mile after mile in the folds
under Haytor

And finally I'd be left
With hardly a street lamp under me

Walking on the dark

10
From the wrecked byre
with dungheap
and periwinkle bed
two narrow fields
fall between woods to the cliff

To one side the stream
cuts under them faster
twisting through water gardens
to a rough cleft where sea shows
then a fall

On the other
the old beach path
mossy and walled in
turns off under the wood

I see the trees hung over it
coming into leaf
a line of them

This is how it was
when first I started with poetry

They are already
three-parts idea

The Six Deliberate Acts

1

Today
let us think
and the smoke rise from the pan

Come in together
with what's behind us
leaning at our backs

Gentle eye can see
débris stuck to the burner
shoot comet tails in gas flame
and crumble away red

Paper resembles skin

On skin comes linen

Pale walls without much echo
out along the passage

2

Emptying his bowel
he sat in a small outside toilet
among dustbins and fire escapes
at the back of the new shops

His turds were dry enough to rattle
but no kind of trouble

The shops were high on a shoulder

built up from dumped ash

and the view from the jakes door
he held open and peered round
dropped over the concrete walkway
straight into the dip

where there was a field of kale
stinking and muddy

Past that the double road
went curving off below

There was a row of leafless poplars
and beyond them hoardings

Across the scene
the railway
went out along a cutting
bridge after bridge after bridge

And clanking into space
hoppers from the brickworks
swung out over the road
on a cable track
down into the sidings

Some way off
on a hillside
the Rehabilitation Centre
had its lights on in the afternoon
and over against the skyline
under blue drops of early streetlamps
a housing estate
filled in the outlines of a farm

Squatting up over the land
backed by the betting and pie shops
hearing the launderette
it was cold with the door open
but high

3

To see the film you buy a ticket

Some say it's just a room you pass into
with air outside

Some say the ticket makes it dark

Got from a woman behind plate glass
with a stokehole at the bottom for the money

The coins come into the light
and through the glass

They pass to the woman on the stool

Shoe grease and touch of nickel
smoky mirrors in anterooms

The edges of the dark are scuffed

But clean as a whistle
the black middle of the pit

4

The only target
is the eyeball

Isolated in its fringe
staring concentric at itself
in a round glass
on a peppermint wall

Copper hair
quivering in the light

she pops the first lens in

Things will move on

The glass when it goes
leaving a dirt-rimmed paler disc

a flat eye

5

Emptying his bowel
in the toilet behind the shops
he looked out across the landscape

A plain ground as if white
stretching away nondescript
set out with tracks
and heaps of things
all made of marking

The more he looked
the more he saw

Hedge-marks
smoke-marks
roof-marks

Until it balanced
and tipped the flush
just as he reached for it

6

He is going to the woman
and he is right

Well past the middle of his age
the sun paler than lemon

Dampness in the flat gardens

He starts to go to the woman
when he starts his journey

There are buses
a bus ticket

There is trajectory of the sun

He will arrive with himself

Diversions

1

Trouble coming, on a Saturday or a Monday,
some day with a name to it:

staining the old paths trouble knows,
though I forget them.

2

Walk through, minding the nettles
at the corner of the brick path —

don't feel sorry for language, it doesn't bear
          talking about.

3

Built for quoting in a tight corner —
The power of dead imaginings to return.

4

Just beside my track through the dark,
my own dark, not to be described,
the screech-owl
sounds, in his proper cry
and in all his veritable image —
you would know him at once.

Beyond him
a dissolution of my darkness
into such forms
as live there in the space
beyond the clear image of an owl:

forms without image;
pointless to describe.

5

I saw what there was to write and I wrote it.
When it felt what I was doing, it lay down and died under me.

6

Grey weather beating across the upland,
and the weather matters.
Grey weather beating easily across the upland.

7

Crooked–angle wings
blown sideways
against the edge of the picture.

8

Roused from a double
depth of sleep, looking up
through a hole in the sleep's surface above;
no sense of what's there;
a luminous dial
weaves along the dark like a torch.
There's somebody already
up and about, a touch-paper crackle
to their whispering.

9

The kites are the best sort of gods,
mindless, but all style;

even their capriciousness,
however dominant,
not theirs at all.

Lost from its line
one flies steadily out to sea,
its printed imperturbable face
glinting as it dips and rises
dwindling over the waves.

The crowd on the shore
reach out their hearts.

10

Leaden August with the life gone out of it,
not enough motion
to shift old used–up things.

A bad time to be rid of troubles,
they roll back in.

Dead troubles take longer than live ones.

11

The pilgrim disposition –
walking in strung-out crowds
on exposed trackways
as if ten yards from home:

domestic to-ing and fro-ing
uncoiled and elongated
in a dream of purpose.

12

Then some calm and formal portrait
to turn a level gaze
on the milling notions,

its tawniness of skin denoting
tension maybe, a controlled pallor;

or a blush of self-delight
welling softly from its intelligence.

13

Periodicity: the crack
under the door of this room
as I stare at it, late at night,
has the same relation to its field
as – what?

The corner over the curtain-rail
in a room I was in one night
forty years ago and more.

The light and the height are different,
and so am I;
but something in the staring
comes round again.

So I stare
at the single recurrence of a counter
I expect never to need.

14

Sliding the tongue-leaved
crassula arborescens
smartly in its pot and saucer
from one end of the windowsill
right down to the other

alters the framed view, much
as a louvred shutter would.

All my life I've been left-handed.

15

Here comes the modulation.
Elbows in, tighten up:
a sucked-in, menacing sound,
but full. The space is narrow,
the time marked out,
and everybody's watching.

16

The woman across the lane
stoops, hands on knees,
behind out, black and grey hair
falling forward, her nose level
with the top of a four foot wall
under a huge shaggy bank of privet.

Nose to nose with her across a saucer,
his tail lifting into the privet shadow,
a big dark cat with a man's
face marked out in white.

Quietly,
in a good, firm Scottish voice,
set well down,
she tells his story:
                    how
when his owners first
moved another cat in on him
then moved out altogether,
he ran wild for three years,
haunting back once in a while,
a frightener.

After that
for a year and a half
she'd set for him daily,
slowly drawing him in

as near as this;
she didn't expect more.

She talks, and the cat drinks.
He turns his mask to me,
sees me, and without pausing
vanishes.

         Later, from a distance,
I see the two of them again,
a saucer apart. The cat
with his enormous guilt
and importance;
            the fortunate cat,
to have such a calm Scots lady
to understand his importance.

17

Out to one side
a flight of shops
turning towards the sun,

each one a shallow step higher,
white and new and good.

And there's the ultimate in shops;
the gallery.

Somebody can be stood –
can elect to stand –
in fresh clothes but barefoot
on a slate ledge, in the place of a pot,

fastidious
beyond the flakings of the skin,
the vegetable variants of body-form,
the negative
body-aura,
that shadowy khaki coat.

Can stand, and receive attributions
of pain and excellence.

18

Everything cast in iron
must first be made in wood –

The foundry patternmaker
shapes drains, gears,
furnace doors, couplings
in yellow pine.

His work fulfils the conditions for myth:
it celebrates origin,
it fixes forms for endless recurrence;
it relates energy to form;
is useless in itself;

for all these reasons it also attracts
aesthetic responses in anybody
free to respond aesthetically;

and it can be thought with;

arranged on trays in the Industrial Museum,
it mimes the comportment
of the gods in the Ethnology cases.

21

Outlines
start to appear
on the milky surface.

Points first,
quickening into perimeters
branches and dividers;
an accelerating wonder.

Arrest; try lifting it away
before the creation
diversifies totally
to a deadlocked fission:
diamond–faceted housebricks
in less than light.

The thin trace lifted off will drop
into a new medium and dissolve.
On the bland surface
will appear new outlines.

Both these ways are in nature.

20

A world
arranged in zones
outside and into
this waterfront café.

A strip of sky
misty with light,

a deep band of
dark hazy mountainside,

a whole estuary width
foreshortened almost to nothing,

a quay,
a full harbour;

then a pavement,
a sill,

the table where I sit,
and the darkness in my head.

Everything still along its level

except the middle zone, the harbour water,
turbulent with the sunlight
even in calm air.

It Follows That

1

Mainly what
hurts the mind: a few idylls
protected in it. Times
where there's no term
for *might-have-been*,
may even yet, elsewhere, then.

'Go on.' I won't

2

The car fights into the wind
along the moor top. Keeping pace
at a run and hidden by the dry stone walls,
the eternal unseen crow-flinger
shows what he still can do.

3

Last thing I want to do is invent something, particularly a building or a structure
of any sort. It's a risk.

A fetish without the power to excite! Turning up. Hanging about. Floating in.

I could do with being restrained from inventing an opaque liturgy. With brass
mountings.

If I were to invent a groin, maybe it wouldn't stay. They have a tendency to
be moving off – *There* you are! Behaviour! Conduct. Coming and going. The
swim. And it's away. Narrow squeak.

4

Medium-sized town
will do. Filled with nuisance,
clothing, bedding, bores.
Every last thing in it
loose as the day it arrived;
flying past my ear but not
leaving.

5

So much gone. Recollections of it
posters of the present
papering rooms the gales yank.

6

Began to sleep. And soon in sleep came
Work; System with ivory lips
nostrils and ears; Forgetfulness
forever startled into remembering.

And the new place, learned rapidly before erasure:
loose treads, warm corner, how
to wash and conceal your cup.

7

Crushed phials and muddy patches of a winter
where a membrane not laminated
peels itself apart
to a pair of split skins
their inner surfaces
bared to the light of a Spring
that creaks like Doomsday,
rears up to dry, all promise, no more
running back home. Habitual
broad-nosed walk on the ring road
by the cleared-out brassica field,
ticking past medallioned railings
to where they corner to cage in
a sodden unnameable black
bole, sawn off
so low it sprawls into a beast.

8

There is a wallpaper,
dusty-patterned, faded red-brown on
faded yellow, the back
of an old playing card.

Shut in with the pattern, you can ride it,
feel it lift off, made ready. Then
It will proceed to move undeniably
through time, shuttling
forward and back with experimental
conviction. In themselves the journeys
show nothing.

9

How the hotel
can ever expand to imagine itself –
lodged, an oracular shell,
in the curve of the Square
where a statue rises over the toilets,
and dedicated steadily to Change. One
public entrance and one only.
A limited range of deals going on.
But the idea of the place,
roofless, chaotic, infinite.

10

Hulk
slides down the night
sky in a strong
forward descent. As good
as finished. There've been no
onboard warning lights. And the monster
never had a self to be sorry for.

11

In brooding,
balance, pleasure,
power. Brooding is voiceless
image stored with no bodily
trace; recoverable only by
strenuous and dense
translation. I don't like writing.

12

Under the wet
mountain at sundown,
the small mountain,
dark, a burnt cone,
December holding the ash-poles
separate and cold,

I'm talking in the water,
slender runs from the sky
into glass panels
and sidelong out. Small
mountain sits in the valley floor,
on the water in the soil,

black pyramid of absence, tilted
fields outlined on the dark.

All the fingers of a hand
grip, twist and with
the fingers of another, wring
the soak-water out,
running on the asphalt strip
that hikes a sky-glint
over the river.

What's
been the sun, sliding all day
unseen above the cloud-lid,
gleams without form from a gap
at the horizon; gleams
a long while, picking up water.

13

Thinking straight thoughts
year in year out
shortens the temper. Bending
the world brings bliss
somewhere the other side of
boredom at having to bend so.

14

Scratched in the plaster where the wallpaper peels:

The lean years follow the years of need –
they write, that will not read –
St Priapus be our speed!

15

Maybe there's been
a new moon. Visible
from the Pennine edge, far off
across the whole dark plain of Cheshire,
a huge curved horn, glowing yellow,
rears over Merseyside
and draws itself in.

If it's the moon, good.

Metamorphoses

1

She sleeps, in the day, in the silence. Where there is light, but little else: the white covers, the pillow, her head with its ordinary hair, her forearm dark over the sheet.

She sleeps and it is hardly a mark on the stillness; that she should have moved to be there, that she should be moving now across her sleep as the window where the light comes in passes across the day.

Her warmth is in the shadows of the bed, and the bed has few shadows, the sky is smoked with a little cloud, there are fish-trails high in the air. Her sleep rides on the silence, it is an open mouth travelling backward on moving waves.

Mouth open across the water, the knees loosened in sleep; dusks of the body shadowed around the room. In the light from the window there is the thought of a beat, a flicker, an alternation of aspect from the outside to the inside of the glass. The light is going deep under her.

Enough depth. To clear and come free. There is no taste in the water, there are no edges under it: falling away, the soft mumbled hollows and mounds of marble, veined with brown, a lobby floor gone down into the descending levels of a sea-basin. The sleep comes naked.

Rising through the clear fluid, making their own way, the dragging wisps of brown that were secret hairs or the frame of a print on the wall. And light that cracks into the bubbles near the surface, lighting them like varnish bubbles, breaking them into the silent space between the surface and the curved roof, threaded with moving reflections of water light.

Water lights crossing and combining endlessly over the inward membrane of the roof, rising in a curve, almost a cone, to the round lantern with its dirty panes. The water lights beating silently under the steep slates of the case, under the painted frames of the lantern's windows and the domed lead cap, holding into the sky a two-foot fluted spike.

2

The cat's glinting face as it stared up between its paws from the odd soft position, near-supine, into which the other cat had rolled it. The other cat was already indifferent, turned away to lick its upthrust leg, but this cat, for the moment, had no next thing.

The cat's glinting face, all mask, no signal, was an old face: on a man it would have been frozen, the defiance of something contemptible. It was framed in soft paws. It stared indiscriminately up at the lights. The cat's eyes, further away than eyes look, more distance in them, no cat. Running in to the distance there's a dull aluminium strip of road, tall skies, flat horizons, with scattered elms and poplars picked out in colour by the sun.

All the green fields are cold, the bright afternoon deserted. Faces look out of the cars that go by; that is what they do, those faces. There is a tower among the trees, a white drum on legs, and a road turns off beside it, sweeping down to a cinder patch by the river where the field-tracks join and cars can park. A path, much mauled and trodden, leads through the elders, and at one place, where it crosses a marshy dip, a sheet of corrugated iron has been wedged, balanced on a springy root and half earthed over.

3

How does he come to be wearing that suit, clay-coloured, with a hang-off jacket and flapping trousers that make him seem to jerk? He's making for the ferry; no he's not. He stands a while and goes somewhere else.

A man among the puddles with his shoes on the pavement and his head in the clear air, his nervous system shrouded in loose, dried-looking clothes. His trajectory leads these arrangements he has to a pause, then takes them past it. While he is there and after he's gone, the shut car-park kiosk remains unwaveringly present.

For a few seconds in the centre of a rigidly composed scene, its elements stopped in the act of crossing from left to right or right to left, there is, maybe in the name of freedom, maybe in the name of compulsion, an unidentified capering, that leaves no trace after it has gone. The pavement gives place immediately to the air above it; there was the sign of a thing like a man in the air, an eddy across the scene.

No system describes the world. The figures moving in the background stop and wait in mid-step, the sound-track cuts out: the projector motor runs on, the beam doesn't waver. Among the whites and greys of the picture a golden shade is born, in the quiet, rippling slowly, knotting itself and suddenly swelling into a cauliflower head, amber and cream cumulus outlined in blistering magenta, erupting out of itself and filling the screen before shrivelling off upwards to leave a blank screen and a stink of fire.

4

Red beans in to soak. A thickness of them, almost brimming the glass basin, swelling and softening together, the colour of their husks draining out to a fog of blood in the water.

The mass of things, indistinguishable one from another, loosing their qualities into the common cloud, their depth squashed by the refraction and obscured in the stain, forms pushed out of line. Five beans down it may be different.

Down in the levels, it's possible to think outward to the edge; with a face to the light, there's no looking out, only hunching before the erosion. Back!

In the midst is neither upward nor downward, head nor foot has precedence or order. Curved belly rises above, warm and shining, its navel out on surface with the vestige of a lip. One eye is enough, to distinguish shape from shadow, paired eyes would fix too much. To be fixed in the midst is suffocation.

So, in the thick of the world, watching the moon whiten the bedroom floor and drag the print of the window nets higher and higher across the wall; thinking how the world would have had a different history if there had always been not one moon in the sky, but a close-set pair. It is said there are two breasts; it is said there are two sexes. That's as may be.

Out in the moonlight is a short street with only one side; houses on it, and walled forecourts. Over the way is a white pavement, and a blackness where the hill falls away. The blackness goes grey with looking, and the valley is full of shapes.

5

Crumpled clothes come slowly off and fall to make a heap on the carpet. In this daylight, the nakedness is theirs: pulling his shirt off, letting his belt snake out of its loops and drop, he is closing inward, tired, to his own body's shadows, while the white underwear faces up to the light from collapse.

The clothes are falling to make a different naked body, loosing the bands that wrap him in; he draws himself into his shade, everything is outside him; the nakedness of his belly crumples out on his shirt.

Seams and bands that contained him are falling away, in shapes to suit themselves, different shadows, different surfaces. Not dispersed from one another, they move into a scheme that frees him and does without him.

It frees him so he can feel it go from him once the clothes have gone, as if a membrane webbed over with straplike lines was parting across his belly, his breast, the fronts of his thighs, winding off across the daylight, that comes to back it with chalky aquamarine, and slowly turning off-centre as the twisted straps float out, and show themselves in blotted-down tapestry blues and reds.

They trail in the greeny blue, where there are dark dried fragments of clover: a stone coping at the edge of the blue has the colour of mushrooms cooled and cut after scalding till they flush, a matt fair skin scattered with wide freckles, thickly over the sun-reddened base of the throat and the stretch beneath, but more and more rarely as it rises pale and smooth to the nipple.

107 Poems

(Pentameters for Eric Mottram)

A scraping in the cokehouse. One red car.
Imperfect science weakens assurances
but swallowing hard brings confidence: fall soft
through to a sunlit verge. Another vision:
stretched out like one expecting autopsy
or showers of sparks across a polished hall.

Swallow all down, to mudstains on the glass;
surmounted by the working, come upon
a sweet for Auntie; for the withdrawn and hurt
something comes sloping upwards, tilts the guard,
then goes across another way: surprise
relaxes from a sideboard in a bottle,
rocks to and fro a while, scores up another –
bottle between the lips – is comforted
into a pointless trip and passes out
finally between two stations, wrapped in yellow.

Sepia slippers in a sepia print,
venerable truth again: it comes direct
and broadens as it comes, is beautiful
if truth is what you want; lies in the blood
and lives on without taint. Magnificent
gorges at sunset! They knew how to live.
They draw us in their footsteps, double-tongued.

To drive under the fog again, and to it,
park by red lights along the road gang's ditch;
changes of *Satin Doll* are getting smothered,
two trumpets and a rhythm section working
carelessly through a roof under the ground;
at twenty past the hour they hit the dirt,
go on across the talk, hit it some more;
a silver surface rears up, wonderful;
somebody scared runs in and turns it over.

Squatting resigned among the rest of it
there's cut and come again; eat anything.
Demolished streets make foregrounds to good skies;
warm hands at rubbish fires, or on a keyboard.
But brightness picks out streaks of signal red,
it's morning. Rumpled, nobody can cope.

What leaks through rotted pipes into the gutter
leaves a long stain that tired arms cannot move,
dispirited by sickness and privation
when peaceful hours have coal dumped under them,
a last delivery, ferried in through sleet.

What's newly made gets treated tenderly;
damage is easy while the aconite
first shows under the window's overhang
and looks well. In the cold light is a refuge,
lying back after breakfast to see birds
flash down the pale grey strip beyond the roof;
and it's a lime-green tent where everything
is fugitive and found, and luminous,
with shadows of a dark track off the calendar
into a depth of sky. Hanging there free,
spiralling down, the ink-trails in the water
that reach the floor and spread. To be well-treated –
a café with net curtains where they bring
coffee or coca-cola to the bedridden –
something to recall on a beleaguered common.
Roads open in succession, windows break;
if both your legs get tired, find a good stick;
slow before lunch, but in the afternoons
Olympic stars perform for invalids
and dark brings in harsh winds and roadside breakdowns;
better to hear of rain on other roofs
or technicolour wrongs worked by hard men.

No choice left but to run, and into it
and back again each time, that being where
the way goes anyhow – so, running
brings it round so much faster, the same dream –
daffodil plastic, various laminates,
children released in yards then sucked away
into an unseen hall; enormous tolerance
somewhere about, and for immediate sky,
hand-lotion-coloured plastic overhead,
the first thing in the world; and back again.
Walking across to the cars in the night air,
everyone slows and vanishes. There'll be
familiar movement when the season dives.
Watch ampelopsis redden the tarred wall;
go straight, and not so fast. The inner sky
is coloured plastic – none the worse for it.

Somewhere the copper pipes a pale gasfitter
left unsecured under the floor tread loose.
The new face might look younger were it not
too harried and too sleepy: there's no time.
Old people go so childish you get scared
thinking about it: someone's moving out.
Under the trees, headlands of alyssum
break through a spring where danger without risk
develops to a style and loses body,
loses its ear for trouble. Ride again.
Desolate sunlit foreshores, visited
and photographed, lie doubly far away;
one more red car gets dealt into the pack;
one guest is laid to rest in his own nature,
his to resist if it should overcome him
travelling in the tracks of a clay lorry
or when the powercut lets the dark back in.

Exhausted, by a different route, twice blessed –
they seem like wooden roses, without yield –
draining the glass again, whatever remains,
past all surprise, repeatedly and strong
though without strength, except to head on out,
surrounded by a street, braced up to feel,
ready for thunder, inescapable change,
the healing of the injured; some idea
of what tradition numbers like these are benched in.

Five Morning Poems from a Picture by Manet

1

Wells of shadow by the stream
and the long branches
high over pools of gold light in the grass.

A drift of morning scents
downward through pines,
dazzled, to hang on water finally;
the road's deserted curve; beyond,
blue town-smoke standing.

Schoolboy in the scarlet cap,
leaning across the wall
motionless –
will you feel the moment end,
a dead scale sliding from a fish?

Plain-featured boy, cast in a pose of beauty.

Wells of shadow spread the stream
so dark it glides invisibly
and leaves his coat-cuffs dry.

Slant eyes that shine too deep a brown
to show time, or to tell
what tautens
stillness round him to a fine
film that shivers, glazed and sombre:

the scents, maybe, that sting.

or ironstone in the water, the taste of April.

So dark it glides invisibly
the moment takes its form
out of his smile, that rests on turbulence –
there have been tears, there could be greed.

Someone has given him cherries:
untouched upon the wall
they spill from yellow paper, crimson-heavy;
glossy, their soft skins burst.

High over light-pools in the grass
and still boughs, a bronze shadow
gestures behind my dream,
a god, polished to nothing by our thoughts:

plenitude, rising at the heart's pace to noon,
that shadow turns clear waterglass of light
to amber, and extinguishes
the last white flecks of agitation.
Music of the generous eye,
swelling, receding on my breath.

Here are the golden distances;
deeper than life the stream goes in the shade.

Cool trees. Clarity. Dreaming boy.
Fat cherries and a scarlet cap;
water under the thin smoke of morning –

music of the generous eye.

    2

Nowhere. Hear the stormy spring
far off across the racks of quiet. Nothing.
Suddenly, a leaning fence-post daubed with rain.

It rots into the day. Cold lights
swell from the clouds, then take their death away.

Some ceremony lets fall its links:
a glistening fence-post suddenly encountered;

iron trumpets in the sky.

All in the flooded meadow, ankle deep,
the lately dead, the tidy men and women
walking with steps like flakes of agony.

Accurate as the trumpet-notes they go,
with polished shoes in the gunmetal water;
they tread on loss as once they counted money.

All in the meadow. Flakes of agony
walking with marble steps to iron trumpets.

Ceremony to wear away the world.

Barbaric news for someone about to die:
each footfall muffles breath, each iron grace-note
stoppers the heart with heartless beauty.

A world freezing apart, where a movement
cracks the glass veins of music in the flesh.

Islands of understanding float, confused:
rain-smears on rotting wood, the sheepish dead
who stand amid the floods, bright stems of glass
shattering by inches; lakes of misery –

The iron trumpets wear away the sky.

   3

Death music sounds for a boy by a stream,
urgent as waves, as polished shoes,
though amber screens of light shade him from time.

Ironstone in the water, tasting
coldly of April pleasure, yet
embitters like brass the pools of golden morning.

Trumpets of iron shake the sky;
in chains of ceremony they spill
out of the music of a generous eye.

Over his quiet they wear away
all to a frigid emphasis
on lines that form his child's flesh into beauty.

Slowly comes the polished step,
cut marble agony to blight
the charm of cherries and the scarlet cap;

to drag the forms of beauty till they gleam
dully on lakes of misery
rising from wells of shadow by the stream.

   4

Looking for life, I lost my mind:
only the dead
spoke through their yellow teeth
into the marble tombs they lay beneath,
splinters of fact stuck in the earth's fat rind.

324

The privet glittered with noon; the hill
slid its green head
down from the sky to try me. I was still
as the evil-shaped dark leaves.
Then I heard what the corpses said.

Muttering, they told me how their lives
from burial
spiked back at the world like knives
striking the past for legacies of wrong –
the fiction of understanding worst of all.

I saw a vase of familiar flowers,
behind it, a tray
of thin pale brass with patterned borders;
the troubling taste of an alien mouth not figured
even in fantasy.

5

Walking beside the wall towards the stream
where flickering water-lights
lick amber tongues quickly across stone,
with a yellow bag of cherries, an old jacket,
a red cap crumpled on thick hair,
thought, an uneven slime;
gravel underfoot, the wall's rough edge;
stub fingers sliding over pads of moss.

Stout morning walls the sun walks down,
smoke bursting slow into invisibility,
the tight sky broken among banks of trees;

sounds vanishing through worn patches on the road,
dark silence dropping from the ledges of the pines.

Flat heads of stone amid the turf. The shadowy stream.

Three Ceremonial Poems

1

Metallic sheath
derelict, that resounds

laurel bars, enamelled
with laurels, the bronze
on matted hair, blades
designed on guns, sharp leaf

blue brick framing a door,
further, medallion,
fallen;
gallon can,
shield's mark on water,
the rusty flow

fold upon fold, so stiff
and out of the clay-track
out of it
to walk and bed on flags,
damp bundles,
padding the stone

salt crust,
crystals break out and part,
open on flesh; in frost
leaf, sharp curled,
like leather, sticking fast
where wheels were down

sunset and dusk mark it,
and the pulling away,
fold on fold,
from matted places

Covering of the stacks; by twilight
live mask plated over

warrior, the stopped man.

2

Absolute
Pity
advancing

out from the grove
of parsley elms
on those that wait
staining
suit-knees
with grass juice.

In the concrete rank, a panther cage.
the panther hates, at morning and at midday;
lies in the dust and stifles the sunbeams.

– But turned inward,
studying one's very own:
this curious corner –

a urine-softened wall
meets an impervious hard one;

clay, cut like butter,
drags at the trowel,
in cold sweat subsides;

and golden drops
shake, and fling
from the body, brightness

trembles the window,
dark strands
lick outward down the arms.

Fading
short
and sudden when it comes,
white flash
lost under the anvil cloud;
dark dust of shame

raining down
deep in the brickwork,
changes its face;

and falling
in the open,
left out among the trees.

3

Oh yellow head,
crust of deception;
pale over wheatfields, the sun.

To the Memory of Wyndham Lewis

1

A trellis of clean men and painted steel
straggles above the tide lines. Autumn day;
an eastern shingle beach
where, caliper-wise, sour schemes confront the surf.

Under the clouds' rebellious plain
drab uniforms peg out their barricades;
like the squat lorries, noon hours pass.

As moorland bushes take the wind
thoughts lean all day pale-eyed towards the sea;
spikes of dune grass stand lithe,
flickering beneath the searchlights' stone-blind gaze.

In the raw, bloodless rampart,
humanity, a turbid stream,
runs dark amid the diagrams and the helmets,

while along oiled steel grooves,
in cruel harness with the uneasy hours,
systems advance on night.

2

The white mare rolls on the pebbles at the edge of the sea.
Searchlights banked behind helmet rims
burn roads across the shelving beach.
The rolling-mill of the night
endlessly sucks the dark in from the land
with a finger of foam to its disappearing lips,
while the white mare on the brilliant pebble shore rolls,
helmet-bowls converse, and in
the red shadow of the dune-grass bayonets
glint on the thought of blood petals.

The horse's stony teeth are young and perishable
as ripples vanishing searchlit among rocks;
the soldiery smoke-stain her coat: to be
near them yellows white; their presence taints
the metal flood rising beyond the surf.

O sepia-blooded soldiers with tobacco coats,
you have waited long; your armoured heads
no more seem to be moving by the bright beams.

The middle darkness is seething round you fast
into the foam; and the mare will not be still
down on those stones you have made glisten so fiercely.

3

The captain to the white mare. 'Handsome thing,
our crescent net entraps you; waves that freeze
thunder along the shore between its horns.
Soldiers tire, hours sag;
the toothed wheel of a stopwatch wakes the rifles.
You will be torn and shattered; we shall rake
with bayonets in your body.
What's left of you will be, by morning,
shovelled into the sea. We shall remember you.

'I think your blood will rot the world from under us,
melting into an ordure of decay —

'Enough. That I'll survive. I see
rising above that filth a scaffolding:
Expediency. There at the last I'll wither.'

4

Her eyes like staring lamps of stone,
she charged the ramp, cantered on flying pebbles
to rear magnesium-white in searchlight rays.

Everyone scattered. The lights blinded the mare,
till slowly, unguided on aimless silent bearings,
they flared their square weight down along empty strand.

Then she was gone, thudding in fronds of dark,
beyond the buttoned hearts of soldiers
who stood all ways, dull basin-hats
tilted askew, their round eyes frozen beads.

Flung into stupefaction by her flight
their taut-strapped faces gaped
in the long concrete jaw of the sea wall;
great bars of yellow light still striped the beach,
the sea teasing and wrenching at their tips.

Voices. Bayonets clattering in the dunes;
brown greatcoats looming; light-beams
snapped into nothing. Vacant order forming.

At No Distance

Antiphon: Two Parts for the Same Voice

It has disintegrated,

                the world across the bay
                silk dress with crayons
                cistern paint;
                        desired
                and remembered things

and everybody's like me

                Over the bay
                at evening raised steam
                silently in a far pool
                sun on the orange
                clouded water

central to ourselves

                the dress wrinkling,
                somebody wearing it
                lying prone across
                stretched to collect
                from the floor the scattered

There,
under that labyrinth
of roofs they're the same –

they see
lead paint fresh-run
on rivets, blobbed
paint-skin to be broken
by anybody,
smelled on the fingernail

                Enamel, coating
                the brown pencil crayon,
                nicked through
                to the wood

                fingers smell of it
                a woman's smile like

Lake, rocking high-bodied
under wood chips,
cold boats bucking

>   and streaks of wax pink
>   across the penknife blade
>   brown and viridian

>   sliced through then
>   to the lead colours.

Some things always close:
giant iron
casts, no dream, and
gantries I have made into
arches that bear sense
are no distance from me

>   the black leather
>   male shoe

or from other men

>   worker-prison

Old Krupp
in the fireproof Villa Hügel
moving from room to room
ceaselessly as he felt
his presence foul the air

>   the colossal woods
>   banked up behind the lake
>   sunlit;

>   there are things men own
>   ample enough
>   to weigh heavy
>   in longing's belly

The dress, cold
wrinkles under the breasts,
no distance
from freckled skin beneath

>   though smelling of himself
>   must have thought

freedom from his own foulness
a metaphor: mountain air,
lake water, gunsmoke

Old Krupp, fearing
his own fires, his own lead

in bad weather
behind the windows
a woman gathers herself in
close to herself,
whoever longs for her

whoever owns

Wedgwood, too,
built his dwelling
a brick barrack
from where he could look down
and watch Etruria
making it

there's
our bright cloud again
swelling far off

glancing from the works

up across the meadow and the water
showed him, distanced, his
rectangular domestic peace

what the imagination calls
power: to own what's longed for
and play both ways –

Grotesque hermaphrodite,
groin without orifice,
that can own what, and whom,
it doesn't even desire –

crayons
sharpening to brown
pink and viridian,
smelling of coloured
leads and cut wood

landing stages across the bay,

nondescript spot –

        unfastening down the back
        and crumpled more
        fallen away round
        freckled skin –

yes, conscious of itself
centred like all of us;
even like Krupp.

        From far in memory
        the red cistern
        freshly painted

Someone else had done it
one sweaty day

        that part
        beyond all distance

It was already done
when I found it

        one various world
        beckoning infinitely
        to make me dream

to make me do;

or many worlds

        someone bought
        the forest behind the lake

collide, precipitate

        cold afternoon
        paper and crayons

making one
various world

        the view across the bay

looked at
from anywhere on it.

Stopped Frames and Set Pieces

As he heaved himself backwards into the water, arms above his head, and went under, for an instant the refraction in the broken water shattered the shapes of his belly, torso and bearded face, blurring and magnifying the whole so that it looked like a crucified Christ coming apart like a cloud figure. That was for half a second: then as the shape, sinking and waving, showed a shade more tranquil, it was more like God Himself, uncomfortably waking.

The god Mercury, plump with winter, flew steadily through the black, gritty dawn, among the pigeon-spattered cornices of one of the cities of Germany.

Furious, the boxer dog leapt in pursuit and was brought up short by its lead while in the air, only one foot touching the ground. The strength of its impetus, the whole weight of the body yanking on the strap, distorted it: the head seemed as if it was being twisted off, and the creature for all its heaviness and force had no more stability of shape than a slug hurled at a paving slab.

In the second the dog's form was destroyed and before it reconstituted itself a fallen scrambling dog, it had an alternative form of paroxysm, a sudden precip-itate out of energy, a bigger payout than was budgeted; dog-sized, big enough to remember, bursting out from the subsiding animal, twisting on into the world, detaching itself, a single plasm, weightless and self-determining.

A small broken Indian statue, of about the thirteenth century. The figure of a girl dancer, or, rather, the torso, for the head and neck are missing, both arms are cracked off just below the shoulders, and the legs are both lost, the left finishing just above the knee, the other a little higher. The right breast has been smashed, the nipple of the other worn away.

Even without the extremities that will have shown what it was intended to mean, the body, with its long supple waist and round thighs, is graceful. The shoulders are held a little way back, and the belly is thrust forward, swung to one side. There's no temptation to guess at the positions of the vanished head and limbs.

It is clothed only in festoons of decorations, metal and stones against the soft flesh which now, its stone polish transformed by age into myriad roughenings and craters, looks porous and sleepy. There is a broad collar with heavy pendants, one of which, a triple rope of what seem to be pearls, falls sidelong to the waist. A necklace of similar design is cast loosely about the shoulders and falls through the deep hollow of the bosom. Just above the break in the left upper arm there is a tight circlet that rises in the shape of a crown. The hips are circled by a low deep belt that reaches to the loins: it starts with a tight flat band, of gold maybe, chased with circling patterns and then loosens into thick swathes and bands, of intricate design, falling low at the front and gathered up neatly at the hips. From this belt hang a central tasselled loop, heavy with baubles, that passes freely between the legs, and also the decorations of the thighs, pendants of beaten metal stretching down toward the vanished knees. Dangling between these and the belt are heavy braided loops, hung with medallions, several bands of them, the higher ones loosely curved, the lower clasping the limbs more closely.

Without gestures or face, this body is dominated, not by its single breast, but by the large and beautiful navel, thrust out and held up into a pout by the constricting belt that curves close beneath it. It is very slightly oval, stretched not upwards, but out across the belly. If the figure were life-size, the palm of a hand could only just cover its hollow, that begins very gradually, then plunges evenly into a deep shadow, ridged at the upper edge by a last flat fold of skin. This is the only feature the body possesses. It is eye, or mouth, or anus, or ear: all the body's orifices. In itself it is useless, a scar crater, an insigna of coming into life; a gross and handsome decoration riding among the goldsmiths' ornaments.

The spray of bullets had struck across the people walking on the pavement. Most rushed for shelter and a few lay still. A big man in a tight suit, lying in the gutter with no apparent injury, began to sit up, clearly conscious of his terribly exposed situation.

The big man in the gutter was up on his feet and tiptoeing across the sunlit pavement. The gunmen, if they were still there, let him go, treading in other people's blood, to get to a shop doorway.

Encouraged by the big man's example, men and women were picking themselves slowly up and stumbling for cover without looking round. From the dead there were long runs of blood, right down into the gutters. Its brightness was astonishing, the gaiety of the colour.

A bare isthmus of ash projecting into the bay, and ending in a little mountain of the most ominous shape, quite shallow, a flat-topped cone, almost a simple geometrical form except for the slight tilt to one side of the platform at the top. The sides sloped evenly down into the motionless and slaty sea. There was no vegetation anywhere about. The sun was just below the long black perfectly horizontal cliffs across the bay.

Along a little causeway a strange domed house had been built on piles in the water. It had balconies of cast iron lacework and big windows, most of them now broken.

The Gentleman's Patent Reducing Bath was a polished cabinet lined with zinc and mounted on legs like a stool. On one side of the cabinet there was an opening, shaped rather like a proscenium, from which hung not a curtain but the legs of a kind of rubber bloomers, bonded to the zinc inside the cabinet. The gentleman, stripping himself naked, would step from a chair into the cabinet, easing himself down until his legs, thighs encased in the bloomers which gripped firmly above the knee, projected through the opening and he was able to rest his feet on the ground. His servant would then pour jugs of warm water into the cabinet. The legs of the gentleman's drawers would fill first; and so on, until he was immersed from knee to waist. A stout wooden cover, the two halves of which fitted together to leave a hole like that of a lavatory seat only larger, completed the apparatus, giving him a dry rest for his elbows and preventing him from dropping his book into the water.

As he stood there in the sunlight, his body placid, the judge's robes and wig were unruffled, by even the least breath, and his heavy face was at rest. Yet this face was set as if in a gale that tore across it from right to left, pulling at the flesh, distorting the eyes and mouth.

The snow turned into the mist; the horizon was so close they couldn't see it. The other four came out of the mist, grey and bearlike. Edmonds was dancing along with the great orange balloon over his head, pretending it was carrying him along; Ray, recognisable by his movements, was waving his arms, praying to it as if it was the sun.

The landlady noticed, while showing them the room, that they seemed rather distant. The man – and she had never seen a fatter one for his age – stood hat in hand, leaning on the post of the huge brass bed and looking out of the window across the marsh, the light catching on his gold-rimmed glasses and picking up his pearl-grey suit. The woman, dressed a little primly in a dark walking suit with a pull-on hat, paid no attention to the bed or the view, but was chiefly concerned to know whether the tasselled bell-pull beside the bed worked or not. On being told that it did, she turned her attention to the wallpaper, and did not speak again during the time it took for the landlady to conclude her agreement with the man and leave them.

Whether the old pig was hungry or not, or belching or yawning, or not, it still laughed at him. Whether or not it laughed at him he was still humiliated in the last degree.

The dank valley below was stopped with mist: the clearer slopes, if there were any, could not be seen. In all directions the ground was deep in pulpy vegetation, probably many feet deep and rooted only in a morass. There were no tracks, no rocks; the terrain seemed to shift in waves as it was looked at. The only colours in it all were the darker greens and the darker shades of rot; everything fresh was bedded on the wet decay of what preceded it. All of the growths seemed monstrous, and some were gigantic. From the middle of the valley floor a single huge tree, many-headed, thrust itself up through the mist, through tangles of vegetation that fouled its trunk, to divide into three or four great giraffe-necks, that stretched out many yards, quite bare except for the clotted growths, big as houses, they each carried at their ends. These were horned, bearded masses like pineapple-tops, bison heads, with sickly white trailers hanging down for yards under them.

Treadgold's electioneering speeches were wretched affairs. He spoke from the horse-drawn landau that belonged to his brother's brewery, and could hardly be heard. He was very tall and thin, with a drooping moustache and downcast eyes. He wore a long black coat, folded his hands in front of him where his belly would have been, and hung his head down sanctimoniously. It was tempting to imagine the horses spurred on, the carriage driving away and leaving him dangling, in just the same posture, from a noose.

At closing time, Lily Maskell and Mr Morris sang a duet, almost nose to nose, with their arms round each other's necks, Lily's coat open to show her high white satin blouse, little pearl studs at her ears and her black hair drawn in tight; Mr Morris not quite her size, crop-head held back to look through his little glasses and down his nose at Lily, who was almost bearing him back.

Works and Days

Onions are frying in a better world
much as they do in this. The metaphysic
flips a mess of onions in a pan
back and forth between worlds
as if it owned it. Even the best shoes
from the pile in the bottom of the cupboard
are not what they were
and the tale of the food litter
on the cellar steps they come down
thickens overnight.

A present mood
some other mood at its shoulder
pulling away
not to replace it
merely dislodge
the same sky
the same grating
the same word
the same cabbage.

By no means identical in appearance the days
group and part and regroup
as if they had foreknowledge
or hindsight they understood
as their pillars go bobbing
along dark oil.

And another new song this morning —
they just keep coming.
Rattle and knock of wood, old
guitar body against piano. A fresh
puff of piano-dust off the felts.
As he reads the lead sheet over my shoulder
his breath, magnified and fleshly
not wholly turned into music
smokes as exhaust gas
out of the saxophone. Smell
my new song. It is
the story of a cigarette.

Gritty dawn overcast
lasts all day. Against it
on any such day so many
separate unforgettable events
come to so many
as if they owned them. Everywhere
those dawns go looking round
for more of their own kind
and without remark or even
a taste from the tap
seamlessly join them together.

Dreams build streets from need
the *schema* of a common town..
But as to how every space
in an old gas-mantle factory
void on a summer evening
but for the echoes of boots on the stairs
and an out-of-tune canteen piano
could come to reek wholly of sawdust
and oil; how the sloping
iron and glass arcade
the tale builds in the middle of town
always has leather on its breath –
something's afoot again.

The Muse, implicit, latinate,
long-legged, literate,
neither unattainable
nor attainable,
all the tastes of her essence
filtered away
in litanies of metaphor
to leave it denatured and pure:
she's such a dodger I feel
I'm starting to get her measure.

What can my tribe have been, that I should
stand for the last time, eyes alert,
nostrils dilated, on the platform
of the Northern Line in the foul-breathed
duct below Euston? No threat to me there
but what the place had to say
for itself. Not being superstitious

I could tell I was right. I'd
had all the lessons.

It could be time
to unpack the amygdala
life's little almond
stuffed with cautions and come-ons.
Cavernous mouthy speech over
a dun gravy, thickening it
in the other world not far
from dead green lily-stems
slimed with the water in a darker
green metal vase in a cemetery.
And clearing a coalhouse back to the brick
beyond the beginning. Gas, oil, coal:
the economy, what else? Empires.
Wars. Spittle.
There's a song
called *The Stoker*
that can settle me. Rough
music. Scrape. Clank.
Battering home to drink and eat
with assurance, love with less.

VIII

Inscriptions for Bluebeard's Castle

(with Ronald King)

The Portcullis

Beyond me the common daylight
divides

The Castle

The furthest journey is the journey that stays still
and the light of the sky has come from the world
to be packed for a journey

The Instruments of Torture

Man conceived us, men made us. We work
almost with perfection and we feel no pain.

The Armoury

Provide. That their mouths may bleed into the cinders.
With bronze and steel, provide. With beauty, provide.

The Treasure House

What
the sun touches
shines on forever dead
the dead images of the sun
wonderful

The Garden

Whose is the body you
remember in yourself?

The Land

The light. The rain. The eye. The rainbow –
horizons form, random and inevitable as rainbows
over bright fields of change

The Lake of Tears

Day has turned to a silver mirror
whose dead extent the weeping
eyes could never see

The Last Door

Moonlight the dead image of the day –
here by the light of that last coin
we are alive within an eye:
when the eye closes on us all
it is complete

Correspondence
(with Tom Phillips)

I have a book, it has grown
from spots in the back cover
right on up
through the bank
to the surface of Page One

Words are lying there
arrived
Nowhere to go
but off the edges

Sooner or later
all things
have to be obeyed

– Caught sight of myself
in the monitor

The world looked like itself
I looked like it too
not like me
as if I was
solid or something

– Solid pushed through the curtains into the grove
for the thousandth time

His world

huddling him
front and back

It's not hard to look busy
from behind

– For *him* the cleared smoke
came back with its warrant
and back with its warrant

For him the sky inched open
the hewn beams rolled

– Far away now
from my home town
down in the monitor

Top Down, Bottom Up

(with Ronald King)

The neighbours' pair of goats,
lodging with us for a while,
breaking bounds,
supported the big horse-chestnut
as high as heraldry

could take them, and higher still,
erect on stretched hindlegs, throats
vertical, mouths upthrust, the pious
and guilty eyes oblique in their heads
as they ate the tree,

baring the white wood
to the curve of a back
patterned with progressed teethmarks;
ducking their skulls to force the bark-line
down to within an inch of the grass,

then once more rising, ripping
into the thick bark,
nibbling a tidy edge to the wound
and quietly subsiding with straight stares
though distant eye-slots.

The old tree, dying already from the top,
dies faster, with bolder strokes
that take whole branches out
to hang hooked up and bare to the sky

when all the others tip their fresh
leaves down by handfuls and lift
blossom-cones through the shade.

What's living rises by sinuous
rivers of lichened bark, inaccessibly
turned in the complex trunk,
too deep to be devoured; what's dead
comes reaching down to touch

with naked wood, sculpted and
signed by active young
goats, one already long dead
the other long gone away.

There'll be
years more of this, the worked object
altering passively as it must; a black
bough at a time,
a few more claws
clear of the canopy each spring.

Five Pilgrims in the Prologue to *The Canterbury Tales*
(with Ronald King)

Knight

He bore himself, or the self he had was borne,
through great indignities and darkness
inviolate in a glass braced with silver.
It was as small as that.

In Lithuania, spars and foul fabrics
prised out of black silt with a frozen crack;

elsewhere, excrements rolled in sand;

scattered all across the back of beyond, seedy nobility,
mincing and cheating, and getting cut to pieces.

As often as he set forth, he would find himself
returning through strange farmlands
in incomprehensible weather.

Webbe

Risen by weaving works to this
abstraction: something at the same time
rich and dry about that trade,
a station on the road to pure money;
stretching resources till the patterns glow.

Dyere

Even in the pools
and vats, even in the steamy
swags and folds and leaf-stinks
stuck in the nose at night
there's always been someone's white finger
waving above it all.

Tapicer

Base yourself on these,
Lords. I have slipped
the carpet in under your foot,
the cushion beneath your buttocks;
the walls are all taken care of.

It is with this sort of confidence
you can look me in the eye.

Cook

Slow cooking in a world on the move.
The hours are slow, the pies live a long time;
cooling and warming, they ride the bacterial dumb-waiter.
A cook goes in and out of focus many times as he learns.

On the bright side, the ulcer's almost forgettable,
and the flies loose in the shop don't irritate,
being mostly middle-sized and black, and in no hurry.

Figures from Anansi Company

(with Ronald King)

Dry Skull

Just to be with you, I've been
getting myself ready.
Shaved my cheeks and chin
closer than close.

.

No trouble.

.

Now, we can always
be closer than close.

Trouble. Trouble.

Chicken-hawk

It's the length of the drop
and the weight
and build of the client. For pay,
chickens are ideal. Thank you.

Three-and-a-quarter
seconds of wing-shadow
is the absolute
maximum the client experiences –
unless there's an intermediate
transportation element involved.

Yes, I do private commissions. Yes.
Transport and Dump? Ah,
Terrify, Transport and Dump.
1 should think so. Distance times weight
times fright. Let me quote you.

Rabbit

Sidekick Other side.
kick. Sit still. What's up?
Ears. Can't

sleep with ears up,
never could, never will, not
my way. There's nothing
up. Odd. Don't like it. If
selected I won't run because I won't
still be there. If I was, I
would, though. Kick up, dig
down, get under, kick back and
up and out. Sidekick and
off.

Snake

See my head? It's packed with
electronics.
It's the Service Module.

It goes wherever the Body
steers it
dangles it
slides it
in. The lenses
are always open when not
shuttered. The whole
capsule cranks back
to monitor the sky while the Body
feeds.

I can bite head, and
head, and head. But can't
nobody never kick ass on me.

Tiger

Amateur dramatics, amateur
sport – one day
you professionals are going to give us a run
for our money. Call me Tim. What's
my profession? Oh,
call me a farmer. Of sorts.
Live off the land. Bit of this
bit of that. Livestock, forestry...

Everybody knows me. So –
anything you need, just
mention my name. Belch. Excuse me.
Why not call me Tiny.

Parrot

YAM PRANK RAPPED.
MAD YAMS LASH TOP CAT.
SNAKE'S HEAD-BITE DODGE GOES TO POT.
IS PARROT PRETTY BOY? NEW PROBE.
THUMBS DOWN FOR SPIDER'S CAT-FLING BID.
NOISE ROW: RAT-BATS HIT BACK.
CHIMP 'CHUMS' SLAM TREE-TOP SEX-ROMP SLUR

NEW SKULL THREAT LOOMS.
TOP CAT'S LOST NUTS: HOPES FADE.
NEWSBIRD SAVES ANT FROM CHAT-SHOW HOST.
HAWK'S 'JUST DROPPED IN' CLAIM QUIZZED
TIGER-TALE TALKS: FRESH TERMS.
COURT TOLD OF BEES' TIGHT SQUEEZE.

HUNT IS ON FOR KILLER STOOL.
PARROT IN RAT-BAT SMEAR DENIAL.
HAWK'S PLUMMETING SKULL FEAT.
OWL: NUDE GRAN IN MERCY DASH.
'I WAS DUPED' CLAIMS BEDROOM RABBIT.
PARROT'S NEW BISCUIT PLEA.

ANGER OF TOPLESS MUM-TO-BE.
HELP NEWSBIRD FIGHT OFF NEWS-FUN CRACKDOWN.
PLUMMETING SKULL: FRESH FACTS
MEDIA BIRD SIGNS TOP BOOK DEAL: SPIDER TELLS ALL.
BOOK TO REVEAL WEB PAIR'S ROMP SECRETS
TIGER DENIES HORSE CHARGE.
FUNBIRD TO GET OWN SHOW – OFFICIAL.

Cat

I say my poem
To myself: it goes,
'When hunger gnaws remember that
Hope springs eternal in the human cat.'

I turn over
And say it again.
And then I say this one:

'In my end is my
beginning. In my eye
is my arsehole.'

That's a *lovely* poem.

Rat-bat

Please be quiet. You can't always hear
us, but we can certainly
hear you. It's painful,
I make this gesture so that you can know
what system means. No,
we don't pee up our own noses
when we're asleep. We're
organised for that, too. The entire
Typing P... the entire Resource Interface
is making, through me, exactly
the same statement. Please listen.

Turtle

Read my
lips. Read
my lid. Read
my expression: now you
see it now you don't

Where were we? Ah.
It's all about coming in
first, right? You
go on ahead then. I'll catch you
up.

Dog

Ouf. Ouf. Ouf. Ouf. Ouf.
Ouf. Ouf. Reload. Ouf. Ouf.
I Ouf I always Ouf. Ouf. Ouf.
Reload. I Ouf. Excuse me Ouf. I
just must Ouf I say, do any of you Ouf.
I've just heard the most amazing Ouf Ouf
Reload. It's all right I won't Ouf. Bite.
Just let me Ouf. Just let me tell you
this one Ouf. No choice. Over and Ouf

Cock

Hey! What you stare at then?
I've got my interests. And here's
two out of the three of em.
So, Up Yours, Cocky!

The Half-Year Letters

(for an alphabet book designed by Ronald King)

Half-year starts out of the quarry. Candle and salt after bread

Better be bloody careful. After booze bodies can break beds. Burnt sugar and blunder to London, lie frog-flat under a black pall. Wake in the after-smoke, a huge bee at the window

Trick of the candle catching the smoke from cigarettes. Fit on a cincture and it clings:unclasp it. Twilight and pictures in confusion with the candle.

Blundering in deaf through the door.

End of the fiesta. Booze, bread and the prize of a breath that ends the candle. Glisten with sweat. And teach how in another year under the veil of a woodland shelter Jonathan Edwards crept to vex himself with prayer.

There's a belief to fix. It feels strong. It feels far off. There is faith to defile by fragmentation: to fit into half-faiths or less

Vigil glistens through into the night under a veil of vagueness. Still left in it there's a virginity that won't tell the time

Half-reconciled, half-healed: but two different sets of halves that won't match

Introducing – Interrupted by Anniversaries. Swift importunate India glistens in her wild veil of tricks, but the prize vigil is among high shoes, tight skirts, pianos, pizzas, a sit-in on *Liza*.

Ear-jewels catch a glint. Floor shine. Journal of what's favourite, a hand laid on its page. Hand-jewel rings true. No job there for jealousy

Klonk! The smoker's trick, foot in the door, acting thick-skulled and frank, asking quickly for a bath without thinking of the risks of refusal. Everywhere sick with old smoke

Half-hearing, half in a veil, to lope and blunder, wild and dull. Medical lights in a glistening inflamed ear. Cochlea, balance, half-circles of canal. Healing for a while in a vigil over a valley set with lamps falling to candlelight.

This is The Rider Who Must Not Materialise. The smoke blows far away. We manage. By empty morning roads to a hump-backed bridge. In a book of marked megaliths the spirals of the snail shells I found in the dawn, scattered in the carbonised stubble of the charred canal bank at Swanbach: some shells burnt white, others still patterned, a glisten of mucus left at their openings

Open season for old wounds, odd jobs. Loping from door to door, hovering, hamming it up, on the booze

Open again, a kids' pub with Space Invaders. Pace in the car park. Then get behind and push for a prize that's not without pain

A queasy request in the mail. The enquiring quill strikes in. So, into the peaceable quarry. Quilted. No disquiet

A burnt year. Trick riders blunder about the concrete without quarry or prize. There's battery trouble. There's no bread left at the door

Pressure in the dusk beside the swan's glistening canal at the summer's end. Smoke, shifting and swift

A thesis to turn a trick comes swiftly to trial. The fate that fits it is to be burnt. After that, in the glistening rain, watch the tendrils wave and retreat

Then in hard-blown sun to the uplands above the used-up quarries and burnt houses

Vigil of a voyeur, more than enough, feeling the vision of others vex the air but not break the veil. Lie out and read the spiral grooves carved in venerable rock

Thinking of the swan, its white streaked with orange rust, then going swiftly into the wild that blows in

Swift exposures fix me in the box: I, who thought *vixen* was a plural. Then the downpour dries out into a huge exuberance

It's not tufty with scrub nor yet quite barren; the year sways past the edge of the quarry

And the prize comes to the cerebral, booze notwithstanding. What are simple necessities for some still amaze one in a dozen

Also
(with Derrick Greaves)

also there was another story/   a bird suddenly crossing a frame of sky to alter/   I had no window, the darkness moulded me/   it said the messages were settled/   we must be crossing a frame of sleep, the sunlit screen over the matted shadow where the cloud had fallen and gone down lost among the folds/   and searching for loss more faint than the first loss/   and then to alter everything by passing it by, asking nothing, expecting nothing to alter/   alter/ /also there.

IX

Studies

1

Convalescent
to get along the shop fronts
far as a butcher's awning.
In the wind and sun, pause.

Quiet afternoon
to be powerless
held up by clothes
muffled
from the empty bright world
unrecognised
near home.

Library books
mostly about mountains
Kangchenjunga
in the silver crust
hanging on the gulf beyond Darjeeling;
Godwin Austen in the silver crust.

Deep sky between the fragile
clouds
backing the library weathervane
set on a cupola of green.

2

Civic water
with lilies and flies.

Men extend a trellis. It
opens across a flowerbed
to enclose –

Boats recede
shouts
tade among the olive
green expanses
The sense of it all slides
faint-tasting
outwards from pain
low in the body
in the registers of the body,

among the all-but-kicked-against
fencing of split birch-logs,
the pergolas –

Even these sometimes leave it,
the discomfort
to be without present image:
body
trying to walk itself off
to a memory of health;

or at times
hope
when the water's seen to move;
a fleck of light on the ripple.

The Badger's Belly-mark

Up from the Fork Dale crease
clear of the first wall, then
twisting through unmown pasture
the badger's belly-mark
grooved in the grass widens
an inch to pass under the gate

makes an event in the tangled
verge and vanishes
over the tarmac

strikes up again to a gate
not quite opposite
wallows under it
and loses itself on the open
hill. No guessing
which way after that.

Still in the night
along the same mark
the belly nobody sees
goes home damp
or dusty or snowy. Heavy.

The House on the Border

Late on a summer evening the news comes blue,
blurred, brown, a transient green,
emitted more than received, the channel
left open for what could happen.

And the sun burns from the horizon
along the faraway carpark of, and into
the windows of a single-deck outlet for plastic
floor-covering, where all, for a few hours,
have left the chill cylinders deserted.

As the news wobbles, its mouths
sprawl and jig. The rooms hang
straight and dinner has turned out
to be restrained moist white
bread with firm cheese chunks
that carry a whiff and a kick. Nothing
to do but get it down, finish the day.

Far from their centres
two edges fuse, and backfill
the meadows that were between, levelling
dips, culverting streams, the streets
facing only inwards, walls closed on
bony bodies with soft skin, short
hasty bodies signed with unique hair.

The Burning Graves at Netherton

This is a hill that holds the church up.

This is a hill that burned
part of itself away:

down in the coal measures
a slow smoulder

breaking out idly at last
high on the slope

in patches
among the churchyard avenues.

Netherton church lifts up
out of the falling land below Dudley;

on its clean promontory
you see it from far off.

Not burning. The fire
never raged, nor did the graves flame
even by night, the old
Black Country vision of
hell-furnaces.

A lazy dessication. The soil first
parched, turned into sand, buckled
and sagged and split. In places
it would gape a bit, with soot
where the smoke came curling out.

And the gravestones
keeled, slid out of line,
lifted a corner, lost
a slab, surrendered
their design; caved
in. They hung their grasses
down into the smoke.

Strange graves in any case;
some of them edged
with brick, even with glazed white
urinal brick, bevelled

at the corners; glass
covers askew
on faded green and purple
plastic diadems of flowers.

Patchy collapses, unsafe ground.
No cataclysm. Rather
a loss of face, a great
untidiness and shame;

Silence. Absence. Fire.

Over the hill, in the lee,
differently troubled,
a small raw council estate
grown old. Red brick
flaky, unpointed,
the same green grass uncut
before each house.
Few people, some boarded windows,
flat cracked concrete roadways
curving round, and a purpose-built
shop like a battered command-post.
All speaking that circumstance
of prison or institution
where food and excrement are close
company. Concrete, glazed brick
for limits. A wooded hill
at its back.

Silence. Absence. Fire.

The Running Changes

Driving northward in February once
on the run, to be clear of the Midlands
in a panic and ruin of life,

I heard the telephones ring in the air
for the first hundred miles.

But in the afternoon rain I found Sedbergh
and threaded on through it,
a silent close stone lock
which let me pass but barred my trouble;
I feared only it might be gone on ahead
to lie in wait for me by the Tyne. Then
the look of the road up to Kirkby,
the plainness and dark of it, settled
my stomach; and the sight of Brough
Keep, black as could be, risen in the fields
by a change of road, made me for that day
my own man, out over cold stripped Stainmore.

Another year,
coming down in peace out of Durham
in a late snowstorm towards sunset,

I met the lorries, headlamps full on,
thrashing their way up over Stainmore
in spray-wave of rose-tinged slush,
cloud-world behind and below them
filling the valley-bottom,
rolling, shot through with pink,
in the side-valleys breaking apart
to lance the pastures right across
with sunlight from no sure source:

and under the last trail of the cloud,
the vanishing up of its blush
into the grey, and the snow thinning,
there, once again, was Brough Castle
marking the turn southward,
and being dark.

Cut Worm

You're the invention
I invented once before –
I had forgotten.

              I need to invent you now
more than you need to be remembered.

Promenade on Down

Against the crowds that push up from below,
their mouths the chief things about them,
teeth revealed, teeth covered, breath
taken and surrendered without advantage,
young men, young women, well-to-do. Downward

against the updraught and the bodies, one
civilised man with all his
appetites on him. On such a paper as this
there can be only one. More would turn
to a chorus, a clique, a college. Elated

all across his body, appetite
the seeds of coriander freed from their soapy
coating and the drooped foliage hung
dry above soil, appetite the varnish that tautens
wood lifted to the light. Passing then

by a god working out a term
as Exarch of the Steps, a blue stain all
about him. Air-blue above, deep
earth-blue under him. Most happy god!
He can take it. Propped on a lower level,

beached figure, aghast,
hollow with longing and old adventure.
Full heads float by, glance
at the live and the dying equitably. Padlocked
doorways, facades for rubble. Going on

down. Bearing up. Death's a shallow
box with a sound bottom, life's
the lid. Good to be riding its patterns,
incised, painted. Enlaced animals, shining
women, stuffed warriors. Twining plants

with flat leaves, printed
to give a harmless bitter taste. Or
breaking alive from knuckles in a wall
close by a pavement where many
poor popes go briskly about their business.

A Poem To Be Watched

Coming into the world
unprepared

and being then always –
in honour of that
birth and to stay
close to it –
under-provided

and driven to exhibit
over and over again
unpreparedness

habitually
unready to be caught
born

Noted

Helplessly judgmental
in spite of myself – am I
supposed just to grin at all this?

Foul-mouthed and equable
among the disappearing hills, mind
grown skeletal with experience.

Keep a late lookout for Normans, notice
death now and then across the garden
tidying this and that.

I can draw now.
I can draw clouds as well as the next man,
any amount, in naked unbroken
English. I've looked at plenty.

Often seen them as they're not to be seen,
edge-on, their arrivals
flakes of mica.

The Least

The least, the meanest,
goes down to less;
there's never an end.

And you can learn
looking for less
and again, less;
your eyes don't get sharper.

For there is less
eyesight;
and no end to that.

There is you,
there is less-you:
the merest trace –
less-eyes will find it.

A Grammar for Doctrine

Not what
neutralises by balance
or by extension cancels –

This is the cleft:
rate it how you will,
as an incredible thing
with tangible properties, even.
But without doubt
the thing that is
shown to people.

Real emphasis
only in the plainness of the signs
for what's known;

mystification itself,
eternal sport,
opens a coloured arch,
plastic to the core,

and a tram with little decoration

sends courageous Gaudi to Avernus.
Entry is quick, you never sense it,

return by way of what's known;
entry is quick, you never sense it,
however you repeat it, or hang by a hair.

The Elohim Creating Adam

Blake drew the guilt of God,
showed him at his compulsion
in plain view. Past the moment
of holding back and not
forcing the universe
to break into matter from the void;

by the very act obliged
for a while to be
imaginable, all the world
hurrying into being
and looking on

Blake, on behalf of Adam,
put the secret question everybody has:
'How was it, that particular
minute when I was made?'

And stained Eternity
with common answers: 'Troubled.
At cross-purposes. Recklessly aware
as to consequence. Streaked through
with the sense of something
suddenly and forever lost.'

Leaving July

Low crippled clouds drag on a naked sky
over night leaves that point
ravines of darkest green down steeply
from the pale plateau of glaucous twilight;

the sky flattens on the land and gazes
back up into itself with rainwater eyes
out of blue rutted sockets on a builder's site:

it levels along the wires and the stump arms
of telegraph poles, almost at cool-tiled house-height;
where long roofs make a floor for shallow midnight.

As He Came Near Death

As he came near death things grew shallower for us:
we'd lost sleep and now sat muffled in the scent of tulips, the medical
        odours, and the street sounds going past, going away;
and he, too, slept little, the morphine and the pink light the curtains let
        through floating him with us,
so that he lay and was worked out on to the skin of his life and left there,
and we had to reach only a little way into the warm bed to scoop him up.

A few days, slow tumbling escalators of visitors and cheques, and something
        like popularity;
during this time somebody washed him in a soap called *Narcissus* and mounted
        him, frilled with satin, in a polished case.

Then the hole: this was a slot punched in a square of plastic grass rug, a slot
        lined with white polythene, floored with dyed green gravel.
The box lay in it; we rode in the black cars round a corner, got out into our
        coloured cars and dispersed in easy stages.

After a time the grave got up and went away.

Photographers' Flowers

When old men get well-known again
and interviews come to the cottages,
the dachas, the garden corners,

there are pictures taken away:
well-known old men. Daylight
from the side and the hard old head
thinking about daylight. Silver
stubble, hands let still.

There's a secret that keeps them going.
Each has beside him at all
times, in a wineglass
or a scrubbed-out fishpaste jar,
his flower. That's how they stay alive,
quietly seated, each with his dried
seed head or spirited weed.

– So the photographers say;
searching the dresser for a glass,
the yard for a flower.

Magritte Imitated Himself

I looked out of the window
once too often
(you'll stick like it)
and on a cold Sunday
afternoon of the Seventies
in Birmingham
stood, for the first time, disaffected,
on the aerial concrete
approach-platform of the new
Library, reared over the ghosts
of Widman and Dodd, Civil
Military and Ecclesiastical
Tailors, and Mason College, the old
Arts Building. Glancing to one side
I saw a skyline of certain
venerable cornices
in form of a frameless window
printed on the world.

Lost window, persistent world:
the place where I stood in the wind
was a sort of same; the space
where my customary seat in the first-floor
English Theatre used to be. They had
torn down all my support, removing
the very street beneath, then
raised it somehow up again, that
my attention could once more
wander. Starlings
used sometimes to fly about during lectures
and would look
ill-at-ease, time-travelling.

Last Poems

Thinning of the light
and the language meagre;
an impatient shift under the lines

maybe to catch the way
the lens, cold
unstable tear, flattens and tilts
to show codes of what may be flaring
at the edge and beyond.

Absence of self-pity suggests
absorption in something or other
new, never to be defined.

But in all those years before
what *was* his subject?

Report on August

How do I sleep? Well, but
the dreams are bad:

filled with accusations
small but just.

These slack summer dawns
that fail of sunrise

there's a relief at falling
awake and into comfort,

becoming once again
four people, watching

from pillow level
my boys' khaki heads bustle about.

Over breakfast I see,
staring at the garden,

how the times have fed:
under heavy leaves and low sky

in profile the bold woodpigeon
walks the lawn.

Beats of a shadowy fanblade
tick through from behind,

time going; ignored,
nobody measuring time, so much

constant, the weather unchanging,
the work I do filling days

so that they seem one day,
a firm framework, made

of the window where I sit
(or lie, slumped, feet on the desk,

waved to by passers-by
like a paraplegic)

a window-shaped guise of myself
that holds what few events come round

like slides, and in what seems
capricious sequence.

Continuity

In a covered way along the outside of the building,
a glazed lean-to with the panes painted over,
there's nothing but the light, falling across the quarries
from the lamp in the wall above.

Purpose? No purpose. Apparitions? None.
Where the lamplight peters out across the yard
two shallow plant pots swim the night.

There is smoke folded into the waters,
the fish-trap gives the waters form,
minimal form, drawn on the current unattended,
the lure and the check. So much free water.

Long clouds are lined.
Over the level-crossing ramp.
Faces behind car-glass painted with reflection,
pressed in the seats, warm bodies;
and the exhausts patter on the dirt
stained through with oils, sterile with gases.

When they pull away across the ballast
dirty Nature claims her own.

Tongues of grease in rings of light.

The towns are endless as the waters are.

On the Open Side

On the open side, look out
for sun-patches of sea-blue:

if you see them
it's beginning to shift
with factory towers along the edge,
chalk-white and silver,
empty even of machines

– the other life,
the endless other life,
endless beyond the beginning;

that holds and suddenly presents
a sunny day twenty years ago,
the open window of a train
held up on an embankment for an hour:

down the field there were children playing
round a concrete garage.
That was all. Something the other life wanted –
I hadn't kept it.

       But look out
for the sea-blue patches.
They'll not make problems.

Rudiments

One half-dark night my father
hoisted me, a three-
year-old illiterate,
on to a parapet to look at
a thing he called *The Barge* –
a pun of shapes from *The Prelude* as it turns out,
deranged with long transmission
and still a few years early for encoding
in what were to be Klee's last paintings:

projecting motionless
down there between the bridge supports
there was a dead black *V* in the murk,
gapped, with its bad face upturned.
Behind us, the biggest thing I'd ever seen,
the dark gas-holder
filled up the sky.

One hot afternoon he led me
to a broken plank in a hoarding, then
showed me, pointing straight down,
The Canal itself. A black
rippled solid, made of something
unknown, and having the terrible property
of seeming about to move,
far under our feet. I'd never
seen so much water before.

Mystery Poems

1

Sloping and tapering away,
form of a dog's head, slick
to the eye but dry and
silky, polished with graphite-
black all across the prevailing
soapy khaki; and grown
from around its rocky shoulder
the side of a red brick
town after an afternoon shower,
the painted old iron frames
wet and a blind greenish-pale
reflection all along
the upper windows of Burton's.

2

Irish cheekbones and close-set eyes,
but not Irish, a man
sits at a loss in a farm kitchen,
looking at a higher chair as if
at a Labrador that's sitting on it
and knowing all the answers. But
only as if.

3

The upper corner – probably
battered concrete – from which
it all depends, is a comfort
by being in a form of order, and
boundless terror through being
inscrutable beyond the top of an upright
and the beginnings of a cross-beam
somewhere in the sky. Whatever
it is that takes this corner
as given
is infinitely flickering and free,
being shreds of primeval
dawn sky, patterned
by the moving parchment-coloured
twists and tatters of a square-rig sail;
blazons and insignia are
breaking away at speed and reforming differently,

as is peeled skin
picked at by curious hands made
in a painted-wood-sculpture style that
seems alien, even when they're gone.

Custom

A head kept somewhere in a pub,
luck of the house – others
in farmhouses around?

Something to think about, a head
in a wall-cupboard round the back.

Old head. Hundreds of years, it's
safer to say. Not just
anybody's. Somebody's. No name,
no story.

By the niche, a label:
The Thought Stops Here.

The Intruder

As I think of yellow,
    a deep shining yellow
that plunges down with white enfolding it,

and as I think of a certain
    stretch of roadway
with a small river beside it in a stone-built channel,

I see, quite clearly, a young girl
    black-haired and quiet
doing some household work, a couple of generations ago.

Her face is broad, like a filbert,
    the features small;
I can see where the colours lie on her skin.

I can see plainly, through the brown varnish
    sentiment lays on the scene
the fat lips and the inexpressive eyes.

A dark body-scent disturbs the air
    but not enough
to persuade me that she and I might sympathise.

She means so little to me, one way or the other
    yet seems so real
it's as if I had walked into somebody else's imagination.

But whose? None of my friends', I think.
    And what will come of it, what
way shall I be involved? The wisest thing

seems to be, by way of the road with the little river
    and the deep shining yellow
to retire discreetly, and leave the sulky bitch to it.

The Flight Orator

Said:

'Little birds live in this park. There are sparrows. There are starlings. They rummage in the grass and among the roses.

'They have their young, and they care for them; and the young grow big and go away. The old ones fade, dry up and die. All little lives, quick lives; soon over.

'Do the cats have all the dead sparrows? How many live sparrows does one see? Countless. How many dead ones? A few. Where are all those small brown birds? Are they sunk among the stones, and their feathers blown away? Are their feathers to be found blown among the bushes, like soft leaves in the wintertime, when these small birds die? I never found the scarlet feathers from a robin's breast.

'I find few feathers, few traces of dead birds. There are great vacancies in life.

'There are bigger birds in the park; a few. Ducks. And swans, that seem more free. They can trail their black legs across the sky when the desire moves them and with their outstretched throats can beat along – on wings of hope.

'They fly into yesterday, last year: into a land nobody could bear to be let loose in. With chains of grey lakes under rainy skies, with miles of yellow reeds, that bleach under the storm-clouds like sick hair.

'And through that lonely place the wildfowler with his punt gun crawls, day after day; that pasty man with a black leather cap. ...

'Gulls come here, too, when sleet drops into the dead pond-water. They fall in a flock in the middle of the cricket field, eating at something, going at it like a patch of maggots.

'Those are the biggest birds that stay any time. But there's a bigger bird still to remember: a great mild bird that maybe comes over this land in the night when nobody's awake to see him blotting the stars out. He's a mild bird, a compassionate bird, not a beautiful bird. He's like a great fat thrush: gigantic, thirty feet long or thereabouts, and soft as they come. An uncrowned king. He needs no crown. And what crown fit for him could those little birds, his subjects, find? The birds are poor.

'He flies on, never stopping, never setting his foot on the ground. For he has no feet. The air is his realm and in it he must stay. So he flies on, slowly beating his soft wings, with the small birds darting about him, hearing him sigh. They

381

catch his eye: but he'll not let them pity him. On he goes, through the darkness before the dawn. Imagine him there, across the roofs when everybody's asleep – shadowing their dreams, it may be. He flies low, it's all he can do to keep going: saving his strength for the hills, and the tall forests and the long stretches of water, and the places where he must fly alone.

'The followers who finally leave him, to flutter back to their homes, imagine they'll be the last to see him; but time after time, when red flashes dart across among the night clouds, or a false dawn seems to be coming, there's an excited chatter among the trees. Some bird has sighted him again: he's coming; he's coming! That black shape flapping in low over the water. Time and again this happens, through the long night: it looks as if it might go on for ever. But at last his end has to come.

'Far in the northern woods the ground is hard, like frozen ashes. The trees are sparse, sad grey sticks with fringes of green. Fog hangs in among them. The only buildings are turfcutters' huts, and there are few of those. A hundred miles away across the tundra there may be deserted imperial hunting lodges with snow and ice on their stone staircases, but no matter. There's a clearing where the woods thin out. A few rocks break through the thick yellow moss and turf. There are dead branches. All is exhausted. The last men to come here, long ago, abandoned a 'small cannon: it's not quite overgrown.

'At last, in he comes, down over the treetops, lower, lower: in among the trees where they thin out he manages to avoid colliding with their trunks; he just keeps his great eyes open. His beak gapes for breath. His breast touches the ground and for a moment he looks like an enormous baby cuckoo. Just a few little birds are there to see. He lifts his head and looks at them with dignity. They cry out in their distress and fly desperately up and down; slowly and remorsefully he shakes his head. For he's beginning to sink down into the earth, through the turf and moss, like a majestic foundering ship. Down he goes, conscious to the last.

'And as his eyes reach the ground they close, each squeezing out a huge tear that shakes among the grasses beside his disappearing beak. Soon all is gone. The tears trickle away into the disturbed earth above his head before they have time to freeze. The little birds, distraught, fly away to spread the news. He may be dead; he may be struggling under the ground for a long while. Nothing can reach him. Nothing of this will ever be repeated.'

Why They Stopped Singing

They stopped singing because
they remembered why they had started

stopped because
they were singing too well

when they stopped they hoped for
a silence to listen into.

Had they sung longer
the people would not have known what to say.

They stopped from the fear
of singing for ever.

They stopped because they saw the rigid world
become troubled

saw it begin
composing a question.

Then they stopped singing
while there was time.

The Trace

Although at first it was single
and silver

it travelled as ink falls
through cold water

and gleamed in a vein
out of a darkness

that turned suddenly on its back
and was dusty instead

letting go forth as it must
a plummet of red wax

from whose course when they lost it
rings of dull steel

like snake ribs in a sidelong curve
twisted away and lifted

to clamp on to a concrete
precipice broken with rust

and with shrubby growths
clustering under it

their leaves
shading and silvering

in the currents of light
draining among the branches

to where it was sodden
full of silky swallowed hair

that dried and was
flying in a fan

air flickering from its ends
collecting silvers

as it twined itself
into the gauze

then scattered as many
mercurial bolts

all through the chamber
darting everywhere

in under the roof-keel
with its infinite brown decline

its warp
unmistakable as it reached

down into the daylight
with a sidelong wooden nose

biased like the set
of a rudder and pulling in

everything that could raise
a bright wave against it

making colours print
themselves on to planes with the effort

one plate of red enamel
dominant and persisting

even through a grey
sleet that scored its face

running away as water
welling downwards

through a raised irregular
static vein

moving only by rills
within itself.

NOTES

NOTES

The Dow Low Drop *(22-26)*

Dow Low is the steep but backless hill that rises behind my house in an upland valley near the headwaters of the Derbyshire Dove. It is part of a line several miles long, formed from limestone of exceptional purity and until recently topped for some three thousand years by many grave mounds of Bronze Age dignitaries, set so as to be clearly visible from their farmlands to either side. Most of those hills have now lost their eastern slopes, and with them their graves, to quarrying for cosmetics and other chemical products and present a line of chasms and vertical cliffs.

A Furnace *(49-85)*

PAGE 58: *Gradbach Hill.* In North-West Staffordshire close to Three Shires Head, where Derbyshire, Cheshire, and Staffordshire meet. Facing it across the Black Brook is the rocky cleft called Lud's Church, a place whose supposed connection with the composition of *Gawain and the Green Knight* I am willing to believe in.

PAGE 59: *'Like dark-finned fish...'* etc. Quoted from J.C. Powys, *Maiden Castle* (Macdonald, 1937).

PAGE 63: *M. Valdemar.* Suspended for months on end in the moment of death, in Poe's story.

PAGE 74: *Barnenez.* Ancient tumulus on the Kernélehen peninsula in Brittany, no great distance from the village of St Fiacre.

PAGE 75: The German Grand Fleet surrendered at Scapa Flow after the First World War, and was then scuttled by its crews. Pictures of the raising of the ships were some of the most awesome images I saw in childhood.

PAGE 77: *The brain-birth of 1818.* The brain was Karl Marx's.

PAGE 79: *Knowlton.* In Dorset. An abandoned Christian church stands in the ring of an enclosure previously sacred to earlier deities whose ground it was tactically sent to occupy.

PAGE 80: *Axe Edge.* In Derbyshire, and reaching down to Three Shires Head. Within a mile or so of one another, on or under Axe Edge, rise three rivers: the Dane, flowing west into Cheshire, the Dove, flowing east, and the Manifold, running close to the Dove and eventually joining it.

PAGE 82: *Blackshaw Moor, Hen Cloud.* An upland plain in North-West Staffordshire and a crag overlooking it.

PAGE 85: *Ampurias.* Extensive Celtiberian, and later Roman, mercantile settlement in Catalonia.

The Cut Pages *(87-104)*

An improvisation but not an experiment. When I wrote it early in 1970 I had reasons for working as closely as I could to the elements of my language and its immediate fields of association, well below the levels of models that imaged the self and its extensions.

And on That Note: *Six Jazz Elegies* (215-16)

This poem commemorates some musicians, now dead, in whose company I used to work: Dick Wellstood, Bud Freeman, Duncan Swift, Bruce Turner, Wild Bill Davison, Archie Semple.

Handsworth Liberties (270-77)

In this sequence I decided to confront and investigate a habitual synaesthesia whereby many familiar pieces of music would inevitably conjure visual recollections of particular though apparently inconsequential locations in the district of Birmingham I grew up in.

Texts for a Film (285-94)

Commissioned for the documentary film *Birmingham's What I Think With*, producer and director Tom Pickard.

INDEX

signs will appear,
converging
on the senses
point the way to something.
somewhere.

Then decay
settles in like a hangover
drawn out for years,
decades.
still a lingering presence
when the memory
of the journey has slipped on disk on the bones celebrae
and the place it suggested
disappeared.

Rust feasts
on its own mixed figures
sign becomes a relic,
icon,
world-not-there which once was
and soon could be

if only imagination
can read the signs

Index of titles and first lines

Poem titles are shown in italics, sequences in capitals, and first lines (some abbreviated) in roman type. Dates in square brackets show the year/s of composition of poems or sequences.

this heartbreak sprawl
spiders web of —
huge wave of
concrete